*vibrator nation*

D1563938

# vibrator nation

## HOW FEMINIST SEX-TOY

## STORES CHANGED THE

## BUSINESS OF PLEASURE

Lynn Comella

*Duke University Press    Durham and London    2017*

© 2017 Duke University Press
All rights reserved
Printed in the United States of America on acid-free paper ∞
Text designed by Mindy Basinger Hill
Cover designed by David Drummond
Typeset in Minion Pro by Tseng Information Systems, Inc.

Library of Congress Cataloging-in-Publication Data
Names: Comella, Lynn, author.
Title: Vibrator nation : how feminist sex-toy stores changed the
business of pleasure / Lynn Comella.
Description: Durham : Duke University Press, 2017
Includes bibliographical references and index.
Identifiers:
LCCN 2017000630 (print)
LCCN 2017006456 (ebook)
ISBN 9780822368540 (hardcover : alk. paper)
ISBN 9780822368663 (pbk. : alk. paper)
ISBN 9780822372677 (ebook)
Subjects: LCSH: Vibrators (Massage)—United States. | Sex toys—
United States. | Female masturbation—United States. | Female
orgasm—United States. | Sex-oriented businesses—United
States. | Feminism—United States.
Classification: LCC HQ447 C66 2017 (print) | LCC HQ447 (ebook) |
DDC 338.4/730670973—dc23
LC record available at https://lccn.loc.gov/2017000630

*To all the sex-positive pioneers.*

*You make the world a better place.*

# CONTENTS

Acknowledgments ix

*introduction*   The Making of a Market   1

*one*   The Business of Masturbation   15

*two*   Out of the Therapist's Office, into the Vibrator Shop   43

*three*   Living the Mission   63

*four*   Repackaging Sex   88

*five*   The Politics of Products   113

*six*   Sexperts and Sex Talk   136

*seven*   Selling Identity   161

*eight*   Profitability and Social Change   188

*conclusion*   Grow or Die?   211

*appendix*   Studying Sexual Culture and Commerce   229

Notes   235

Selected Bibliography   257

Index   267

# ACKNOWLEDGMENTS

I conducted my very first interview for what would eventually become this book in 1998, long before the slow scholarship movement emerged. This research approach involves slowing down and letting ideas percolate, emphasizing quality over quantity, and taking the necessary time to write, rewrite, and, ideally, get it right. There was no way I could have known back then that I was embarking on a research project that would span so many years. In an academic world in which the mantra "publish or perish" is a constant refrain, time is indeed a luxury. For this book, it was also indispensable.

When I began this research in the late 1990s, feminist sex-toy stores were a loose network of like-minded businesses that were part of, but also somewhat peripheral to, the larger adult industry. Not long after I signed my book contract, the economy of the sexual marketplace underwent a seismic shift. By 2008, the women's market for sex toys and pornography was being heralded as a major growth market and feminist sex-toy stores seemed to hold the key to how other businesses could appeal to this newly significant and highly sought-after demographic. To tell the story I wanted to tell, the focus of my book would need to expand; so rather than winding down my research, another phase of data collection was just beginning, ultimately adding years to this project.

I am extremely indebted to all of the feminist sex-toy store owners, employees, marketers, manufacturers, educators, cultural producers, and customers who took the time to speak with me over the years and who always, with enthusiasm and thoughtfulness, shared their experiences and expertise. This book would not have been possible without them, and I am immeasurably grateful for their support.

I am especially thankful to Aileen Journey, the former proprietor of a small, feminist sex-toy store in Northampton, Massachusetts, who was the first person I interviewed for this project and whose contributions sparked my thinking in significant ways.

Babeland cofounders Rachel Venning and Claire Cavanah took a chance on an unknown PhD student when, in 2001, they welcomed me into their fold as a researcher, with no conditions or limitations. I am forever grateful for their openness, generosity, and belief in this project and in me. I was fortunate during that time to be surrounded by a remarkable group of Babeland employees who accepted me into their world with sincerity and kindness. A very special thank you to Dan Athineos, Dana Clark, Ducky Doolittle, Alicia Relles, Felice Shays, Saul Silva, and Jamye Waxman, and a big shout-out to Christine Rinki for her wry wit, keen intellect, and years of friendship and support.

Living with a project for so long means that many of my research contributors have become valued friends and interlocutors. I am grateful for the support of Kim Airs, Metis Black, Susie Bright, Coyote Days, Greg DeLong, Roma Estevez, Charlie Glickman, Carol Queen, Shar Rednour, Jackie Strano, and Tristan Taormino. I also want to sincerely thank retailers Ellen Barnard, Searah Deysach, Matie Fricker, Laura Haave, Nenna Joiner, Jacq Jones, and Jennifer Pritchett for their numerous contributions and invaluable input.

Sadly, not everyone who had a hand in shaping this book is alive to see it come to fruition. Dell Williams, the founder of Eve's Garden, died in 2015, and Joani Blank, who founded Good Vibrations and helped so many other entrepreneurs start their businesses, died following a brief illness just as I was putting the finishing touches on the manuscript. These women helped lay the foundation for sex-positive feminism long before it had a Wikipedia entry, or even a name, really. I hope this book serves their memories well and does justice to their pioneering visions, which have inspired so many others to follow in their feminist footsteps.

I am immensely grateful to the archives that helped me historicize the growth of the women's market for sex toys and pornography. Dell Williams and Joani Blank both invited me to rummage through their personal papers, regaling me with stories in the process and giving me duplicate copies of things they thought might be useful, from early mail-order catalogs and advertisements to photographs and corporate memos. I am thankful for the Lesbian Herstory Archives, the GLBT Historical Society, and the Center for Sex and Culture, which provided valuable primary source materials that greatly enriched my analysis. I would also like to express thanks to the Kinsey Institute at Indiana University, and Cornell University's Human Sexuality Collection, especially Brenda Marston, who has worked diligently to acquire the papers of numerous sex-positive innovators.

Ken Wissoker, my editor at Duke University Press, has been an unwavering champion of this project since its early days. He believed that this was a story that needed to be told and was exceedingly patient, not to mention extremely encouraging, as the manuscript slowly took shape through multiple drafts and iterations. I am deeply grateful for his guidance and support. I would also like to thank senior editor Courtney Berger, assistant editor Elizabeth Ault, editorial associate Olivia Polk, and project editor Danielle Houtz for their enthusiasm and help along the way.

I received a number of fellowships and grants over the years that helped make this research possible, including from my home institution, the University of Nevada, Las Vegas. These include a Faculty Opportunity Award, a College of Liberal Arts Summer Research Stipend, research funding from the UNLV provost's office, and a semester's research leave at the William S. Boyd School of Law, the last of which helped me cross the finish line with a renewed sense of academic vigor and enthusiasm.

I am extremely thankful for the research support I received during the early stages of this project, most notably from the Sexuality Research Fellowship Program of the Social Science Research Council, with funds provided by the Ford Foundation. I am enormously indebted to the SRFP and its director, Diane DiMauro, for giving me the opportunity to be part of an exciting, interdisciplinary community of sexuality scholars, many of whom have gone on to become leaders in the field. A year-long research associateship at the Five College Women's Studies Research Center at Mount Holyoke College allowed me to be part of a lively group of feminist scholars during the initial stages of this project. I am also grateful to the Graduate School at the University of Massachusetts, Amherst, for a dissertation fellowship that provided much-needed financial support.

The spark for this book was kindled at the University of Massachusetts, Amherst, where I received a doctorate in communication. My doctoral committee embraced this project at a time when research on the adult industry was hardly the norm and showed me that it was possible to push academic boundaries and pursue research agendas that went against the grain. Lisa Henderson encouraged my research on feminist sex-toy stores from the moment I wrote my first seminar paper on the subject. She had an expansive definition of what counted as communication scholarship and made sure that the politics of sexual representation were part of that conversation. I have benefited enormously from her mentorship, intellectual rigor, generosity, and words of encouragement. Janice Irvine's brilliant insights and friendship strengthened my scholarship and, by extension, this book. Sut Jhally's mentorship sharpened my thinking and helped me become a better scholar.

I loved the years that I spent at UMass, in large part because of the wonderful people I met there. The communication department was a special, vibrant place. I want to thank Michael Morgan, who, as chair of the department during my time there, cultivated a wonderfully collegial and lively environment. I was fortunate to enter the graduate program at a time when there was a small cadre of students working in the area of sexuality and queer studies. I am thankful to James Allan, Vincent Doyle, Viera Lorencova, Eve Ng, and Katherine Sender for their camaraderie, support, and friendship during those years and beyond. I also want to thank Melissa Click, Andres Correa, Alpha Selene Delap, Esteban Del Rio, Janice Haynes, Nina Huntemann, Ann Johnson, Alicia Kemmitt, Kembrew McLeod, Eric Morgan, Saila Poutiainen, Lisa Rudnick, Michelle Scollo, Cindy Suopis, and Rebecca Townsend for helping to make graduate school so much fun.

Terrific colleagues both near and far have sustained me over the years, including a network of sexuality scholars whose work has inspired me. Many thanks to Peter Alilunas, Feona Attwood, Heather Berg, Kevin Heffernan, Danielle Hidalgo, Giovanna Maina, John Mercer, Mireille Miller-Young, Constance Penley, Diana Pozo, Teela Sanders, Clarissa Smith, Whitney Strub, Georgina Voss, Ron Weitzer, and Federico Zecca. I spent two years in the Department of Gender Studies at Indiana University surrounded by some of the best colleagues I have ever had. I would like to thank Colin Johnson, Jen Maher, Brenda Weber, and Mary Gray for their collegiality and friendship. A special thank you to my colleagues at UNLV, past and present, including Christie Batson, Sheila Bock, Barb Brents, Manoucheka Celeste, S. Charusheela, Georgiann Davis, Marcia Gallo, Joanne Goodwin, Kate Korgan, Elizabeth MacDowell, Emily Mann, Kelly Mays, Ann McGinley, Bill Ramsey, Ranita Ray, Peg Rees, Anita Revilla, Addie Rolnick, and Danielle Roth-Johnson.

I would like to express my sincere appreciation to the anonymous reviewers at Duke University Press whose detailed and insightful reader reports strengthened this book in countless ways. Felicia Mello brought her professional editing chops and keen storytelling ability to this project, and I am a better writer as a result. Thanks also to Crystal Jackson and Rayette Martin for research assistance, and Alecsandria Cook and Kirby Stolzoff for input and copyediting. A very special thank you goes to Carol Queen and Shira Tarrant for reading the penultimate draft of the manuscript and providing invaluable feedback. I am eternally grateful for their unconditional support and friendship.

I developed some of the ideas that appear in *Vibrator Nation* in previous publications. I was very pleased to be included in *New Sociologies of Sex Work*, edited by Kate Hardy, Sarah Kingston, and Teela Sanders. Portions of that chapter have been revised and appear in this book. I was similarly honored to have a chapter in *Commodity Activism: Cultural Resistance in Neoliberal Times*, a cutting-edge collection edited by Roopali Mukherjee and Sarah Banet-Weiser. Some of the ideas that I discuss there about profitability and social change reappear here. Finally, I first developed my thinking about the importance of the customer feedback loop in my contribution to *The Feminist Porn Book: The Politics of Producing Pleasure*, a groundbreaking volume of essays edited by Tristan Taormino, Celine Parreñas Shimizu, Constance Penley, and Mireille Miller-Young.

Numerous friends and family have sustained me over the years. Wendy Sweetser Ferris was there at the start of this project, and her easygoing nature and sense of humor were always a welcome relief after a long day of writing. I want to thank Emily West and Kevin Anderson for friendship, food, and wobbles in western Massachusetts. I am deeply appreciative of my in-laws, Marie and Ron Olbrysh, who have never shied away from asking me about my academic work or this book, and especially my sister, Kristen Comella, who has always cheered me on. But most of all I want to thank my husband, Ryan Olbrysh. He read every word of this manuscript and never complained as my research materials slowly began to migrate out of our shared office, eventually taking over almost every surface of our home. He kept the candy jar filled with jelly beans and, after long days of writing, always found a way to make me laugh; and if he had a dollar for every time I said, "Can I read you something?" he would be a very rich man. My cats, Buddy, Mama Catt, and my beloved Schishy (1993–2013), supplied much-needed snuggles and comic relief.

The influence of my grandmother, Wilma Talcott Kitson, is everywhere in this book. Born in 1910, she studied library science in college and worked for many years in the Cleveland Public Library system. She was a voracious reader, a consummate researcher, and my heartbeat. When I started this research project in the late 1990s, she would clip stories about sex-toy stores, or about Dr. Ruth, from the newspaper and mail them to me. Once, during a research trip when I was worried about the data I would not have time to collect, she said, "Don't worry about what you don't have. Use what you have and use it well." She died in 2011 at age 101, and I miss her every day. I know she would be proud of this book.

# THE MAKING
# OF A MARKET

———

Women-run sex shops are the little pockets of sanity around
the country where women can go and get sex information . . .
and get their toys and vibrators. This is where feminism —
if there is such a thing — lives if you want to deal with sex.

BETTY DODSON

The seminar room at the Sands Expo and Convention Center in Las Vegas was
filled to capacity. Onstage sat six women. They were porn producers, sex-toy
retailers, product buyers, and CEOs, all of them respected industry leaders who
had been asked by the organizers of the 2008 Adult Entertainment Expo — the
largest adult entertainment showcase in the United States — to answer what
for many had become the million-dollar question: "What do women want?"

As people in the audience listened intently and took notes, the panelists
outlined what they saw as the key ingredients to marketing sex toys and pornography to women. Women want products that are made well and look good,
and this includes packaging, said product buyer Alicia Relles. "Women are
willing to spend a little more money for something that is beautiful and works
well . . . and that will last a long time." They also want information. "If you
have a flagging retail space," Penthouse Media executive Kelly Holland told
the audience, "I'd start doing workshops." Industry veteran Kim Airs agreed.
"Having an educational component benefits retail stores because it makes
your store a resource center, not just a store," she emphasized.

The panel discussion illustrated a gravitational shift taking place in an industry long dominated by men and viewed by many as antithetical to feminism.
The newly christened women's market for sex toys and pornography had become what many analysts considered the adult industry's hottest growth mar-

ket. "Women have dollars, believe me," Holland told the crowd at the expo. "And they love to spend [them] on things they feel enhance their self-esteem, their intelligence, their sexual lives." Ken Dorfman, the national sales manager for Doc Johnson, one of the largest sex-toy manufacturers in the world, used dollars and cents to make a similar point: "One guy shopping alone—average sale $8. Two guys, $12. But one female shopping alone—average sale $83. Two females shopping together, $170."[1] In an era when profits from pornography had declined precipitously, the result of piracy and free Internet video sites, these numbers told a powerful story: the marketplace was changing and adult businesses needed to change with it.

Even the convention's infamous parties mirrored this change. Later that evening in a suite at the Venetian Hotel and Casino, high above the Las Vegas Strip, feminist sex-toy retailer Babeland hosted a party to celebrate the release of the SaSi vibrator by Je Joue. Billed as one of the most innovative vibrators to hit the market, the SaSi was touted as a marriage of sleek design and customizable technology. While the product's designers huddled around the prototypes they had brought with them from the United Kingdom, others, including Babeland cofounder Rachel Venning, milled around the room, sipping the evening's specialty cocktail, the SaSitini. Transgender porn star Buck Angel lounged on the bed while, across the room, feminist author and filmmaker Tristan Taormino signed copies of *Chemistry*, her award-winning porn series.

This was not your father's porn industry party, and it reflected the growing power of a women's market that until fairly recently was regarded as a relatively small and somewhat inconsequential part of the larger adult industry, a specialty niche more likely to elicit a playful wink than any serious consideration. In recent decades, due in part to the popularity of television shows like *Sex and the City*—which introduced millions of viewers to the Rabbit vibrator—and the runaway success of *Fifty Shades of Grey*, women have acquired newfound economic and cultural cachet as sexual entrepreneurs and consumers.[2]

Many adult entertainment companies, from sex-toy manufacturers to retailers, are recalibrating their business practices with an eye toward wooing female shoppers. Traditional brick-and-mortar retailers, for example, are removing their video arcades, painting their stores to make them lighter and brighter, hiring female staff, and placing a greater emphasis on stocking quality products and offering attentive customer service. They are softening the edges of their businesses and taming the often harsh and in-your-face representations of sexuality customarily associated with the adult industry, all in the hope of appealing to women and their wallets.

A 2009 study conducted by researchers at Indiana University found that close to 50 percent of women have used vibrators and, of those, 80 percent have used them during partner sex.[3] These results prompted condom-maker Trojan to cash in on the growing popularity of sex toys by developing its own line of vibrating products.[4] References to sex toys abound in popular women's and men's lifestyle magazines, and vibrators can now be purchased at many neighborhood Walgreens. Even female celebrities have jumped on the sex-toy bandwagon. *Real Housewives of Atlanta* star Kandi Burruss teamed with sex-toy manufacturer OhMiBod to create her own line of sex toys, Bedroom Kandi, and pop star Macy Gray grabbed headlines after writing an ode to her "battery-operated boyfriend." Mainstream media, for its part, can't seem to get enough of discussing women's role in igniting a sex-toy revolution. "Are sex toys a woman's best friend?" asked one *Huffington Post* writer, while another reporter declared, "Sex toys are hot," pointing to an industry that, according to one frequently cited number, purportedly grosses upward of $15 billion annually.[5] Although accurate sex-toy sales figures are difficult to pinpoint—businesses keep their numbers extremely close to the vest and virtually no reliable adult industry data exist—there is little question that interest in, discussions about, and sales of sex toys have grown exponentially since the 1970s, with women leading the way.

## The New Sexual Sell

It was not always the case that women's sexual satisfaction and orgasms commanded such public interest. The 1950s, the era documented in Betty Friedan's groundbreaking book *The Feminine Mystique*, were, for many women, a time of profoundly felt ambivalences. The book's 1963 publication exposed deep fissures in the cult of postwar domesticity, which had produced a generation of unhappy, bored, and listless suburban housewives who had not found fulfillment in their roles as wives and mothers. Magazines, advertisements, pop psychology, and higher education had all colluded to convince women that their greatest achievements would come from waxing the floor, baking casseroles, and running the PTA. Many white, middle-class women, whose lives revolved around their children, husbands, and homes, faced a crisis of identity that left them wondering, "Is this all?"[6]

When it came to sex, these same women received extremely conflict-ing messages. Although the romantic fantasy of marriage and motherhood loomed large in 1950s popular culture, other competing currents were also at play. Alfred Kinsey, the Indiana University sex researcher, let the cat out of the bag in 1953 when he published *Sexual Behavior in the Human Female*. Kinsey's findings, according to historian Sara Evans, revealed that a quiet sexual revo-lution had been percolating for most of the twentieth century.[7] Women mas-turbated and had orgasms; they engaged in heavy premarital petting and sometimes intercourse; they had extramarital affairs; and many indicated they were not exclusively heterosexual. Kinsey's discoveries exposed a "vast hidden world of sexual experience sharply at odds with publicly espoused norms."[8]

The same year that Kinsey's volume on female sexual behavior was released, the first issue of *Playboy* hit the newsstands. Author Barbara Ehrenreich has argued that *Playboy* was a "party organ of a diffuse and swelling movement" that promoted male rebellion rather than responsibility.[9] *Playboy* encouraged young men to reject the traditional roles of husband, father, and breadwinner in favor of remaining single and indulging in the finer things in life, including the company of beautiful women. Thus, a decade before Friedan unmasked the deep discontent that many suburban housewives felt as a result of rigid gender role expectations, and years before the sexual revolution of the 1960s was in full swing, Kinsey's research and Hugh Hefner's *Playboy*—and later, Helen Gurley Brown's *Sex and the Single Girl*—challenged sexual attitudes in ways that "loosened the straitjacket of domestic ideology."[10]

Women were witnessing more open cultural portrayals of sexuality all around them in movies, magazines, and novels, from the 1956 *New York Times* best-seller *Peyton Place*, which told the story of unbridled lust in a fictitious New England town, to erotic lesbian pulp fiction that could be easily pur-chased at newsstands and corner drugstores; and yet it was also the case that women lacked socially sanctioned outlets and occasions where they could freely discuss their sexual desires, fantasies, frustrations, and pleasures.[11] It is not surprising, then, that Friedan, in conducting interviews for *The Feminine Mystique*, encountered women who, according to her, "would often give me an explicitly sexual answer to a question that was not sexual at all."[12] That these white, middle-class women wanted to talk about their sexual adventures, many of which involved men other than their husbands, surprised Friedan and also seemed to puzzle her. Was this preoccupation with sex the cause of the "problem that has no name" or an effect? How was she to make sense of what she regarded as the "frustrated sexual hunger of American women" at the very moment when many women had retreated to the home in pursuit of domestic bliss?[13]

While even Friedan—who would go on to help found the National Organization for Women in 1966—could not point the way forward to the types of discussions women wanted to have about their sex lives, by the time her book was published, a sea change in sexual attitudes had already begun. In 1960, the Food and Drug Administration approved the birth control pill. By 1964, it was the most popular form of contraception in the country, becoming "an important tool in women's efforts to achieve control over their lives."[14] The pill, so tiny and yet so groundbreaking, was not only a symbol of women's growing sexual autonomy but also a powerful indicator of the increasing commercialization of sexual freedom. Author David Allyn has argued that the sexual revolution would never have "gotten off the ground without the free market."[15] Pharmaceutical companies invested in the pill because they saw dollar signs; the Supreme Court handed down decisions in the 1950s and 1960s that redefined obscenity in large part, according to Allyn, because the "market demand for sexual materials was so high."[16] By the end of the 1960s, there was ample evidence to suggest that American society, aided by the values of consumer culture and shifts in sexual attitudes, had become more visibly sexualized.[17]

Women's forays into the sexual marketplace in the early 1970s, as both entrepreneurs and consumers, took place against this backdrop. Their increasing economic independence from men facilitated a growing sexual independence, producing what authors Barbara Ehrenreich, Elizabeth Hess, and Gloria Jacobs have described as a "new consumer class for the sex industry."[18] A new kind of female sexuality was being produced through marketplace culture: "In this consumer arena female sexuality functioned differently than it had previously in mainstream society: it was unattached to reproduction, motherhood, monogamy—even heterosexuality."[19] But more than this, they argued, the sexual marketplace had a democratizing effect, helping to spread the sexual revolution to women who "would never have attended a feminist conference on sexuality or perhaps even have read one of the new sex manuals."[20]

Meanwhile, second-wave feminists, aided by the growing visibility of the gay and lesbian liberation movement, were dramatically reshaping cultural understandings of gender and sexuality. They challenged the patriarchal status quo that had taught women to see sex as an obligation rather than something they were entitled to pursue for the sake of their own pleasure. They wrote essays about the politics of the female orgasm, attended sexual consciousness-raising groups, and positioned masturbation as a decidedly feminist act. In feminist rap sessions, workshops, and sex therapy groups, and on the pages of books like Betty Dodson's *Liberating Masturbation*, the clitoris assumed new-found importance. Women were encouraged to masturbate as a way to learn about their bodies and take control of their orgasms.

Not everyone viewed the expansion of the sex industry as a sign of sexual freedom, however. In October 1967, Congress declared traffic in obscenity and pornography to be a "matter of national concern" and established an advisory Commission on Obscenity and Pornography.[21] President Johnson appointed an eighteen-member committee to marshal evidence to determine whether the reputed smut industry was wreaking havoc on American society. The report, released in 1970, found no evidence suggesting that pornography was harmful. Instead, it claimed that "much of the 'problem' regarding materials which depict explicit sexual activity stems from the inability or reluctance of people in our society to be open and direct in dealing with sexual matters."[22] The findings caused outrage. The Senate rejected them by a vote of sixty to five and Spiro T. Agnew, speaking on behalf of the Nixon administration, assured the American public that "as long as Richard Nixon is President, Main Street is not going to turn into Smut Alley."[23]

Feminist opposition to pornography was also intensifying in certain corners of the women's movement. The 1972 release of *Deep Throat* put pornography front and center on the national stage and ushered in the era of porno chic.[24] *Deep Throat* told the story of a woman whose clitoris had mysteriously migrated to a location deep inside her throat. If she wanted to experience the peaks of sexual pleasure and orgasm, she would need to perfect the act of deep-throat fellatio. For many women, the film highlighted the failures of the sexual revolution and the inability of the culture to take women's pleasure seriously. According to media scholar Carolyn Bronstein, *Deep Throat* was feminism's aha moment, one that encapsulated the "painful truth" about what men really thought about women.[25] Although it would be several more years until an organized antipornography feminist movement emerged, alarm bells were already ringing.

And it wasn't just the availability of pornography that was fueling concern. In 1975 legislators in Georgia amended the state's antiobscenity clause, criminalizing the sale of "sexual devices" and creating a legal template that would serve as a model for other states, including Texas and Alabama.[26] Vibrators were suddenly at the center of courtroom battles regarding an individual's right to sexual privacy versus the state's interest in regulating public morality—a concern that many critics argued unfairly targeted women. (For years, the standing joke was that it was easier to buy a handgun in Texas than a vibrator. To fly under the radar, woman-owned Forbidden Fruit in Austin adopted a highly coded language that masked the sexual uses of products, thereby insulating itself from legal repercussions.)[27]

Into the roiling waters of these cultural debates waded the pioneering feminist entrepreneurs who are the subjects of this book. Dell Williams, who founded Eve's Garden in New York City in 1974, the first business in the United States devoted to women's sexual pleasure and health, and Joani Blank, who opened the Good Vibrations retail store in San Francisco in 1977, boldly reimagined who sex shops were for and what kinds of cultural spaces they could be at a time when no business model for women-friendly vibrator stores existed. Theirs were the first businesses to bring an unapologetically feminist standpoint to the sexual marketplace, helping to establish what Babeland cofounder Claire Cavanah has described as the "alternative sex vending movement."[28]

Williams and Blank began their businesses at a time when places for the average woman to comfortably buy sex toys, or even talk openly about sex, were scarce. Conventional adult stores were not designed for female shoppers; reputable mail-order businesses that sold so-called marital aids were few and far between; and women walking into a department store—or any store, really—to buy a vibrating massager risked encountering a male clerk who might say, "Boy, you must really need it bad, sweetie pie."[29]

Blank, a sex therapist with a master's degree in public health, grew Good Vibrations from a cozy hole-in-the-wall in San Francisco's Mission District with macramé on the walls into a company with a national reputation as a clearinghouse for sexual information, becoming a standard bearer for quality in an industry that had few standards. Along the way, she infused her business with a noncompetitive ethos, happily sharing the company's financial records and vendor lists with entrepreneurially minded interns who would go on to found similar stores of their own.

Today, decades later, a sex-positive diaspora of women-friendly sex shops based on the Good Vibrations retail model exists in cities across the country. Businesses such as Babeland in Seattle and New York, Early to Bed in Chicago, Smitten Kitten in Minneapolis, Self Serve in Albuquerque, Sugar in Baltimore, and Feelmore in Oakland have made quality products and accurate sex information cornerstones of their retail missions, demanding in the process that women—as well as queer-identified and gender-nonconforming people—be taken seriously as both sexual agents and consumers.

*Vibrator Nation* tells the story of feminist sex-toy businesses in the United States and the women who pioneered them. It chronicles the making of a market and the growth of a movement, detailing the intertwining domains that shape the business of pleasure and the politics of business. In the chapters that follow, I draw upon extensive ethnographic and archival research, including more than eighty in-depth interviews with key retailers, manufacturers, and marketers, to discuss the history of sex-positive retail activism, including its highly gendered and class-specific nature; the relationship between identity politics and feminist entrepreneurship; and the ongoing—and perhaps irrevocable—tension between profitability and social change. This is a book about feminist invention, intervention, and contradiction, a world where sex-positive retailers double as social activists, commodities are framed as tools of liberation, and consumers are willing to pay for the promise of better living through orgasms.

## Let's Talk about S-E-X

I conducted my first interview on the topic of feminist sex-toy stores in 1998 while I was still in graduate school. At the time, I was taking a seminar on fieldwork methods in cultural studies that required I conduct a small-scale ethnographic project. I was interested in the relationship between sexuality and public culture, and wanted to know more about those spaces and places where representations of women's sexuality assumed an unapologetically public presence as opposed to being relegated to the privacy of the home.[30] As luck would have it, a sex-toy shop geared toward women, Intimacies, had just opened in the small college town where I lived. I have, time and again, returned to the initial interview I conducted with Intimacies owner Aileen Journey because my experience at her store was so influential to the development of my thinking about the history and retail culture of feminist sex shops. It also provided me with my first eureka moment as a researcher.

Journey saw her business as a "feminist way to support women's power" and told me that she had based her store on the Good Vibrations model. Good Vibrations had even supplied her with a list of sex-toy distributors for a nominal fee of $50 because the company's founder, Blank, wanted similar shops to open in cities across the country—and hers, Journey emphasized, was not the only business Good Vibrations had helped. According to Journey, the Good

Vibrations model included an emphasis on creating a comfortable and welcoming retail environment that did not have a lot of "porn hanging around." It was a place where women and men of all gender identities and sexual orientations were positioned as sexual subjects, not objects, and where merchandise was openly displayed so people could pick items up and be "encouraged that this stuff is okay." Intimacies was also a resource center, Journey explained, a place where people could ask questions and get information about sex.[31]

I spent hours at Intimacies observing the interactions between sales staff and customers in an effort to better understand what made this business different from typical adult stores ostensibly aimed at men. "This is so liberating to come into a store and talk about this stuff!" one female shopper remarked. Another noted, "I get braver every time I come in here. The first time, I looked over my shoulder, afraid that someone I know would see me. The second time, I blushed when the salesperson explained how things worked. This time, I parked illegally and strutted right in!"

As a researcher, I was captivated. I soon realized that this was a story not only about one feminist sex shop, but also about an entire network of businesses across the country that had all adopted a certain way of selling sex toys and talking about sex that blended sexual commerce and feminist politics. I knew then and there that I needed to turn this small pilot study into a much bigger research project that could more thoroughly amplify and illuminate the history of the Good Vibrations model and its travels. What were the sexual vernaculars, ways of doing things, ideologies, challenges, and paradoxes that had shaped these businesses? I wanted to know more.

The project especially resonated with me because I had become a feminist at the height of the feminist sex wars in the 1980s when heated debates about pornography, BDSM, butch-femme relationships, and politically correct sexual expression polarized many feminists. While I was an undergrad, I saw firsthand how competing values and political commitments could fracture a group of feminists when several faculty members in the women's studies program at my university stopped speaking to each other as a result of their opposing positions on these issues. My understanding of feminism, and indeed my own sexuality, was deeply intertwined with these battles over female sexuality and its public expression, clashes that often pitted women's pursuit of sexual pleasure against the perceived dangers of male lust and violence.[32]

Around the same time, I discovered Betty Dodson's celebratory treatise on female masturbation, which advanced the idea that masturbation was an essential stepping-stone to female liberation. Several years later, on my first trip to San Francisco in the early 1990s, I visited Good Vibrations, a store I had learned about from reading Susie Bright's column, "Toys for Us," in *On Our Backs* magazine. It was my first visit to a sex-toy store, and while I didn't buy anything, it felt like a rite of passage, entrée into an altogether new world of sexual imaginings and possibilities. In retrospect, it is difficult to envision what my own sexual journey might have been like if I had not had access to various "sex publics"—women-owned sex-toy stores, how-to guides, literary erotica, and feminist pornography—which allowed me to imagine myself in new ways.

These discoveries felt all the more significant because I did not have easy access to sexual information growing up, nor did I come from a family in which sex was openly discussed. My parents taught me that sex was something reserved for marriage, that good girls supposedly didn't, and that one's sexual reputation was worth protecting at all costs. I learned at an early age that sex was risky: it could lead to pregnancy, disease, and a bad reputation. Perhaps not surprisingly, these lessons did not inspire a sense of teenage sexual exploration or experimentation. Instead, they produced a fair amount of confusion and angst. As I got older, publicly accessible forms of sexual culture piqued my curiosity and gave me permission to explore my sexuality in ways that were personally transformative and deeply meaningful.

I found myself on the front lines of the movement to reshape sexual culture in the early 2000s, while conducting dissertation research at feminist retailer Babeland in New York City.[33] I was trained to work on the sales floor as a staff sex educator, a role that allowed me to participate in, and gain insider knowledge about, the range of activities that constituted the daily life of the store. I talked to hundreds of customers about their sex lives, sold my fair share of dildos and vibrators, attended staff and marketing meetings, stood on my feet for hours at a time, and crossed my fingers that my cash register balanced at the end of the day. It was an ethnographer's dream, my own golden ticket into the inner sanctum of a feminist sex-toy store with a national profile (see appendix).

My position as observer and participant, ethnographic researcher and vibrator clerk, meant that I was located squarely within the talking sex phenomenon that is so central to the experience that Babeland and other feminist retailers pride themselves on offering customers. I talked with shoppers about the G-spot, strap-ons, and vibrator use; I recommended books, such as *The Good Vibrations Guide to Sex*, *The Multi-Orgasmic Man*, *The Ultimate Guide* to *Anal Sex for Women*, and *The Survivors Guide to Sex*; I peppered my tours of Babeland's video library with facts about the history of pornography, from *Deep Throat* to *Bend Over Boyfriend*. I dispensed information about sex, dispelled common myths ("Can I become addicted to my vibrator?" The answer: No), and reassured nervous customers from all walks of life that there was nothing wrong with wanting more sexual pleasure in their lives.

I noticed that others now perceived me as a particular kind of sexual interlocutor, a quasi-expert with both academic credibility and practical know-how about sex. The subject of my research was often a topic of discussion at social events and dinner parties. "Tell them about your research," the host would say, or, "You will *never* guess what she is writing about!"

An especially memorable encounter took place one night at a party, when the host beckoned me into her bedroom. There, I found a group of thirty-something women casually piled onto her bed. One of them was holding a copy of *Bitch*, a feminist magazine dedicated to smart critiques of popular culture. As I moved closer, I realized they were looking at an ad for the Rabbit vibrator. "She thinks this is for the butt, is it?" one of them asked. "Is it a vibrator?" another inquired rather incredulously. One question led to another, and I soon found myself on the edge of the bed talking with a group of strangers about vibrators and the history of women-run sex shops.

For me, the field was potentially everywhere: the sex shop floor, adult industry trade shows, social gatherings and dinner parties, magazines and blogs, panels and invited speaking engagements, and, over time, social media platforms such as Facebook, Twitter, and Instagram. There were no clear boundaries demarcating which occasions might yield useful data, or when I might encounter people willing—and indeed eager—to talk about sex. Simply wearing a Babeland T-shirt in public became a magnet for strangers who wanted to talk about their experience shopping for sex toys at Babeland or a similar store.

These seemingly random conversations and serendipitous encounters were actually data points, snippets of talk that revealed something meaningful about Babeland's brand recognition and reach; they also spoke to the ways in which the talking sex part of its mission extended far beyond the limits of its retail stores and website. And finally, these moments also said something about me, and the degree to which I had internalized the idea that sexuality should be talked about and studied as we would any other social phenomenon.

## The Cultural Production of Sexuality

*Vibrator Nation* can be situated within the larger research tradition of studies of cultural production, an approach that has historically "sought to make concrete the universe in which designated 'cultural producers' (TV writers, broadcast journalists, filmmakers, etc.) do what they do."[34] Scholars have analyzed the making of television shows, consumer markets, magazines, and organizations, revealing the broader institutional contexts, practices, and processes that give rise to specific cultural texts and meanings.[35] In the field of sexuality studies, there is a growing body of scholarship that draws on these traditions to examine how sexual commerce and culture—the pornography industry, legal brothels, strip clubs, and BDSM clubs—are produced and organized.[36]

The focus of this book is brick-and-mortar feminist sex-toy stores, those physical spaces where customers can interact directly with sexual products and the people who sell them.[37] Like other forms of popular culture, retail stores are made; they are produced by social actors—store owners, managers, sales staff, and marketers—who cultivate specific kinds of shopping environments with particular audiences in mind.[38] Through the careful design of their retail spaces, the types of inventory they carry, the strategic display of merchandise, and their direct appeals to consumers on the basis of gender, race, social class, and cultural taste, feminist sex-toy retailers actively cultivate ideas about sexual identity and the role that consumption plays in people's lives. They also produce what French philosopher Michel Foucault has described as a "proliferation of discourses concerned with sex"—specific messages about sexual empowerment, education, and well-being—and a corresponding set of retail practices aimed at transforming the sexual self.[39] As one staff sex educator at Babeland explained, "We don't just sell products. We sell information; we sell education; we sell our mission [which is] making the world a safer place for happy, healthy, sexual beings."[40] In other words, feminist sex-toy stores produce a particular understanding of what it means to be a happy, healthy, and sexually empowered individual, and offer a consumer-oriented agenda for how this might be achieved.

At the center of this retail universe is the discourse—and, one might argue, sexual ethic—of sex positivity. Sex positivity is a way of conceptualizing and talking about sexuality that seeks to intervene in a culture overwhelmingly shaped by the belief that sex is a dangerous, destructive, and negative force.[41] Longtime Good Vibrations staff sexologist Carol Queen explains that sex positivity is both a social critique and a "cultural philosophy that understands sexuality as a potentially positive force in one's life. . . . It allows for and in fact celebrates sexual diversity, differing desires, and relationship structures and individual choices based on consent."[42] This includes the idea that the more encouragement and support people have around their sexuality, the better; that everyone deserves access to accurate information about sex; and that people should not be embarrassed or ashamed for wanting more sexual pleasure in their lives. Sex positivity functions as an ideological matrix that informs virtually every aspect of the Good Vibrations retail model, from marketing and advertising to product selection and customer service.

Today, feminist sex-toy stores sit at the epicenter of a growing network of sex-positive cultural production and consumption, serving as sites of distribution for sex toys, books, and other products aimed at enhancing people's sexual lives and relationships. Good Vibrations has also served as a launching pad for a number of sex-positive writers, educators, and pornographers who have impacted the broader culture in significant ways. Author Susie Bright was working at Good Vibrations in the 1980s when she helped found *On Our Backs*, a magazine for the "adventurous lesbian"; Marilyn Bishara started Vixen Creations, a silicone dildo manufacturing company, in 1992 when she was plugging away as a computer programmer at Good Vibrations; Jackie Strano and Shar Rednour, the creative forces behind lesbian porn company SIR Video, conceived the *Bend Over Boyfriend* series of instructional sex videos while working on the Good Vibrations sales floor in the late 1990s; and filmmaker Shine Louise Houston, the founder of Pink and White Productions, an award-winning porn company known for featuring queer people of color, credits Good Vibrations for teaching her about sex positivity. And the list goes on.

This book brings the history of feminist sex-toy stores to life. In the chapters ahead, I detail how, since the early 1970s, sex-positive feminist retailers in the United States have used consumer culture as an instrument for sexual consciousness-raising and social change by imbuing sex toys and sex-toy stores with new kinds of cultural and political possibilities. A number of cultural critics have argued that radical politics are at odds with or hostile to consumer capitalism.[43] Others suggest that the sex industry is the epitome of crass commercialism and gendered exploitation, a male-dominated sphere that is inherently inhospitable to women.[44] My research challenges these perspectives. I argue that feminist sex-toy stores have created a viable counterpublic sphere for sex-positive entrepreneurship and retail activism, one where the idea that the personal is political is deployed in the service of a progressive—and potentially transformative—sexual politics. And yet, as readers will see, there is nothing self-evident about how discourses of sexual education, empowerment, feminism, and consumer capitalism mediate and rearticulate each other within these decidedly commercial spaces. The tension between defining and advancing a feminist mission in these stores and ensuring their financial success has led to sharp debates among owners and staff—at times threatening the stores' very survival. As store owners have attempted to define what it means to be a successful feminist business in the context of capitalism, they have come up against a number of related questions. What do they describe as their brand of feminism and who is included? How do they legitimize their businesses in a culture where sex is seen as dirty without resorting to stereotypes about race, class, and gender? What possibilities, moreover, do commercialized versions of feminist politics enable and what might they foreclose?

Cultural theorist Michael Warner argues that sexual autonomy requires "more than freedom of choice, tolerance and the liberalization of sex laws. It requires access to pleasures and possibilities, since people commonly do not know their sexual desires until they find them."[45] Warner suggests that although people do not go shopping for sexual identities, they nonetheless have a stake in a culture that enables sexual variance and freely circulates knowledge about it. Without these things people have no other way of discovering what they might or might not want when it comes to sex.

My research on the history of feminist sex-toy stores in the United States and the growth of the women's market for sex toys and pornography suggests that many people do in fact go shopping for sexual identities and information, and the range of practices and possibilities that such knowledge enables. This book is my attempt to detail how feminist entrepreneurs are redefining the sexual marketplace and redrawing the boundaries between sexual commerce and politics—one conversation, one vibrator, and one orgasm at a time.

# one

# THE BUSINESS
# OF MASTURBATION

———

> We are tired of being confronted . . . with the idea that the vaginal orgasm, no matter what any woman says, is the real orgasm. We are also tired of being told that we should be sexual objects, but we should not be sexual beings. For these reasons, we decided that we would like to hold a sexuality conference. . . . So, we come together in the spirit of individual feminism and individual identity and decision-making, to define, explore, and celebrate our own sexuality, each of us in our own ways, and hopefully sharing this with our sisters.
>
> JUDY WENNING
> "President's Remarks," National Organization
> for Women's Sexuality Conference

Betty Dodson stood stage left and looked out at the sea of women in front of her. Her dark hair was cut short, her body taut from yoga. Behind her, a six-foot-tall color slide of a woman's vulva was projected onto a large screen. It was June 10, 1973, the final day of the National Organization for Women's (NOW) groundbreaking conference on female sexuality at P.S. Intermediate School 29 on the Upper East Side of Manhattan. Dodson's slide show, "Creating a Female Genital Aesthetic," was making its debut in front of a packed room of conference attendees.

Dodson, who had been running masturbation workshops for women out of her Manhattan apartment for the past year, was convinced that women needed to see images illustrating just how diverse and beautiful vulvas actually were. She knew what it was like to grow up feeling ashamed of her body and had encountered many women in her workshops that felt the same way. It wasn't until she was in her mid-thirties—after seeing her first "beaver magazines"—

that she realized just how varied women's genitalia were. "I didn't want other women to suffer what I had gone through—struggling to have vaginal orgasms and avoiding oral sex because I believed there was something wrong with my sex organ," she wrote in her memoir.[1]

The previous day at the conference, Dodson had talked openly about her relationship to her vibrator. "I'm probably hooked on my vibrator," she declared. "I'm probably going steady with it, but I'll worry about that later."[2] She had also taught a workshop called Liberating Masturbation and Orgasm that was so crowded it spilled out into the hallway. Now, she was talking about women getting to know their genitals as an important first step in sexual self-discovery. As the slide show progressed, she pointed to the different shapes, sizes, and colors of the vulvas projected onto the screen. "This is a classical cunt," she said about one image. "This is a baroque cunt," she remarked about another.

The audience was quiet at first, unsure what to make of the larger-than-life vulvas displayed in front of them. Some women giggled nervously, while others stormed out, offended by Dodson's use of the word "cunt." One attendee later recalled, "I started out watching [the slide show] with a huge 'Ugh! Cunts look revoltingly unaesthetic . . . no, ugly, to me.'"[3] But as the slide show progressed, the woman's attitude began to shift. She forced herself to look at each slide, and as she listened to Dodson's running commentary about the beauty of women's genitals, she became what she called a "cunt-appreciator."[4]

The NOW Women's Sexuality Conference was one of the first events of its kind. According to reports, more than a thousand women and nearly a hundred men attended the two-day conference, which featured more than forty workshops for women on topics as varied as older women's sexuality, lesbianism, race and sexuality, sexual fantasies, and nonmonogamy, with a separate series of workshops for men. Although previous feminist conferences had addressed issues such as sex roles, marriage, and women's health, the NOW event was heralded in the popular press as the first major conference "to concentrate on . . . 'physical liberation' and sexual pleasure," and to explore what it meant to be both sexual and a feminist.[5]

The conference opened with a stirring "speak-out." Borrowing from the tradition of feminist consciousness-raising, in which women shared their personal experiences as a basis for political analysis, a number of women took turns at the microphone to talk about their sexuality. While Dodson joked about her vibrator, others spoke candidly about open marriage, swinging, bisexuality, childhood sexual abuse, and heterosexual power dynamics. They

Betty Dodson at the 1973 NOW Women's Sexuality Conference in New York City.
Courtesy of Betty Dodson.

shared stories about sexual exploration and expressed frustration about the sexual double standard. "I am thankful to the people in the women's movement and in the gay movement who have paved the way to loosening the shackles on sexuality," said one speaker. "I'm optimistic that, by sharing our experiences, ridding ourselves of myths, by exploring our sexuality, by conferences like this, [and] most of all, by talking honestly with each other, we will all be able to enjoy our sexuality more and more fully."[6]

The event was not without moments of controversy and dissent, a sign that not all feminists were on the same page when it came to sexuality. Some women objected to the presence of men; others felt that the image that Dodson had drawn for the conference flyer and poster was too masculine in appearance. Despite these dustups, the conference organizers and attendees alike considered it an overwhelming success. Laura Scharf, one of the event's key coordinators, described it as a "marathon consciousness-raising experience" and claimed that for many women it was the "first time we could verbally explore our feelings about our sexuality, confront our doubts and questions, cut through the traditional rhetoric handed to us, and establish our own priorities and definitions."[7]

The NOW conference created a space for women to come together and talk

Betty Dodson discussing vibrators at the 1973 NOW Women's Sexuality Conference in New York City. Courtesy of Betty Dodson.

about their sexuality at a time when there were few opportunities to do so. It also presented female sexuality in explicitly political terms, a part of women's lives that intersected with power in ways that feminists needed to take seriously. As conference coordinator Dell Williams wrote in the proceedings, "If freeing ourselves from sexual imprisonment is not a political issue, I don't know what is." The real sexual revolution, she predicted, "will begin in the women's movement."[8]

By the start of the 1970s, many women who had been active in and influenced by the social movements of the 1960s, including the so-called sexual revolution, had become disillusioned. Sex outside of marriage and non-monogamy may have offered women new ways of thinking about their sex lives, but open relationships did not bring an end to the sexual double standard, and the freedom to sleep with whomever they wanted did little to eliminate unequal power dynamics between men and women. Suddenly, according to historian Ruth Rosen, "peer pressure to say yes replaced the old obligation to say no."[9] Many women saw the sexual revolution as a decidedly male revolution that had left sexism largely in place. "Most of us found out [the sexual revolution] was not liberation at all, but only a different game," NOW's Judy Wenning recalled. "We were supposed to be performing well and we no longer had the option of not performing."[10] As a response, women began participating in sexual consciousness-raising groups and openly discussing the benefits of masturbation. They were challenging the idea of the vaginal orgasm and, in some cases, working with sex therapists in an effort to become orgasmic. Women were sharing information with each other and developing an expressly political language for talking about sexuality.

The history of sex-positive feminist activism and entrepreneurship in the United States has its roots in these heady days, when female masturbation and orgasm were being framed as fundamental ingredients of women's liberation. What was for many women a search for the elusive orgasm helped produce new kinds of cultural spaces—feminist sexuality conferences, consciousness-raising groups, and vibrator shops—where women could learn about their bodies and talk openly about their sexuality. The first wave of sex-positive feminist entrepreneurs in the 1970s combined elements from a grassroots, do-it-yourself liberal feminism with key tenets from humanistic sexology, the latter of which asserted that women had a fundamental right to sexual information and pleasure. Pioneers such as Betty Dodson and Dell Williams placed sexual liberation at the forefront of their feminist agendas, helping to establish a foundation upon which future generations of feminist entrepreneurs would build.

## The Politics of Female Orgasms

Feminist writers and activists of the early 1970s were beginning to develop a radical analysis of sex and power that upended traditional ways of thinking about female sexuality. Sexuality was not just a matter of biology, they argued; rather, it was a set of practices and beliefs firmly embedded in and shaped by a complex web of social arrangements, scientific discourses, and gendered power relations that supported the patriarchal status quo.

Feminists took off their gloves and took aim squarely at Sigmund Freud and his theory of the vaginal orgasm. Freud had popularized the idea that the vaginal orgasm was an essential part of a healthy female sexuality. In Freud's schema, the clitoral orgasm reflected an infantile sexuality, whereas the vaginal orgasm represented a more mature and therefore desirable state of female sexual development. "With the change to femininity from an earlier stage of development the clitoris should wholly or in part hand over its sensitivity, and at the same time its importance, to the vagina," Freud wrote.[11] Women who failed to achieve vaginal orgasms through sexual intercourse were labeled as frigid, a condition that was thought to require psychiatric intervention and even medical treatment.

Anne Koedt, a founding member of the New York Radical Feminists, railed against Freud in her influential essay, "The Myth of the Vaginal Orgasm." Koedt argued that Freud and those who subscribed to his ideas defined female sexuality almost exclusively in terms of what pleased men. "Women are fed the myth of the liberated woman and her vaginal orgasm—an orgasm which in fact does not exist."[12] Koedt denounced Freud's theory of the vaginal orgasm, which, she argued, had caused undue distress for countless women who either "suffered silently with self-blame or flocked to the psychiatrist looking desperately for the hidden and terrible repression that kept them from their vaginal destiny."[13] Women's sexual situation could be vastly improved if people engaged with facts instead of fiction: The clitoris, and not the vagina, was the center of female sexual pleasure and orgasm.

In "Organs and Orgasms," writer Alix Shulman wasted no time declaring that the term "vaginal orgasm" must go. "The penis and the vagina can either make babies or male orgasms, but very rarely do the two together make female orgasms."[14] According to Shulman, a concern with female sexual pleasure was nowhere to be found in the male-oriented definition of sex: "The word about the clitoris has been out for a long time, and still, for political reasons, society goes on believing the old myths and enforcing a double standard of sexuality."[15] Women's bodies were not failing women, she asserted; society was.

Feminists drew on the work of Alfred Kinsey and Masters and Johnson to bolster their claims about the primacy of the clitoris in female sexual response. A zoologist turned sex researcher, Kinsey was one of the first scientists to approach female sexuality as a topic worthy of serious inquiry.[16] According to sociologist Janice Irvine, "Kinsey discussed [women's] sexual pleasure, separated the concept of sexual pleasure from reproduction, cited the pleasures of masturbation, and regarded women as sexual agents."[17] He challenged many taken-for-granted assumptions about female sexuality, including the idea that sexual intercourse was the primary source of female sexual pleasure. Kinsey also took psychoanalysts to task for minimizing the importance of the clitoris: "Some of the psychoanalysts and some other clinicians insist that only vaginal stimulation and 'vaginal orgasm' can provide a psychologically satisfactory culmination to the activity of a 'sexually mature' female. It is difficult, however, in the light of our present understanding of the anatomy and physiology of sexual response, to understand what can be meant by the 'vaginal orgasm.'"[18] Kinsey maintained that far too many women had been needlessly distressed by what he described as a "biologic impossibility."[19] His bold challenge to the concept of the vaginal orgasm, an idea that had held sway for decades, was later described by Irvine as planting a "time bomb that would not explode" until the sex research of Masters and Johnson was published in the mid-1960s.[20]

Masters and Johnson's research on female sexuality corroborated Kinsey's findings and added an important physiological dimension to Kinsey's ambitious sex surveys. Masters and Johnson argued that the clitoris had suffered from decades of "phallic fallacies" that had ignored both the anatomical evidence and the lived reality of women's subjective experiences.[21] The clitoris was the center of the female orgasm and the claim that there were two separate and distinct kinds of orgasms—the vaginal and clitoral—was simply not supported by scientific evidence.

The essays that emerged from within the women's movement about the politics of female sexuality were self-consciously political tracts, feminist interventions into what women's health writer and activist Rebecca Chalker has described as a "male-centered, heterosexual model of human sexuality."[22] Feminists argued that the myth of the vaginal orgasm, as a discourse and a corresponding set of practices, produced a version of female sexuality that was anchored in heterosexual intercourse, a social-sexual arrangement that ultimately benefited men and supported patriarchy. Good Vibrations founder Joani Blank put a finer point on it: "In those days," she said, "when we were discussing vaginal and clitoral orgasms, we used to say that the only people who reliably have vaginal orgasms are men."[23]

Feminists of the early 1970s were beginning to fill in the gaps of missing information about their bodies, which included rediscovering the clitoris. Women took off their pants, grabbed their speculums, and reclaimed their vaginas—and their orgasms—from the medical establishment, all while advancing the idea, popularized by the women's health movement, that knowledge is power. "Using self-examination, personal observation and meticulous analysis," a group of women from the Federation of Feminist Women's Health Centers "arrived at *a new view of the clitoris*."[24] They found that there was far more to the clitoris than just the visible glans and shaft. It was a complex structure with hidden parts under the skin—erectile tissue, glands, muscles, blood vessels, and nerves—that surrounded and extended along the vagina. The fact that women experienced pleasure during sexual intercourse was not surprising, they argued, given just how extensive the anatomy of the clitoris actually was. For once and for all, they declared, we can "put to rest forever the controversy over clitoral and vaginal orgasms."[25]

Feminist writers and activists generated new ways to think about women's bodies and sexual responses that were not necessarily contingent upon what author Ti-Grace Atkinson referred to as the "institution of sexual intercourse."[26] They drew attention to the gendered dimensions of power embedded in the social construction of heterosexuality and made a compelling case for how the theory of the vaginal orgasm supported women's sexual subordination. They also, importantly, expressed women's sexual concerns in explicitly political rather than individual terms. As Shulman noted, "Now that women . . . are beginning to talk together and compare notes, they are discovering that their experiences are remarkably similar and that they are not freaks. . . . It is not they who have individual sex problems; it is society that has one great big political problem."[27] This shift in emphasis, from the personal to the political, and the individual to the social, would prove crucial to feminist analyses of, and interventions into, the patriarchal status quo. In privileging the clitoris as the site of female orgasm, feminists were producing a powerful set of counterdiscourses that would eventually be incorporated into a number of feminist projects aimed at educating and empowering women around their sexuality. Women's sexuality could no longer be reduced to their vaginas. Women had clitorises—complex organs with thousands of nerve endings—and they were encouraged to learn how they worked.

As important as these theoretical contributions were, it would take more than feminist polemics and a nod toward scientific evidence to dismantle widely accepted understandings of female sexuality that had long suppressed information about women's bodies. The stories emerging from within feminist consciousness-raising groups revealed that many women were not having orgasms, had never masturbated, and were deeply sexually dissatisfied. There was a growing sentiment in certain corners of the women's movement that women—and indeed society as a whole—needed to be sexually reprogrammed. Women needed encouragement, especially from other women, to move beyond scientific data and text-based theories of female pleasure and into the concrete realm of sexual exploration and discovery. For Betty Dodson, masturbation was the bridge between an abstract theory of female sexual autonomy and its tangible expression.

## Betty Dodson's Feminist Body Trip

In the early 1970s, Betty Dodson turned the living room of her Manhattan apartment into a feminist pleasure studio and began offering physical and sexual consciousness-raising groups for women. She got rid of her furniture, installed wall-to-wall carpeting, scattered pillows on the floor, and hung erotic art on the walls. Dodson called these groups Bodysex Workshops. Conducted in the nude, the workshops included yoga and deep breathing exercises designed to increase participants' body awareness. They also included an unabashedly naked Dodson demonstrating how to use a vibrator to masturbate to climax. In 1974, Dodson self-published *Liberating Masturbation*, a radical feminist manifesto on self-love that Dell Williams would later describe as rippling "through the women's movement like an orgasm."[28]

Dodson was not always a sexual renegade. Born in Wichita, Kansas, in 1929, she made her way to New York City in 1950 with $250 in her pocket and the dream of becoming an illustrator. She enrolled in art school and fell in love with drawing the human nude. Like so many women coming of age in the 1950s, Dodson felt torn between getting married and having a career. While the more traditional side of her longed to fit into the version of postwar domesticity that dominated popular culture—minus the children—the rebellious part of her wanted to compete with men as equals, including in the bedroom.[29]

The fantasy of marital bliss and financial security eventually won out, and in 1959, at the age of twenty-nine, Dodson got married. She quit her job as a commercial artist and became, in her words, "a professional wife who painted." She soon realized, however, that marriage was not all it was cracked up to be. She had a husband who doted on her but had little interest in sex. Before long, sex had dwindled to once a month and, when it did happen, her husband climaxed too fast and she wouldn't have an orgasm at all. Frustrated, she started secretly masturbating under the covers after her husband fell asleep.[30] Resigned to a sexless relationship, Dodson was quietly relieved when, after more than five years of marriage, her husband left her for his secretary.

It was 1965. The sexual revolution was picking up steam, and Dodson, who was now thirty-five, was single and ready to explore her newfound freedom. Dodson's divorce was a turning point in her life, a new beginning that was aided, in part, by the first sexual relationship she entered following her marriage. Her lover, Grant Taylor, a former English professor, had also recently left a sexually unfulfilling marriage. In Taylor, Dodson found a sexual ally—

someone as hungry and inquisitive about sex as she was. The two embarked on a passionate affair marked by sexual openness and exploration. According to Dodson, they began "mainlining sex."[31] They talked openly about their sexual pasts, which were wrought with guilt and shame, especially about masturbation. "We both knew that masturbation had saved our sexual sanity and we vowed that we'd never again consider it a 'second-rate' sexual activity."[32] Dodson and Taylor incorporated masturbation into their sex life and used it as a way to learn about each other's bodies and sexual responses. Their relationship, which lasted for years, included nonmonogamy, threesomes, and group sex, and created a space where Dodson could begin to sift through the various messages she had learned about sex, love, and relationships. Dodson vowed to make guilt-free sex an ongoing part of her life.

It was Taylor who first introduced Dodson to the electric vibrator. One day, when he was getting a haircut, his barber gave him a scalp massage with a vibrator strapped to the back of his hand. That same day, he went to a barber supply store and purchased one, thinking that it would be great for sex. The device looked like a small cement mixer and Dodson was unsure about having sex with a vibrating machine attached to her hand. It didn't take long, however, for her to realize that vibrators had the potential to "create a more level playing field for women's orgasms."[33] She began experimenting with different models—the Oster, the Panabrator, and the Hitachi Magic Wand—and incorporated them into her group sex parties and, eventually, her masturbation workshops.

British physician Joseph Mortimer Granville invented the electric vibrator in the 1880s as a way to treat nervous conditions of various kinds, including, most notably, female hysteria, which encompassed a wide range of symptomatology, from anxiety to melancholia to insomnia.[34] Vibrators were initially mass marketed as medical technology and home beauty and health devices that could be used to treat any number of maladies in both women and men. A user manual published by the Shelton Electric Company in 1917 extolling the vibrator's virtues listed eighty-six diseases it claimed could be treated by vibration and massage, including asthma, dandruff, impotency, obesity, watery eyes, and wrinkles. With regular use, the manufacturer asserted, the Shelton vibrator would restore "such a wholesome, sparkling degree of vigor that life will present a new aspect to the man or woman who has moped along in a semi-invalid condition for a long period."[35] Although their erotic uses were known, advertisers in the early twentieth century were coy, using coded language to both hint at and mask the vibrator's sexual capabilities. Vibrators

Images from the Shelton Vibrators user guide, 1917. Republished in 1981 by Down There Press. Courtesy of Joani Blank.

began to be openly sold as sex toys in the 1960s, and by the early 1970s, feminists, including Dodson, had recast them as indispensable tools of women's liberation.

It did not take long for Dodson's artwork to begin to reflect her developing sexual consciousness. Her first one-woman show of erotic art, the *Love Picture Exhibition*, took place in a Manhattan art gallery in 1968 and depicted couples having sex. Two years later, she devoted her second one-woman show to the topic of masturbation and, according to her, "all hell broke loose."[36] The four larger-than-life drawings of people masturbating caused a stir the day they were delivered to the art gallery. The director of the gallery initially refused to hang the pictures, and Dodson, who was not one to cave to censorship, threatened to withdraw the show. A compromise was eventually reached when two of the four drawings were hung. A six-foot drawing of one of Dodson's girlfriends, shown naked and masturbating with a vibrator, adorned the gallery's main wall. Many women who attended the show admitted to Dodson that they didn't masturbate, and many men said they had no idea that women masturbated. These revelations bolstered Dodson's belief that female sexual repression was directly related to the social prohibitions surrounding masturbation. In order for women to be truly liberated, they would need to "get a handle on their sexuality" — and this included taking control of their orgasms.[37]

Dodson was not the only person in the early 1970s determined to recuperate masturbation from what one author described as the "twilight zone of the sexual spectrum."[38] Religious authorities had for centuries positioned masturbation as an offense against God and nature; and medical practitioners claimed it caused disease, insanity, and social-sexual maladjustment, especially for habitual masturbators. By the early 1970s, the taboos around masturbation were starting to fade. The sexual revolution, combined with the rise of feminism and the gay and lesbian liberation movement, had produced a cultural climate in which masturbation and other forms of sexual expression were more openly discussed. "For the first time in history," wrote historian Thomas Laqueur, "masturbation was embraced as a mode of liberation, a claim to autonomy, to pleasure for its own sake, an escape from the socially prescribed path toward normal adulthood. It went from being the deviant sexuality of the wrong kind of social order to being the foundational sexuality of new sorts of imagined communities."[39] New cultural discourses about masturbation, and female masturbation specifically, were emerging.

*Our Bodies, Ourselves*, the groundbreaking women's health book, devoted an entire chapter to sexuality, including challenging the idea that masturbation was bad or that it would keep women from enjoying sex with men. Statistics, the authors argued, showed that women who masturbated were more likely to have orgasms than those who didn't. "Masturbation is not something to do just when you don't have a man. . . . It's the first, easiest and most convenient way to experiment with your body. It's a way to find out what feels good, with how much pressure, at what tempo, and how often."[40] Other books echoed this sentiment. In 1972, the National Sex Forum published the booklet *Masturbation Techniques for Women/Getting in Touch*, as part of its Yes Book of Sex series.[41] The authors encouraged women to give themselves permission to learn about their bodies and to say yes to their orgasms. "We want to assist you in learning to masturbate and come by yourself. This is a natural desire and you have a right to enjoy your own body, all of it, from head to toe."[42]

Founded in 1968 as part of the Glide Urban Center in San Francisco, the National Sex Forum aimed to develop educational and training materials that would be relevant to people working in the counseling professions. According to Janice Irvine, the forum became an influential part of the humanistic branch of sexology. Rooted in the human potential movement that had popularized experiential practices such as sensitivity training and encounter groups, humanistic sexology flourished in the 1960s and 1970s, especially in California.[43] With the slogan, "We believe that it is time to say 'yes' to sex," the forum asserted a highly individualistic, do-your-own-thing approach to sexuality.[44] The goal of humanistic sexology was less about advancing a scientific understanding of sexuality in the manner of researchers such as Kinsey and Masters and Johnson, and more about enhancing sexual performance and communication, and celebrating the liberatory potential of good sex.

The National Sex Forum and its Yes series on sexuality employed a basic set of premises in what was arguably an early articulation of sex positivity. Sex, the authors posited, plays an important role in everyone's life; it can and should be discussed casually and nonjudgmentally; individuals have the right to know the facts about sex; everyone has a right to a good sex life; and sex is okay in whatever form of expression it takes.[45] These ideas took shape in and through a language of sexual liberalism that constructed sexual rights as basic human rights, a position shared by a growing number of writers, activists, therapists, and educators in the early 1970s, including Betty Dodson.

Dodson's message was brilliant in its simplicity: If women took control of their orgasms, she argued, they'd be more empowered to take control of their lives. The key to this, according to her, was masturbation: "[Masturbation is] the way we discover our eroticism, the way we learn to respond sexually, the way we learn to love ourselves and build self-esteem. Sexual skill and the ability to respond are not 'natural' in our society. Doing what 'comes naturally' for us is to be sexually inhibited. Sex is like any other skill—it has to be learned and practiced. When a woman masturbates, she learns to like her own genitals, to enjoy sex and orgasm, and furthermore, to become proficient and independent about it."[46]

Dodson took many of the ideas about female sexuality that were circulating at the time and packaged them into a coherent program aimed at educating and empowering women around their sexuality. She brought together the principles of consciousness-raising, which used women's personal experiences as a starting point for feminist theory and action, with guided sexual exploration and body work to create a new mode of feminist praxis.

Dodson believed in the power of images. Most women, she claimed, had no idea what female masturbation or the buildup of sexual tension actually looked like, so they had no reliable way to identify what was happening to their bodies when they became sexually aroused. In her masturbation demonstrations, Dodson offered women an "erotic testimonial" that was designed to give them the visible evidence of female sexual response she felt they were missing.[47] "In my mind, what I was doing was based on pure logic," she told me.[48] One woman who attended one of Dodson's workshops in the early 1970s later recalled that it was "fascinating to see other women come, to realize that women didn't necessarily flip out in exaggerated orgasmic seizures as pornography and literature would have us believe."[49]

Not all feminists embraced Dodson's pro-masturbation message. Many women resisted vibrators because they felt they were too mechanical, while others feared they might become addicted. For Dodson, *Ms.* magazine symbolized feminism's ambivalence about female sexuality in general and masturbation specifically.

In 1971, editors at *Ms.* asked Dodson to write an article about masturbation for the fledgling publication. Dodson submitted a seventeen-page manifesto titled "Liberating Masturbation," in which she described her sexual philosophy, including the belief that women needed to take charge of their own orgasms. According to Dodson, the article sat on someone's desk for more than two years because the magazine's editors feared they might lose subscribers.[50] A heavily edited and much shorter version was eventually published as "Getting to Know Me" in the August 1974 issue.

While editors at *Ms.* may have been nervous about running an article that openly discussed the benefits of female masturbation, Dodson's essay clearly struck a chord with readers. Several women wrote letters to the magazine expressing their appreciation for the essay. According to a reader from Dallas, "The subject of masturbation is so often avoided that even we women who enjoy and accept it often wonder if we are the only ones."[51] "Masturbation is part of knowing oneself," another wrote. "Coming alone is different from coming with another person, but both are dynamic motions and together contribute to a complete experience. Dodson is so right—masturbation is not second-rate sex."[52]

Dodson was a cheerleader for female masturbation at a time when few women were uttering the word, becoming, as Susie Bright would later describe her, "Yoko Ono with a vibrator."[53] Dodson challenged the sexual double standard that maintained that sex was the province of men, but not women, and dismissed the idea that women's sexual pleasure was dependent on erections and intercourse. She made it her mission to teach women about their clitorises and railed against what she described as an "anti-sexual social system."[54] In many ways, Dodson did for sexual dogma in the 1970s what *Our Bodies, Ourselves* had done for medical dogma: she "validated women's embodied experiences as a resource for challenging . . . dogmas about women's bodies and, consequently, as a strategy for personal and collective empowerment."[55] Dodson utilized women's experiential knowledge as a form of sexual pedagogy and encouraged women to become their own experts. But perhaps most significantly, she gave many women the permission they needed to explore their bodies, take control of their orgasms, and make sexual pleasure a greater priority in their lives. One of these women was Dell Williams.

## "We Grow Pleasurable Things for Women"

Dell Williams stood in front of apartment 12B. Her heart was pounding. It was spring 1973, and it had taken her months to work up the courage to attend one of Betty Dodson's Bodysex Workshops. She knew that once she stepped inside the apartment she would have to take off all her clothes. As she stood outside Dodson's door, her finger on the buzzer, she was filled with a mix of curiosity and trepidation. She was fifty years old, and despite her nerves, she realized she was taking an important first step toward having a new relationship to her body and to sex.

"Here I was," Williams recounted years later, "going into a room, having to be completely nude. It was a little scary. When I got to the door, Betty was standing there completely nude, and she said 'hello.' Her honesty and forthrightness . . . didn't indicate any guilt, fear, or shame that most women are prone to when it comes to sex. There she was, pure truth."[56]

Surrounded by other naked women, Williams let go of her inhibitions. Dodson led the group through a series of exercises to build body awareness and confidence. They talked about their relationship to their bodies and participated in a genital "show and tell"[57]—the first time that Williams had ever looked at her own vulva, or anyone else's. But the highlight for Williams was watching Dodson pick up a Hitachi Magic Wand and masturbate to orgasm. Her initial thought was, "How can a mechanical thing make any difference?" But Williams and the rest of the women followed Dodson's lead. It was the first time Williams had ever used a vibrator, and although she couldn't recall whether or not she had an orgasm that day, she vividly remembered the energy in the room. It was "pulsing" from "all the heat that was happening."[58]

"That was an incredible experience," she told me, "and that kind of catapulted me into what eventually became Eve's Garden."

Imbued with a newfound confidence, Williams took a trip to Macy's in Midtown Manhattan to buy a Hitachi Magic Wand. It was an item marketed and sold by Macy's and other department stores as a body massager. When Williams asked the salesman for help, he responded by asking her what she wanted the massager for. His voice was loud and Williams was afraid that others around her might hear him. "I felt like everybody on that floor knew I was buying that thing so I could masturbate with it."[59] Embarrassed, and just wanting to purchase the item and leave, she quietly mumbled, "To massage my back."

Williams's experience at Macy's left her feeling frustrated and angry. Despite her newfound sexual confidence, years of sexual shame had not simply evaporated overnight. The encounter also left her wondering how many other women had experienced similar discomfort and embarrassment when trying to buy their vibrators. Women, she thought, should be selling these things to other women. And so, in 1974, at the age of fifty-two, Williams founded Eve's Garden, the first business in the United States exclusively devoted to women's sexual pleasure and health.

There was very little in Williams's background to suggest that she would one day start a feminist vibrator business. Born Dell Zetlin in the Bronx in 1922, Williams was the older of two children born to Russian émigrés who had come to America by way of Paris. An average student, Williams skipped college and went straight to work after high school. Her real dream, though, was to someday become an actress and singer. Williams joined the Women's Army Corps in 1945 and was classified as an entertainment specialist. Her days in the army were among the happiest of her life. After the army, she moved to Los Angeles, where she took singing and dancing lessons and tried to break into show business. By the early 1950s she was back in New York, working in the typing pool at the United Nations. She was briefly married and subsequently divorced. In the early 1970s, while working as an account executive at an advertising agency, she discovered feminism, and her life was forever changed.

In 1970 Williams joined more than 100,000 demonstrators, including Betty Friedan, Eleanor Holmes Norton, and Bella Abzug, in a historic march for women's rights that filled Fifth Avenue from sidewalk to sidewalk. It was as if a lightbulb had been turned on. Williams jumped feet first into the women's movement and became an active member of NOW. "I was just passionate about our endeavor to change the world and bring about equal rights for women," Williams told me. "I don't know whether younger women will understand the kind of passion and commitment we had for that, because we came from a time where women were conscious of the fact that [we] just didn't have all of the opportunities."[60]

Eve's Garden founder Dell Williams in her New York City retail
showroom, circa 1976. Courtesy of the Dell Williams papers, #7676,
Division of Rare and Manuscript Collections, Cornell University Library.

Several years later, Judy Wenning, president of the New York City chapter of NOW, asked Williams to coordinate the organization's landmark conference on women's sexuality. Before then, Williams recalled, women were talking about equality in the workplace and in the political arena, but nobody was talking about sex.

During the planning stages of the conference Williams was approached by a man who wanted to sell vibrators at the event. She told him he couldn't unless he was part of a woman-owned company. He said he was—Williams would later learn he had lied—and they struck a deal: for every vibrator he sold, he would donate $1 to NOW. Afterward, NOW ended up with $110, and Williams once again wondered why women weren't in the business of selling vibrators to other women.[61]

Williams contacted several feminist entrepreneurs she knew at the time who were selling buttons, T-shirts, bumper stickers, and other movement-based material, and asked if they would add vibrators to their product mix. No one was interested. Perhaps, Williams thought, they were intimidated by the prospect of being labeled the "vibrator lady," or maybe they were concerned that they would no longer be able to advertise in feminist venues, such as *Ms.* magazine. "I thought, 'Well, if nobody is going to do it, I will do it. Why don't I just start this?'" Williams later recalled.[62]

Initially operating part time out of her Manhattan apartment, Williams put together a two-page mimeographed catalog that featured two vibrators, the Hitachi Magic Wand and the Prelude 2. She also included Dodson's self-published pamphlet, *Liberating Masturbation*.

Word about the fledgling vibrator business spread and Williams began opening her apartment on Friday nights so women could shop. Encouraged by the response, in 1975 she placed a small classified ad in *Ms.* (which didn't seem bothered by the prospect of promoting Williams's business). Sandwiched between ads for feminist jewelry, "woman power" T-shirts, and bumper stickers with slogans such as "Adam was a rough draft" and "Sisterhood is powerful," the message was simple and to the point: "Liberating books and vibrators for the sexually-liberated woman."

Women from all over the country wrote to request a catalog, and in no time, orders for vibrators were flooding in. To meet the demand, Williams often stayed up late into the night filling orders, sometimes with the help of her younger brother, Lorenzo. Within a year of starting the business, she had quit her job and moved Eve's Garden out of her home and into an office-showroom in a building directly next door on West Fifty-Seventh Street. She expanded

Early Eve's Garden classified advertisement in *Ms.* magazine, May 1975.

her catalog to include several more vibrators, massage oils, and a variety of books about sexual liberation and women's health, including *Our Bodies, Ourselves* and Nancy Friday's *My Secret Garden*, a collection of women's erotic fantasies. In 1979, Williams opened what she described as an "elegant" retail boutique in another Midtown Manhattan location, where she continued to sell vibrators and promote women's right to sexual self-discovery and pleasure.

Williams considered Eve's Garden to be a tangible expression of the women's movement. "I never thought, 'This will be a great business and I'll make money,'" she explained. "That was never my intention." Rather, Williams wanted to create a world in which women felt empowered to celebrate their sexuality, take control of their orgasms, and feel good about themselves. "My ultimate vision, and I had this vision when I started, was that if women could really express their sexuality, get in touch with their energy, use it in their life and feel good, we can change the world. That was my bottom line."[63]

Williams's philosophy was deeply informed by Austrian psychoanalyst Wilhelm Reich, whose theories about sexuality had greatly influenced the field

Eve's Garden mail-order catalogs (L to R) from 1986, 1991, and 1995.
Courtesy of Dell Williams. Photograph by the author.

of humanistic sexology. Years before opening Eve's Garden, Williams had read Reich's book *The Function of the Orgasm* and was surprised to learn that the orgasm had a purpose other than just producing sexual pleasure.

In *The Function of the Orgasm*, Reich argued that there was a connection between sexual energy and life energy.[64] Orgasmic energy played an important role in the life of individuals and the life of society. Reich maintained that a "satisfied genitalia" was a precondition for social productivity and psychic equilibrium.[65] He believed that sex and politics were "deeply linked" and that sexual repression had dire social consequences.[66]

Williams incorporated Reich's biophysical theory of sexuality, and his views on the function of the orgasm as a vital source of life energy, into her feminist politics and her vision for Eve's Garden. "Aside from making you feel good," she wrote in an Eve's Garden catalog, an "[orgasm] was electrically-charged energy that rippled through the body like an ocean wave, leaving in its bubbling wake a myriad of tingling, undulating sensations that swept away all body tension."[67]

If sexual repression led to the imprisonment of mind and body, as Reich suggested, Williams wondered how this had affected women who, as a group, had been sexually repressed for thousands of years. She came to believe that women's lack of social power was directly related to sexual repression, and that in order to dismantle patriarchy, women needed to be empowered sexually. And yet it was also the case that Williams failed to interrogate the ways in which sexual disempowerment and its effects did not necessarily mean the same thing to all women, relying instead on the collective "we" of a presumed universal sisterhood. Nevertheless, she encouraged women to channel their erotic energy not only into their orgasms, but also into projects related to social transformation. As Williams would tell me years later, "I always saw the orgasm as part of the context of the energy of the earth. So yes, I am trying to empower [women] and my motivation is not only for her, me, and all women to be free sexually and take responsibility for their own bodies, but I knew in some sense it would give women the power to change the world."[68]

Williams was convinced that women's erotic energy could be harnessed for the greater good of humankind. "We don't think of our sexual energy as being productive and beautiful and creative, and all of those things. We think of it as only sexy, and that's kind of limiting," she said.[69] She believed that if all the energy in the world was connected, from orgasms to oceans to world peace, a shift in women's erotic energy had the potential to affect other kinds of energy in the universe. In other words, unleashing women's sexual energy would release their creative power, which would lead to a domino effect, one ripple of change producing another and so on. Despite the fact that it takes more than orgasms to eliminate structural problems such as world hunger, poverty, and racism, Williams maintained—with a sense of wide-eyed optimism and unyielding political idealism—that women who had orgasms could change the world.

Eve's Garden quickly established itself as a feminist institution, joining the ranks of other for-profit and not-for-profit feminist organizations that had begun to emerge in the early 1970s, including women's health centers, feminist bookstores, credit unions, and rape crisis centers. These institutions became what historian Alice Echols has described as "islands of resistance" in a patriarchal culture that was often hostile to women, creating opportunities along the way for feminist consciousness-raising and community building.[70]

Williams founded Eve's Garden in the hope of empowering women around their sexuality, and she did this by catering to what she perceived as women's unique sexual sensibilities. These sensibilities, however, closely mirrored her identifications as a primarily heterosexual, white, professional woman. Indeed, Williams's understanding of female sexuality was rooted in a version of feminism that was largely one-dimensional, focusing on women's supposed commonality and what she saw as their shared "erotic sisterhood"—views that shaped how she thought about and marketed her business. Williams originally carried a very small selection of products and books that she personally liked and felt comfortable selling, and avoided ones she did not. In this respect she was both a retailer and a tastemaker, someone who was establishing hierarchies around specific kinds of sexual products and practices. Williams initially declined to carry any bondage gear, because she found BDSM's message about power to be "off-putting."[71] And she considered herself "too fancy" to say "butt plug," preferring instead to refer to these items as "APD"—which stood for "anal pleasure devices."[72] For years, Williams refused to carry dildos, because she personally didn't like the way they looked and figured that other women didn't care for them, either. "Why did they have to look like penises was my big thing," she told me. But customers began to request them, and Williams ultimately realized that feminism's focus on reclaiming the clitoris notwithstanding, there were women who enjoyed the feeling of having something inside of them.

Williams eventually sent a questionnaire to customers asking what style of dildos they might like. Many women wrote to say they wanted an undulating, wavelike design. In the meantime, Gosnell Duncan, a disability rights activist who had been paralyzed from the waist down following an accident, had started to make silicone dildos for his own use. The two began to collaborate on designing nonrepresentational dildos (ones that didn't look like penises) for Eve's Garden customers—giving them names like Venus Rising and Scorpio Rising—ultimately expanding the idea of what women supposedly wanted beyond Williams's somewhat limited sexual tastes and feminist viewpoint.[73]

Williams positioned Eve's Garden as both a feminist outpost for sexual consciousness-raising and a health shop specializing in sex. She hoped her business would become a resource center for the woman who, according to one writer, was "too embarrassed to speak to her neighborhood druggist or family doctor about exploring and expanding her own sexual attitudes and behavior."[74] Williams also reached out to sex therapists. She joined the Society for the Scientific Study of Sexuality and other professional organizations, and attended their conferences, where she would rent a table, distribute copies of her catalog, and sell vibrators.[75] Williams soon established a loyal following of sex therapists and counselors, including Dr. Ruth Westheimer, who routinely referred clients to Eve's Garden.

Williams used her connections with sex therapists in her broader marketing

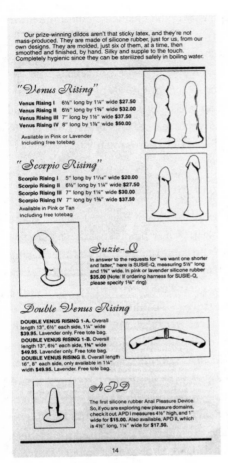

Our prize-winning dildos aren't that sticky latex, and they're not mass-produced. They are made of silicone rubber, just for us, from our own designs. They are molded, just six of them, at a time, then smoothed and finished, by hand. Silky and supple to the touch. Completely hygienic since they can be sterilized safely in boiling water.

*"Venus Rising"*

**Venus Rising I**  6½" long by 1¼" wide **$27.50**
**Venus Rising II**  6½" long by 1¾" wide **$32.00**
**Venus Rising III**  7" long by 1½" wide **$37.50**
**Venus Rising IV**  8" long by 1¾" wide **$50.00**

Available in Pink or Lavender
Including free totebag

*"Scorpio Rising"*

**Scorpio Rising I**  5" long by 1¹¹⁄₁₆" wide **$20.00**
**Scorpio Rising II**  6½" long by 1¼" wide **$27.50**
**Scorpio Rising III**  7" long by 1¼" wide **$30.00**
**Scorpio Rising IV**  7" long by 1⅜" wide **$37.50**
Available in Pink or Tan
Including free totebag

*Suzie-Q*

In answer to the requests for "we want one shorter and fatter," here is SUSIE-Q, measuring 5½" long and 1¾" wide. In pink or lavender silicone rubber **$35.00** (Note: If ordering harness for SUSIE-Q, please specify 1¾" ring)

*Double Venus Rising*

**DOUBLE VENUS RISING 1-A.** Overall length 13", 6½" each side, 1¼" wide **$39.95.** Lavender only. Free tote bag.
**DOUBLE VENUS RISING 1-B.** Overall length 13", 6½" each side, 1¾" wide **$49.95.** Lavender only. Free tote bag.
**DOUBLE VENUS RISING II.** Overall length 16", 8" each side, only available in 1¼" width **$49.95.** Lavender. Free tote bag.

*APD*

The first silicone rubber Anal Pleasure Device. So, if you are exploring new pleasure domains, check it out. APD I measures 4½" high, and 1" wide for **$15.00.** Also available, APD II, which is 4½" long, 1¼" wide for **$17.50.**

14

Selection of dildos in the 1986 edition of the Eve's Garden mail-order catalog. Courtesy of Dell Williams. Photograph by the author.

campaigns. Eve's Garden's early mail-order catalogs, for example, included a page called "What the experts are saying about Eve's Garden." Williams included remarks by psychologist Lonnie Barbach, the author of *For Yourself* ("Eve's Garden has made a very important contribution towards women's affirmation and joyous expression of their sexuality"), and sex educator Shere Hite ("Dell's dedication is tremendous. Her store truly loves women").[76] Eve's Garden's ad copy also made frequent references to the fact that the business's catalog had been "informed by many leading professionals in the field of human sexuality who find our materials helpful in their clinical practices."

Remarks and endorsements from experts within the professional sex therapy community helped legitimize the sale of vibrators to a virtually untapped market of women who, like Williams, were beginning to take control of their sexuality and their orgasms. By emphasizing the business's commitment to sexual health and well-being, Williams was not only distinguishing Eve's Garden from the stereotypically lurid sex shops located just blocks away from her business in Times Square. She was also sanitizing the sale of sexual products in an effort to appeal to, and indeed construct, an entirely different customer base: the sexually curious yet reticent female shopper who needed additional coaxing and encouragement before she would feel comfortable venturing into a vibrator shop—even one owned and operated by a woman.

## What's a Feminist Doing in a Business Like This?

The center of Eve's Garden's mail-order operations during the first year of the business's existence was the kitchen table in Dell Williams's Midtown Manhattan apartment. Each night, Williams would come home exhausted after having finished a long day at the advertising firm where she worked to find more work that needed to be done before she could crawl into bed. Orders for vibrators were pouring in, spilling over onto the stove and countertops.

Many of the orders that Williams received were accompanied by deeply personal letters in which women, and occasionally men, revealed intimate details about their sex lives, shared their joys, and cried with frustration over what they saw as their sexual failings. Envelopes were postmarked from urban centers and rural towns, from one end of the country to the other. Letters were typically handwritten in neatly penned ink—some on floral stationery, others on yellow notebook paper. The correspondents addressed their letters to Dell, Eve, the Gardenkeeper, Ms. Garden, Sister, and, occasionally, Dear Sir or Gentlemen—the latter of which suggested that some people had trouble imagining a vibrator business run by a woman.

Williams read them all and saved many.

One missive arrived in April 1975—a few sentences handwritten on a piece of stationery with a running header across the top, a line from the Equal Rights Amendment: "Equality of rights under the law shall not be denied or abridged by the United States or by any state on account of sex." "Ms. Dell Williams," the note began, "I want to thank you for offering this service to help women fulfill themselves sexually. I know I would never go into a store to buy a vibrator, but thanks to you, I don't need to. All of us are grateful for the help of our sisters in all ways. I am looking forward to receiving my order." In a gesture of feminist solidarity, the letter was signed, "Yours in Sisterhood," followed by a small, carefully outlined woman's symbol.[77] Williams loved receiving letters like this. They fueled her desire to keep going, because they let her know that she was making a genuine difference in women's lives.

People wrote to Williams for any number of reasons. Many praised her work and expressed gratitude that a place like Eve's Garden existed. "Please RUSH my order," one woman wrote. "Just from this step of ordering these items, I feel myself taking greater responsibility for my sexuality." Others sought advice about a specific issue or concern. "My wife thinks she is being too selfish to have such orgasmic pleasure. . . . I could not ask a doctor about this, but could you tell me? Or could you recommend a book which would present only the good, positive response?" one man asked. Occasionally, letters arrived from women who were upset about a product that had failed to deliver the mind-blowing orgasm they had expected. "As soon as I flipped the switch on the Prelude 3, I knew it for a timid, half-hearted wimp of a thing," one woman noted with disappointment.[78]

It is clear from these letters that Eve's Garden made it possible for many women to get the vibrators they wanted while avoiding the discomfort they had previously experienced, or feared they would experience, in more traditional adult stores. "Thanks for the catalog," one woman wrote. "This saves me from having to venture into the Combat Zone and pay my money to people I don't particularly want to support." Another wrote, "I am very glad to learn that a store such as yours exists—an alternative to the sleazy, women-degrading porno joints. More power to you—you are filling a need to access the tools for women's self-discovery, and in my book, that's affirming, in a very good way."[79]

In her catalog and, eventually, her retail store, Williams offered a version of female sexuality that resonated with many women, offering them new forms of identification that enabled them to see themselves as sexual subjects and agents, rather than sexual objects that existed solely for the pleasure and entertainment of men. For some women, however, getting to the place where they could comfortably occupy this subject position—one of sexual entitlement and freedom—was no easy task. Many letters indicated that women felt hindered by a lack of encouragement and limited, if any, access to sex-positive resources:

> Your catalog is wonderful! I was so relieved when I got it—it's so
> warm and positive and accepting and candid and comfortable and
> nurturing! I've been struggling to accept my sexuality and, being single
> and celibate, decided to try to get a vibrator. I suppose the Louisville

"sex stores" have them but I wouldn't be caught dead on *that* street. The catalogs advertised in *Cosmopolitan* looked sleazy and suggestive and had all the implications that women are sex objects — really awful. I got your address from [Lonnie Barbach's book] *For Yourself* . . . and waited anxiously. [It was] such a joy and healing to receive it. I feel like you wrote it just for me. . . . Those of us out here in the Midwest areas, where one cannot admit one is sexual, much less sex positive about masturbation, need desperately to have sources like your boutique. I wish I could come to New York and visit. Not likely — but I am grateful you are there.[80]

By 1976, just two years after Williams started Eve's Garden, the business's catalogs and products were reaching customers all over the country and internationally, too. Many regarded Williams as a resource and a confidante, and credited her with saving their marriages, changing their lives, and helping them rediscover — or in some instances discover for the very first time — their sexual selves. They offered deeply personal testimonials that recounted their sexual awakenings and self-discoveries. "I just finished masturbating with my Prelude 2 and as I did, I said, 'I love you Dell.' This is how I feel about all my sisters, including Betty Dodson, who are positively helping the rest of us," one customer wrote.[81]

Another woman, who had been married for many years and was months shy of turning seventy-five, sent Williams a thank-you note. In it, she explained that she never knew vibrators existed until a friend told her about them a year earlier. "I had always enjoyed sex and having babies . . . but oh, wonder of wonders! Using the vibrator made me understand what orgasms are all about. I had never had any in all my years of marriage. . . . I can now enjoy my body when I am alone and have delightful orgasms."[82]

Although most of the people who wrote to Williams had never met her or visited her retail showroom, they saw her as someone who was accessible, knowledgeable, and sympathetic to their needs and concerns. "It is so nice to share my personal feelings with someone who understands," wrote one woman, who disclosed that she was an incest survivor living with multiple sclerosis and attempting to reclaim her sexuality.[83] "It is so nice to know there is a *real* person who really cares about her customers on the other end," wrote another. "Thanks for listening" and "Thanks for being there" were sentiments frequently expressed in the letters.

Many letters were filled with intimate details: the inability to orgasm, husbands who were impotent or ejaculated prematurely, and the loss of sexual response following a hysterectomy. Those who sent the letters often expressed immense frustration, desperation, and even anger about what they viewed as their underwhelming sex lives and unresponsive bodies. "How can I be so sexually charged and still be non-orgasmic?" one woman asked. "Why is it so hard for me to climax?" another wrote. "Is it a lack of experience? Is it my body?" "I am a lesbian . . . with a non-functioning, if existent, clitoris," wrote another woman. "I am tired of unfulfilling, unsatisfying, incomplete 'sexual' . . . relating with my fully and easily orgasmic partners. . . . It makes me sick, angry and full of rage that she gets hers in a minute, and I am always left feeling 'empty' and without."[84] Their pain was palpable.

In her role as a lay expert, someone customers could turn to for information and advice, Williams was compassionate and encouraging. She often replied to the letters, applauding people's sexual self-discoveries and dispensing practical advice, many times with a folksy wisdom one might expect from an older friend or family member. In her response to a college student who was concerned that she might be "overdoing" her vibrator, Williams said, "I am just hoppin' mad at the doctor that says, 'Well, don't overdo [it]' when it comes to women's sexuality. In my estimation, that is just plain hogwash!" Don't worry about overdoing it, she reassured the young woman: "Overdo all you damn please!"[85]

The letters that Williams received over the years suggested that women, as well as men, were deeply affected by the cultural messages they had internalized about gender and sexuality. Many women were not having orgasms, or not having them reliably. They had never been encouraged to masturbate or learn about their bodies. They had virtually no access to accurate information about sex, and even fewer places they could turn to get practical information that could alleviate their concerns and bolster their sexual self-confidence. In some instances, they expressed guilt for enjoying themselves or for having desires that did not fit with their idea of what a woman, a lesbian, or a feminist should want sexually. Williams was for many people a resource and a lifeline, a tangible expression of sexual possibilities and hope.

Eve's Garden's unapologetically feminist standpoint appealed to many customers. The language of feminism articulated in its catalogs offered them a familiar interpretive framework—one of consciousness-raising and information sharing—that they could use to understand the larger project of sexual liberation and female empowerment that Williams was attempting to advance. As one woman explained:

I just received an Eve's Garden catalog via the mail and I wanted to take a moment to let you know how delighted I am with it. As a woman and active feminist, I greatly appreciate efforts by other women to liberate the minds and bodies of our sisters. I am always meeting women who are caught in a self-defining and unfair cycle; women who wish they could freely enjoy their sexuality, but cannot seem to shake the labels: Slut, whore, hot-to-trot, etc.—relics of an archaic and repressive past. Thank god we are past there! For these reasons, I am grateful that there are caring women such as you to provide us with information and quality merchandise, to help us understand and release the full beauty of our sexuality.[86]

What Williams was doing—running a feminist vibrator business geared toward women—was so unconventional that some women remained deeply skeptical even as they wrote to request a catalog. "I am writing for your catalog," wrote one woman, "but I want you to understand my position. If you are another sleazy sex company parading as a feminist erotica store that is not what I am looking for." Another woman, who had stumbled across Eve's Garden's ad in the classified section of *Ms.*, the mouthpiece for popular feminism during this period, was not entirely convinced that she was corresponding with a legitimate feminist company: "I am sending you a ten cent stamp so that you can send me your catalog. I hope I won't be bombarded with lewd pamphlets and advertising, but that I will receive a tasteful catalog of your products. Thanks for existing." And from another woman: "I am not quite sure what feminists are doing in the vibrator business (it seems rather anti-social and anti-people), but send me your catalog anyway."[87]

Letters like these gave Williams an opportunity to articulate her feminist vision for Eve's Garden. "What a feminist is doing in the vibrator business," Williams wrote in one reply, "is creating space for women to touch base with their potential power which lies in the release of the orgasm . . . the ability to sense more pleasure and change the world from the standpoint of pleasure-based rather than hostile/anger-based power. Anyway, that's it in a nutshell. Hope you dig it."[88]

# two

# OUT OF THE THERAPIST'S OFFICE, INTO THE VIBRATOR SHOP

———

> My mission was simple: to encourage women to take charge of and have fun with their sexuality. . . . I planned to exploit people's interest in sex rather than their anxiety about it.
>
> GOOD VIBRATIONS FOUNDER JOANI BLANK
> "Good, Good, Good, Good Vibrations"

If you lived in San Francisco's Mission District in 1977, a largely working-class Latino neighborhood with a growing lesbian population, you might have stumbled upon a tiny shop about the size of a parking space, with macramé hangings on the walls and a display case full of antique vibrators.[1] Just down the street from a women's café and a feminist bookstore that were part of the burgeoning women's district, the store was gaining attention in the local press for its "head spinning display of exotic-looking implements"[2]—including a line of hand-crocheted "vibrator cozies"—and the disarmingly charming woman who ran it, sex educator and therapist Joani Blank. Whereas Eve's Garden founder Dell Williams was a women's liberationist with an interest in sex, Blank, who had been teaching women how to orgasm at a clinic at the University of California, San Francisco (UCSF), was a sex professional with a level of expertise that recast her vibrator shop as a sex-positive resource center. Despite the store's humble appearance, Good Vibrations would become the standard bearer for a new model of sex shop that brought the techniques of sex therapy and the language of sex education into a retail environment—

Good Vibrations
founder Joani Blank,
1977. Courtesy of
Joani Blank.

eventually inspiring future generations of feminist entrepreneurs to follow in Blank's footsteps.

Blank was convinced there needed to be a sex shop for people who hated sex shops, a place where women in particular could get the vibrators they wanted without the feeling of distaste that often accompanied their visits to more conventional adult stores. She bought a big carpet at a garage sale to brighten up the space and made a display shelf for the small selection of vibrators and books she was selling. At Good Vibrations there was no pornography, no lingerie, and no gimmicky novelty items. Vibrators were plugged into a power strip on the floor so people could turn them on and try them out on their wrists or hands to see if a particular model suited them. Blank even turned the small bathroom into a tryout room where customers could hold a vibrator against the outside of their clothing to test its strength. She got nondescript brown paper bags in case some of her customers wanted to hide their purchases and, just for fun, stamped Plain Brown Wrapper on each one. Blank placed a small ad in the newspaper and, according to her, sat there and waited for people to discover her shop.

News about the little vibrator store spread throughout San Francisco's feminist community, mostly by word of mouth. Three months after Good Vibrations opened, a story in the *Berkeley Barb* painted an inviting picture of the friendly, wholesome vibrator shop and its welcoming proprietress. Blank's warmth and approachability, and her ability to talk about sex with ease, were components of what the reporter described as Good Vibrations' "unique and non-threatening" environment.[3] This was a sex shop of an altogether different order: one with a women-friendly, educationally focused, and unmistakably feminist vibe.

From the start, Blank was interested in serving what she referred to as "various sexual styles"[4]—older people, younger people, single people, married people, lesbians, gays, and transgender customers; everyone from sex workers to suburban housewives. Good Vibrations adopted the tag line, "especially but not exclusively for women," and Blank worked hard to make sure her shop was a welcoming, nonjudgmental place for everyone, regardless of whether they had sex twice a year or twice a day.

Blank's rent for the postage-stamp-sized shop was $125 a month. She invested $4,000 to cover start-up expenses and, on an average weekday, made about $40 in sales. Operations were small and the overhead low. Blank never wrote a business plan and didn't work from a budget for the first ten years of the business's life. "I just sold stuff and then bought more stuff with the money I got from selling the first batch," she told me.[5] What mattered most to Blank wasn't making money or getting rich, but creating a supportive environment where people could ask questions, get information, and talk openly about sex. And if they happened to buy a vibrator in the process, that was great, too.

The daughter of a former schoolteacher and a research scientist nicknamed the Father of Moisturizing for his work in dermatology, Blank was raised in a politically progressive Jewish household in the Boston suburbs along with her younger sister. She attended college at Oberlin, a small liberal arts school in Ohio, where she discovered her love for anthropology. After graduating in 1959, Blank spent the following year traveling the world. She journeyed solo by train through India, with just an overnight bag, her guitar, and a purse, taking Indian dance classes and working at a camp outside of Madras. It was an adventure that, among other things, allowed Blank to sidestep the expectation that many young women of her generation faced to either get married or go to graduate school immediately after finishing college. After returning home, she earned a master's degree in Asian studies at the University of Hawaii and another master's in public health from the University of North Carolina, with an emphasis on community health and family planning.[6]

After graduation Blank began working in the field of family planning. Over time, she became highly critical of the public health discourses surrounding contraception, which presented birth control not as a feminist choice that could expand women's opportunities, but as a duty and obligation, especially for poor women. She also encountered women who were having a hard time using contraceptives effectively, because certain forms of birth control, such as the diaphragm and spermicidal jelly, involved touching their genitals, and too many women were, according to Blank, just "plain uncomfortable with everything about their genitals and many things about their sexuality."[7]

Blank herself was not someone who had always been comfortable with her body or her sexuality. Although she had grown up in what she would later describe as a sex-positive household, she didn't have sexual intercourse until she was twenty-four and she had also never masturbated. It was her first lover who in an indirect way showed her how, she told me. "I didn't know women masturbated at all. You read the books and they talk about boys having wet dreams and masturbating. It just never occurred to me." (Years later when Blank asked her mother why she had never said anything to her and her sister about masturbation, her mother said, "I just assumed you and your sister were doing it all your lives. Doesn't everybody?")[8]

Blank moved to San Francisco in 1971 and began working for the San Mateo County Health Department in their family planning program. One of the first places she turned to find a sense of community was the local chapter of Medical Committee for Human Rights (MCHR), an advocacy organization she had become involved with years earlier. It was there that she met Maggi Rubenstein, a nurse, bisexual activist, and sex educator who cofounded San Francisco Sex Information (SFSI), among several other major sexuality organizations in San Francisco. It was at one of the MCHR meetings that Rubenstein invited Blank to be part of what would be her first feminist consciousness-raising group.

Blank's friendship with Rubenstein opened a number of doors for her in San Francisco's growing, interlocking sex education community. Rubenstein, along with several others, in 1972 cofounded the SFSI switchboard, a hotline for sex information that combined strands of thought from feminism, the human potential movement, and gay and lesbian liberation. According to Blank, SFSI was a new kind of sex information service that emphasized talking honestly and frankly about sex. Blank was part of SFSI's first group of volunteers, and it was through the connections she made there that she met the up-and-coming, now legendary, sex therapist Lonnie Barbach and began working with preorgasmic women at the sex therapy program at UCSF, teaching them how to orgasm.[9]

It was the early days of women exercising agency over their sexuality and figuring out how to have orgasms, and the counseling program at UCSF was offering sex therapy groups for women to help them do just that.

"We didn't start them off with vibrators," Blank explained. "We really wanted them to become comfortable touching themselves with their hands."[10]

> Basically, we taught [women] how to orgasm. We didn't tell them how to do it. . . . It was a Lonnie Barbach thing. She developed this technique; it's a gradual approach. People would tell their sexual histories and then we'd give them an assignment to look at their bodies in the mirror, then talk about how they felt about their bodies. They'd have questions about masturbation, the clitoris [and] partners. It was a group thing—group therapy. If they were having a hard time having orgasms we'd encourage them to supplement with a vibrator. And it was impossible to buy a vibrator in a decent place. So I decided to make it easier for them.[11]

The activities taking place in the treatment program at UCSF, which included encouraging women to learn about their bodies and take responsibility for their own sexuality, closely resembled the do-it-yourself body education workshops that Betty Dodson was conducting in her apartment on the other side of the country (minus the show and tell). However, one was called sexual consciousness-raising and the other was labeled sex therapy, the latter of which repositioned women's sexual self-discovery as a therapeutic enterprise.

What Blank learned about sex therapy and education during this time would eventually become the foundation for Good Vibrations. For example, it was typical for therapists working at the clinic to provide new clients with an informational overview that discussed sexual anatomy, the sexual response cycle, and human sexual variation prior to the start of counseling. This became such a standard part of clinical practice that the counseling program decided to streamline the educational component by holding mandatory workshops once a month for groups of people who were interested in being seen at the clinic. What the counseling staff quickly discovered was that a surprising number of them never returned for additional sessions. The basic information they received during these meetings was apparently enough to "fix" them.

According to Blank, "The facts that would come up again and again [in these sessions] and the information that would come up over and over again mostly had to do with the same kinds of questions teenagers ask: 'Is what I experience normal?'" Once people realized—often to great relief—that what they were experiencing wasn't a sexual problem or dysfunction that had to be fixed, but a routine part of normal human sexual variation, the need for additional counseling seemed to vanish.[12]

For men, these concerns often focused on what Blank described as the "old bugaboo" of penis size or the occasional difficulty some men have getting or maintaining an erection. In the case of women, the most common anxiety was that something was wrong with them because they were unable to achieve orgasm through intercourse alone, or that they felt that masturbation was an activity reserved exclusively for men. Blank discovered that many people had never been told that sex did not always work perfectly, so when a so-called expert told them that what they were experiencing was actually quite common, the effect was often reassuring, if not liberating.[13]

Blank's observations lent support to the idea that a little bit of accurate information about sex could go a long way toward making people feel better about themselves and their relationships.

Blank eventually began conducting sexuality workshops in the Bay Area, and decided, with the encouragement of her clients and other therapists, that writing and publishing books about sex was one way she could reach an audience that might never attend a counseling session or workshop. In 1975 Blank founded Down There Press, which would later become the publishing arm of Good Vibrations.

Blank's first book, *The Playbook for Women about Sex*, began as a calligraphy project for a class she was taking at the time. ("I hated my handwriting, and I decided I could learn to write neatly if I took a calligraphy course, so I practiced with that book," she told me.) Filled with exercises designed to dispel common myths and increase women's sexual self-esteem, *The Playbook* encouraged women to look at their bodies and to list the things they liked and disliked about them. Blank even provided an empty page where women could draw a genital portrait. "Give your cunt a name and put it on the portrait name plate," she wrote. "Use crayons or paints to color your portrait."[14] The book also included an application for membership in the Society of Out-of-the-Closet Masturbators. Applicants were asked about their experience with masturbation, including how old they were when they first masturbated, how often they did it, and in what ways (e.g., "One or two hands, up and down,

The society of
OUT-OF-THE-CLOSET MASTURBATORS
application for membership
~*~

Name (or pseudonym)_____
Rank_____
Serial number_____
Age now_____ Age I first masturbated_____ Age I first called
"that" masturbation_____ Age I plan to stop_____
Reason for stopping, if any_____
Current Pattern
  Frequency (how often)_____
    this is:  ☐ too much    ☐ just right
              ☐ too little   ☐ none of your business
  Method(s):
    hand(s)          yes no   My "special" (describe):
    vibrator         yes no   _____
    running water    yes no   _____
    towel, pillow, teddy bear, etc.    yes  no
    dildo, zucchini, candle, etc.      yes  no
    railing, edge of chair, door, etc. yes  no
    squeezing legs together            yes  no
  How I do it:
    One or two hands____
    This many fingers and thumbs 1 2 3 4 5 6 7 8 9 10
    Up and down____      Back and forth____
    In and out____       Round and round____
    Something in my vagina____ what?_____ or_____

11

A page from Joani Blank's first sexual self-help book, *The Playbook for Women about Sex*. Published by Down There Press, 1975. Courtesy of Joani Blank.

back and forth, or round and round?"). On the last page was a diploma, with a space for the reader to write her name, certifying that she was now a "bona-fide sexually aware woman."

In 1976 Blank published her second book, *Good Vibrations: The Complete Woman's Guide to Vibrators*.[15] Blank struck a similarly irreverent tone as she detailed how these funny-looking mechanical contraptions worked and why women might want to try them. The book was a way for her to share what she had learned over the years about the "art and science of buzzing off," including how to choose between different vibrators—electric versus battery operated—and how to use them, either alone or with a partner. Borrowing an approach popularized by feminist consciousness-raising groups, Blank used experiential knowledge as a mode of feminist epistemology. As she wrote in the book's early pages, "I have conducted no formal research on my subject. I am reporting from my own experience, the experience of other women, and from what I perceive to be vibrator folk wisdom. This is hardly a definitive book on masturbation for women, or on anything else for that matter. It is rather a sharing of information, in the hope that we can all enjoy our sexuality a little more through the exercise of informed and independent choices."[16]

In discussing the benefits of vibrators, Blank drew on the philosophy of sex positivity—the idea that sexuality is a potentially positive force in people's lives—that was gaining traction within San Francisco's sex education community. She had this to say about how to use a vibrator: "You use it any way that feels good. Anything goes. If it doesn't hurt, it won't hurt you."[17] She dismissed the idea that women could become addicted to their vibrators, insisting instead that there were no known detrimental side effects to being a "vibrator junkie." Blank argued that there was no such thing as too much pleasure or too much masturbation. Nodding to the field of sex counseling, she wrote, "Sex researchers and counselors working with women are finding that the more times a woman experiences her own sexual response, the more reliable her response becomes."[18]

In her books, and eventually her small vibrator shop, Blank helped give form to what would eventually become known as sex-positive feminism. She blended the educationally oriented and quasi-therapeutic approach to talking about sex that she had refined as a sex therapist with aspects of 1970s feminist consciousness-raising and humanistic sexology. She combined these ideas to form a new assemblage of discourses that was arguably greater than its individual parts. Former Good Vibrations staff member Cathy Winks summarized it this way: "In creating Good Vibrations, Joani was responding to the need that was being expressed in the preorgasmic women's groups and the workshops that she led: 'Well yeah, you say vibrators are so great and I would be happy to buy them but I just can't find a place where I am comfortable doing it and I don't want to go into an adult store.'"[19] Although Good Vibrations was a retail store and not a therapist's office, the underlying philosophy was essentially the same: Give people the information and tools they need to have more fulfilling sex lives and the world will be a better place.

It wasn't just Blank's sex-positive attitude and philosophy, or Good Vibrations' focus on women, or its "clean and well lighted" ambiance that positioned the business as a different kind of sex shop. Blank was equally committed to running an alternative business, one in which prices were kept low and profits were used to sustain and grow Good Vibrations' educational mission, not just line the pockets of its owner. As the business grew, Blank developed a knack for hiring what one person described as "competent overachievers" who not only shared her passion for sex education but understood her vision for Good Vibrations and were eager to help her bring it to life. Unbeknownst to Blank, she was setting the stage for a sex-positive diaspora that would soon spread to cities across the country.

## Sex Education, Not Sales

Susie Bright was not yet the nationally known author and trailblazer Susie Sexpert when she walked through the doors of Good Vibrations for the first time in 1980. She was twenty-two years old and lived around the corner from the store at Twentieth and Valencia Streets. Bright remembers that initial visit vividly. Honey Lee Cottrell, who would later become Bright's lover and collaborator, was working behind the counter. Cottrell, a butch lesbian with prematurely graying hair, was opening envelopes that contained a single quarter—the amount Blank was charging at the time for an itemized list of vibrators that doubled as the company's mail-order catalog.[20]

Bright watched curiously as Cottrell opened the envelopes and stacked the quarters, one on top of the other, next to the cash register.

"Why don't you just put them in the register?" she finally asked.

"We don't know how to record it," Cottrell replied. "It's not a sale and no one can figure out what it is, so we just pile them up on the side and Joani says she will deal with it later."

There was a quaintness, and even quirkiness, about Good Vibrations in 1980. A large wooden and glass case housed Blank's collection of antique vibrators, taking up most of the space in the tiny store. The product inventory was still very small and included only a few different models of vibrators and a small selection of books. "I loved the attitude and the point of it all," Bright recollected. "And I loved the idea that you could just pick up a vibrator and hold it outside of your jeans for one second and know how you felt about it. You could break through all this apprehension and all this cerebral bullshit that people have about good/bad/I don't like it."[21]

Bright bought her first vibrator that day. She went home and, according to her, had her "own personal revolution." For Bright, using a vibrator was a revelation, a "visceral leap in consciousness" that fundamentally changed how she thought about her body. Until then, she hadn't really understood why anyone would need to buy anything, or use anything mechanical, to have an orgasm. It had never occurred to her to use anything other than her fingers to masturbate (although admittedly it seemed to take forever for her to have an orgasm that way). Vibrators changed that. With a vibrator, Bright was able to have an orgasm in less than thirty seconds—"just like any teenage boy."

"It was so funny," she told me. "I just wouldn't come out of my room. I had vibrator races for about three days [to see how fast I could come]."[22]

Not long afterward, Bright learned that Good Vibrations had an opening

Susie Bright, 1992. Photograph by Phyllis Christopher,
www.phyllischristopher.com.

for a sales clerk. Back in San Francisco after an aborted trip to Alaska, where she had gone to make money fishing, Bright was sleeping in a storefront on Valencia Street and needed a job. She had two job interviews scheduled, she recalled: one was at the Golden Gate Bridge for work putting up traffic cones to mark the lanes, and the other was at Good Vibrations.

Bright was completely captivated by the thought of working at the feminist vibrator store. She recalled that Blank explicitly told her during her interview, "I don't care if you don't sell a damn thing all day. This is about education and it's about providing an alternative place for women to explore their sexual self-interests." Despite their twenty-year age difference, Bright felt she had met a kindred spirit. "I just loved [Blank's] zeal and her determination. And she was charming and charismatic, and a lot of the things she said about how to talk to people and answer their questions were just the kinds of things I would say. We just clicked, and I know it was fun for her to meet a young woman who just 'got it' so delightfully."[23]

Bright got the job not because she was a retail guru, she explained, but because she so thoroughly understood Blank's vision for the store. "I knew that [Good Vibrations] wasn't just some store, the same way that Modern Times wasn't just a commie-anarchist bookstore. They had a bigger purpose," Bright said. "And the fact that they were a retailer was secondary to that."[24]

Blank likely saw in Bright someone who shared her passion and political vision. Bright had come of age at the height of the women's liberation movement in the early 1970s. Feminism, she would later tell me, was "her mother's milk." She cut her teeth on Marxism while still in high school and spent much of her teenage years as part of the American New Left, where she was active in labor and community organizing. She participated in feminist consciousness-raising groups and speculum-wielding women's self-help collectives where performing cervical self-exams to learn about their bodies was de rigueur.[25] Along with her friends, she took over a janitor's closet in high school and turned it into a birth control center. "I thought of myself as an activist and, very earnestly, a revolutionary," Bright explained.[26]

By the time Bright began selling vibrators at Good Vibrations in the early 1980s, debates about pornography, homosexuality, and AIDS were reaching a fever pitch in the Reagan-era culture wars, and Bright soon found herself in the middle of heated feminist battles regarding sexual expression and representation.

In 1976, Bay Area feminists founded Women against Violence in Pornography and Media (WAVPM), one of the first organizations in the country dedicated to fighting media sexism and violence, which quickly narrowed its focus to pornography. The group staged antipornography protests outside the Mitchell Brothers Theatre in San Francisco, a venue known for live sex shows; it also held regular strolls through North Beach, drawing attention to the massage parlors, adult stores, and porn theaters that dotted the neighborhood. The idea that pornography was a tool of patriarchal oppression and gender discrimination was gaining traction among feminists, and calls for legal remedies to mitigate what some saw as its harmful social effects were mounting.[27]

The ascendency of antipornography feminism and its emphasis on sexual violence and danger meant that by the early 1980s there was dwindling cultural space for feminists to talk about—and indeed champion—the more positive and life-affirming aspects of sexuality and pleasure. And it wasn't just pornography that was in the line of feminist fire. As the antipornography campaign gained steam, both in the Bay Area and elsewhere, a hierarchy of good and bad sexual expression was also being constructed. At a time when the New Right was flexing its conservative muscles, the stakes regarding sexuality, especially for women and sexual minorities, could not have been higher.

Samois, a San Francisco–based lesbian-feminist BDSM group, also found themselves in the crosshairs of antipornography feminists, accused of being the bad variety of sex. WAVPM viewed lesbian S/M as eroticizing violence and glorifying the "unequal relations of power fundamental to a patriarchal society."[28] They rejected the idea that S/M could be consensual—even among lesbians. Instead, they argued that patriarchy had conditioned women to think that domination and subordination were natural, even desirable, states. Media scholar Carolyn Bronstein wrote, "For many activists within the antipornography movement, there was no way to reconcile lesbian S/M with feminism."[29]

Even the dildo was a source of feminist debate and consternation, especially among lesbians. According to Heather Findlay, "No other sex toy has generated the quantity and quality of discussion among mostly urban, middle-class white lesbians as the dildo."[30] Some lesbians viewed dildos as "male-identified" and thus fundamentally incompatible with "women-identified" sexuality. As one recalled in an essay in the book *Coming to Power*, dildos were a "no-no" because they were "men's ideas about what lesbians did."[31] Using them, or fantasizing about using them, made you a Bad Lesbian. Feminist sex educators had likely and unwittingly contributed to the dildo's image problem by working so hard in the 1970s to decenter the idea that the vaginal orgasm was the be-all and end-all of female sexuality. Blank, who initially didn't sell dildos at Good Vibrations, noted, "[My view on dildos] wasn't so much anti-dildo as it was proclit."[32]

*On Our Backs* (OOB), a sex magazine for the "adventurous lesbian," offered a radical, pro-sex counterpoint to the antipornography, anti-BDSM, and anti-dildo feminist factions, reclaiming these things as symbols of lesbian lust and defiance. (Indeed, the publication's title was a cheeky spin on the radical feminist newspaper *off our backs*.) "We made a conscious decision to express the political nature of sex in an entertainment format in an effort to put the fun and diversity back into lesbian life," OOB publishers Debi Sundahl and Nan Kinney wrote in an editors' note.[33]

Bright was working as the manager at Good Vibrations when she helped start OOB in 1984. The magazine featured pictorials of lesbians with dildos and strap-ons, dyke leather daddies and their femmes, floggers and nipple clamps, threesomes, vibrators, and public sex—images that defied stereotypes about the kind of sex lesbians were having. Bright also penned a regular column for the magazine called "Toys for Us." Part lesbian *Consumer Reports* and part Dear Abby, the column discussed various issues affecting lesbian lives, from AIDS and safe sex to dildos and vaginal fisting.[34] In the magazine's inaugural

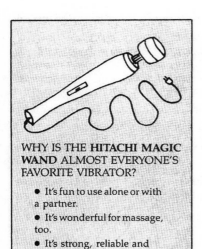

Early Good Vibrations advertisement in *On Our Backs* featuring the Hitachi Magic Wand, 1986.

issue, Bright chimed in on the great dildo debates and offered a particularly memorable bon mot when she wrote that "penetration is only as heterosexual as kissing."[35]

Bright's work on behalf of *OOB* in the 1980s, as both a writer and an editor, was an important node of articulation between Good Vibrations and the wider sex-positive community. *On Our Backs* took its readers into the heart of San Francisco's lesbian and queer sex scene, forming an imagined sexual community among lesbians in far-flung places. As Shar Rednour, who worked at *OOB* and its sister company Fatale Media in the 1990s, recalled, "The reality of lesbian sex—what it actually looked like and the pleasure it could produce—were simply not images that were readily available or accessible in the 1980s and 1990s."[36] The magazine's features, fiction, columns, and pictorials were printed alongside ads for Good Vibrations, Stormy Leather, the Lusty Lady—a well-known San Francisco peep show—and Fatale Video. The magazine helped create a lesbian market and distribution network, and connected readers to many of San Francisco's most culturally influential sex businesses. At the height of the feminist sex wars, OOB was a sex-positive megaphone that didn't shy away from frank discussions and portrayals of lesbian sex or sexual consumerism.

Bright's "Toys for Us" column gave her a platform for talking about sex and sex toys that extended far beyond the borders of sex-positive San Francisco; and, in the eyes of many readers, it also made her synonymous with Good Vibrations. She was a walking, talking advertisement for the little vibrator shop in the Mission.

Bright's contributions to Good Vibrations throughout the 1980s were considerable. She wrote most of the copy for the company's first mail-order catalog, a little booklet with illustrations by Marcia Quackenbush that was published in 1985. The catalog was jam-packed with information about the differences between electric versus battery-operated vibrators, notes about the G-spot, dildo harnesses, and lubricants, and a list of books from Down There Press. It was a far cry from the company's previous single-sheet mail-order form. Together with Blank, she created the Herotica book series featuring erotic fiction from a female point of view, which Bright would later describe as another "shot across the bow." She also convinced Blank to begin carrying explicit erotic videos (see chapter 5) and encouraged her to add quality dildos to the store's product mix. In many ways, Bright carried Blank along with her into a new era of feminist sexual politics. As Bright recalled about her campaign to make silicone dildos a legitimate part of the store's inventory, rather than items that needed to be secreted away,

> I remember this talk I had with Joani where I was like, "You know that I
> stand with you on the absurdity of the vaginal orgasm." It was our cross
> to carry up the mountain. We are never going to shut up about this.
> But honestly, the reason some dyke or experienced sex person comes
> in and wants a dildo isn't because they think they are going to lie back
> and think of England, and have an orgasm; it's because it enhances
> the orgasms they are already having. . . . This is the stuff we should be
> carrying. It is not stupid. It is not offensive. Times were changing and I
> think Joani knew how absolutely strong I was on this point.[37]

During Bright's time at Good Vibrations, where she worked and managed the store from 1981 to 1986, she saw the business's profit margins grow and its vibrator and dildo inventory expand to include more innovative, thoughtful, and colorful designs. Bright's strength, she readily admitted, was not the business end of managing a retail store, like tracking inventory; but she excelled at talking to people about sex and was good at selling vibrators. "I knew what we grossed every day, but I had no idea what that looked like over time. What was the overhead? What was the profit? I couldn't tell you. I didn't inquire." Bright did not inquire, in part, because the business's emphasis was education, not sales. "I considered myself running a sex education kiosk. I didn't have to sell anything, right?"[38]

## The Briarpatch Philosophy

Blank's unconventional approach to running a business, one in which profits were largely secondary, was informed by the Briarpatch, a group of socially conscious small businesses that had its roots in the counterculture values of the 1960s. (One Good Vibrations employee described the Briarpatch as a "loose network of hippies who became business people and wanted to maintain a sense of social responsibility.")[39] The Briarpatch philosophy emerged from a rather gloomy outlook that had developed in the wake of the Vietnam War. Briars believed that large corporations would eventually become obsolete, succumbing to a "business apocalypse" that would render them unable to fuel their voracious appetites.[40] Briars, by comparison, would learn new skills so they could live and thrive on less. They would share resources with others, serve the common good, and, importantly, do all of this with honesty, openness, and joy.

Briars considered greed and competition to be poor models for running a successful business. Instead of being cutthroat, Briars emphasized cooperation. As Gary Warne explained in *The Briarpatch Book*, "One of the important values for a Briarpatch business is that of shared information. Whatever a Briar learns in his or her work and in setting up a business should be available as a resource for others to learn and grow from as they begin their own ventures."[41] For Briars, sharing information with other businesses about their management structure, finances, marketing, and legal and technical strategies was an essential part of doing good business. They believed that if you were in business for purposes other than financial gain, you could sell things more cheaply and treat your employees better.

The Briarpatch philosophy resonated with Blank and provided her with a socially conscious and communitarian framework for thinking about herself as a businesswoman, assuaging some of the long-standing discomfort—and indeed disdain—she had about the world of business. (In high school, she once turned down a blind date with a young man attending Harvard Business School for no other reason than that he was pursuing a career in business, which she found distasteful.) The principles promoted by the Briarpatch philosophy allowed Blank to think differently about herself as a business owner: "If I can do business [the Briarpatch] way, then I can be a businesswoman. If I have to be a regular businessperson—someone who had to go to school and get an MBA [makes disparaging noise]. Or [someone] who has to care about profits? Forget it. I don't want to be a businesswoman. I resisted that. And that's one of the reasons, incidentally, that I ended up focusing on the educational stuff is that it helped me not worry about being a businesswoman."[42]

Blank put the Briarpatch principles of humanistic management, cooperative decision making, and publicly visible accounting into practice at Good Vibrations. Employees set their own salaries and, for many years, Blank employed an open-book policy under which anyone, inside or outside the business, could view the company's financial records. (Bright would later tell me that she regretted never asking to see the books. "It never occurred to me. Isn't that weird?") The company printed its profit and loss summaries in the *Good Vibes Gazette*, its irregularly published in-house newsletter. (The first issue included a statement from January to September 1985 reflecting a net loss of $3,520.) A prominently placed sign in the store alerted customers that Good Vibrations was an open business. "This means that all of our records, including wholesale prices, vendor lists, and financial statements are open to anyone who wants to see them, including the present company," the sign read.

Blank's commitment to the Briarpatch philosophy trickled down to her staff and shaped their views about what it meant to run a successful business. One of the things that Cathy Winks learned from Blank over the ten years she worked at Good Vibrations, from 1986 to 1996, was that it was not only possible to run a socially conscious business and be successful, but that doing so engendered credibility and respect from customers who felt good about shopping at the friendly, feminist sex-toy store and who wanted to pass the word along to others. Good Vibrations increasingly began to play up these things in its marketing and promotional work: "The late eighties and early nineties was a kind of heyday of socially responsible businesses and thought processes around it, and marketing without advertising and cause marketing and so forth," Winks recalled. "And [Good Vibrations] just had this amazing platform from which to grow: women taking charge of their own sexuality, grassroots production of sexual materials with desktop publishing, and the advent

Good Vibrations' do-it-yourself aesthetic was evident even in the business's choice of bags. Photograph by the author.

of video. Suddenly, a lot more alternative voices could be heard and we could be the means of distribution to get them out into the world."[43]

Good Vibrations frequently received fan mail from customers that lent support to the idea that people valued the company not only for what it sold and the information it provided, but also for how it did business. In a letter published in an early edition of the *Good Vibes Gazette*, from June 1986, a customer named Kathryn wrote, "Thanks for the vibrator you sent along with the catalogue. I love all the information on sex, but I especially appreciate the personal info on you and your company. It's nice to know that I'm not just sending my money off to [be] gobbled up by a huge corporation owned by Vanderbilt or Rockefeller. I like the way you do business."

Some customers were less comfortable with how open Good Vibrations was about its finances. In the same issue of the *Gazette*, a different customer note appeared next to the company's financial report: "It's embarrassing to be sub-

Good Vibrations advertisement from 1993 underscoring the business's identity
as a friendly, feminist sex-toy company.

jected to a forced violation of another's privacy. I have no more need or desire
to look at your finances than I do to watch you have sex in your bedroom."
Blank took it all in stride, replying, "Oh well, you can't please all of the people
all of the time."

Blank lived cheaply and had a small income outside of Good Vibrations, including family money and proceeds from the sale of a home, which gave her
the freedom to not be overly concerned about the business's bottom line. This
meant that she could run her business in a way that felt ethical regardless of
the amount of daily sales she recorded. Blank kept the markup on products
low and often carried merchandise with little to no profit margin simply because they were items she thought should be available. She also wasn't afraid to
say why a particular product was not worth the hype. For years, for example,
Blank displayed a pair of Ben Wa balls—little gold-plated balls about the size
of marbles—so she could talk to customers about why they didn't work in the
way their lore suggested. (The idea was that a woman would put the balls in
her vagina and she'd have orgasm after orgasm as they rolled around inside
her. But inserting Ben Wa balls was no more interesting, Blank asserted, than
putting in a tampon.) Blank also had no problem letting customers walk out
the door empty handed. There were occasions, she told me, when men would
come into the store looking to buy a vibrator for their wife or girlfriend, and

Blank would say, "Well, does she masturbate now?" "I don't know." "Does she use her hand or a vibrator?" "I'm not sure." Blank encouraged these men to go home and have a conversation with their partners to figure out what they might like—or better yet, bring them back to the store so they could pick out something themselves. "You would never do that if you cared about profits," Blank noted.[44]

In addition to publicizing sales figures and financial information, Blank was also invested in sharing what she knew about how to run a business with people interested in opening a store like hers. As former Good Vibrations employee Anne Semans recalled, "I remember Joani saying, 'In my vision there is a sex-toy store in every neighborhood, and it doesn't have to be run by us.' And I was like, 'Good for you.' Because in that world everybody just feels great and perfect about their sex lives, and that's what we are all about, right?"[45]

Blank felt there was no reason to fear competition, withhold information, or create an aura of secrecy around the company's business practices. As Winks explained,

> If we share there will be more for everybody, not less for us. Your
> competitors are the people you can compare yourself to and see
> how they are the same as you, how you are better [and] how you are
> different. You should be striving to excel without putting all the energy
> on competing as a race, where you have to adopt devious maneuvers
> to get ahead of the guy. It was very much like, "Sure, you want to open
> your own store like ours? We always say that we want there to be more
> stores like this. Come on in and we will tell you where we buy all our
> products. Let's make this happen." . . . It was very much an open,
> community-creating approach.[46]

This kind of approach was rare in the often-cutthroat world of business—especially in the adult industry, which was notoriously secretive about financial information and resources. Yet there was a sense among many of those who worked at Good Vibrations in the 1980s and early 1990s that there was no such thing as competition in the traditional sense of the word, a view that Blank actively promoted. The dominant belief, according to Carol Queen, who started working at Good Vibrations in 1990, was, "We are all helping each other change the culture and what it expects and what it thinks is appropriate and we will all benefit from that."[47] In other words, if more businesses began doing what Good Vibrations was doing—selling vibrators and talking openly and honestly about sex—then more people in more places would have

Advertisements announcing the opening celebrations for Grand Opening and Toys in Babeland (now Babeland) in *On Our Backs*, 1993.

the opportunity to buy sex toys in a supportive and welcoming environment. Blank took this idea to heart, and in the early 1990s she started a short-lived internship program to train aspiring entrepreneurs in how to run a business like Good Vibrations. The first, and only, two people to complete the internships were Claire Cavanah, who along with Rachel Venning would go on to found Babeland in Seattle in 1993, and Kim Airs, who started Grand Opening in Boston that same year. (Indeed, ads announcing their opening celebrations ran adjacent to one another in the same issue of *OOB*.)

Although Blank wanted the store internships to continue indefinitely, others within the company felt they were too labor intensive and time consuming; they also questioned the wisdom of training the business's competition. (According to Queen, it turned out that nobody but Blank was "all the way down" with the Briarpatch philosophy.) Despite this, Blank's communitarian, noncompetitive ethos—what we might think of as a retail-based version of open source—created a ripple effect of sex-positivity that eventually spread to other cities across the country. As Babeland's Cavanah would later affirm, "We took the Good Vibrations model and ran with it." Good Vibrations' DNA was replicating and with it, a sex-positive diaspora of feminist retailers and cultural producers was beginning to take shape.

*three*

# LIVING

# THE MISSION

———

We are acting on the belief that sexual exploration empowers people.
Getting a dildo or a vibrator may not change the world, but acting
in the interests of your own desire may change you.

BABELAND FOUNDERS CLAIRE CAVANAH AND RACHEL VENNING
Toys in Babeland catalog

It was a midmorning in August 2001 when I made my way up and out of the
dimly lit Delancey Street station on the Lower East Side of Manhattan. At the
height of summer, the day was already hot and thick. I passed the Essex Street
Market, its dumpsters still teeming with yesterday's cast-off produce, made
a left, and walked by a construction site, a leather goods store, and Economy Candy, a confectionery business that had been a neighborhood fixture
since 1937. In just a few short hours, this ethnically and economically mixed
neighborhood would bustle with the sights and sounds of a typical New York
Sunday: people out and about with the *New York Times* tucked under their
arms, cabs careening down narrow side streets, families running errands, and
friends sipping cappuccinos at the neighborhood's trendy cafés.

A block later I was standing in front of 94 Rivington Street, a relatively un-
assuming storefront that was home to feminist sex-toy retailer Babeland. I
rummaged through my bag for my keys and opened the heavy security gates
that guarded the store at night. I unlocked the front door and let myself inside.

I loved being alone in the store before it opened. There were no customers,
no conversations about sex, no whirr of vibrators or cha-ching of cash registers.
In this absence, the space felt like a completely different place, one in which
the social meaning and value of these otherwise inanimate and strangely con-
figured objects were only partially realized. I turned on the lights and clocked

in. What had moments before been silhouettes of sex toys were now cast in colorful relief.

I made my way downstairs to the cramped basement offices. To my left, shelves of inventory lined the walls. There were neatly stacked rows of condoms, vibrators, dildos, butt plugs, cock rings, leather harnesses, floggers, paddles, wrist restraints, books, porn, and more. Directly in front of me was the manager's office. A copy of *The Whole Lesbian Sex Book* sat on a bookshelf. A hand-lettered sign above a desk said, "Positive Sexuality." Near it was a Post-It note with the words: "Order lube." There were other, more mundane signs of retail life: filing cabinets, calculators, deposit slips, rolls of register tape, shipping boxes, and packing peanuts. I grabbed a money box and headed upstairs.

Back upstairs, I went through a series of opening rituals: I transferred money to the register, swept the floor, straightened merchandise, restocked inventory, and checked the display vibrators to make sure their batteries worked. I scanned the daily log for updates about sales goals, new product reviews, promotional campaigns, press coverage, and information about upcoming sex education workshops, such as the popular Sex Toys 101 and Sex Tips for Straight Men. There was fan mail from appreciative customers: "It was my first time in a sex shop and I couldn't have asked for a better experience," read one letter. On another page was a note from the store manager: "Customer Sarah rented the video *Fire in the Valley* and in the case she found *Revenge of the Bi-Dolls*, instead. Please give her store credit for one video rental."

Just before noon, I unlocked the front door. Babeland was officially open for business.

Although Babeland was created with women in mind, its customers come from all walks of life and are drawn to the store by a common quest for sexual information, products, reassurance, validation, camaraderie, and community in a world where these things are often difficult to find. People whose paths might otherwise never cross can be found standing shoulder to shoulder exchanging notes about twirling vibrators with fluttery rabbit ears: guys from the fire station, young queers from Brooklyn, straight couples from Long Island. In the six months that I worked on the sales floor at Babeland, I saw shoppers who just minutes before were strangers form a meaningful — albeit fleeting — kinship on the basis of varied acts of consumption and open conversations about sex.

By two o'clock the small store was crowded. I answered customer questions, retrieved merchandise, and rang up sales. What's the difference between electric and battery-operated vibrators? they asked. Why are silicone dildos more expensive than rubber ones? Can you recommend a good lube? Does the G-spot really exist? Do you have porn for women? Couples? Lesbians? What is this thingamajig and what does it do?

After the throng of early afternoon shoppers had subsided, I made the most of the temporary lull to restore a sense of order to topsy-turvy sex toys. I propped up vibrators that had fallen on their sides, straightened books, and returned butt plugs that had migrated to other parts of the store to their rightful place on what was affectionately referred to as "anal island."

I turned around and noticed a young woman holding a small, pink Hello Kitty vibrator in one hand and the Rabbit — the vibrator that had catapulted to celebrity status thanks to the HBO series *Sex and the City*— in the other.

"I want to buy a vibrator," she said, "but I have absolutely no idea what I'm looking for."

The sheer volume of consumer choice that awaited shoppers at Babeland could be overwhelming, especially for the first-time customer. There were electric and battery-operated vibrators, in all shapes and sizes, made out of various materials, some of which were waterproof, some of which were not, with prices from $20 to $200 and beyond.

I started the vibrator tour by asking how much she wanted to spend, so I could focus on items that fit her budget. My job was not to do a hard sell ("You should buy this $200 vibrator; it will change your life forever") or up-sell ("That $30 vibe is fine, but if you really want to rock your world, I suggest this one for $100. Everyone is buying it"). I was trained to tailor my interactions to meet a customer's specific needs, not only in terms of their budget, but also in terms of information. Was the customer a sexually sophisticated swinger or a shy suburban housewife looking to buy her first vibrator? There was no one-size-fits-all approach for helping people find the right sex toy.

In my capacity as a staff sex educator—which is how management referred to us—I was expected to be constantly learning about sexuality. We were taught that the more knowledge we had about sex, the more sex positivity we'd be able to spread. I was encouraged to attend in-house sex education workshops, borrow videos and books, read widely, and ask my coworkers questions. For reaching sales goals and participating in community outreach events, I also received Babeland Dollars, an in-store currency that I could spend to build my own collection of sex toys and books. While using sex toys and selling them were two different things, it was clear from the start that using them, and knowing how they worked, was an important part of my job.

Every shift I worked at Babeland put me on the front lines of its mission, which was "to promote and celebrate sexual vitality by providing an honest, open and fun environment, encouraging personal empowerment, educating our community, and supporting a more passionate world for all." I was a vibrator-slinging cultural intermediary, a sex-positive go-between whose job it was to be a point of articulation between the production of sexual goods and discourses and their wider distribution. And while I would never say that selling things was unimportant, it wasn't the sole, or even main, focus of my job. I considered myself to be a "sex-positive concierge," someone whose job it was to give people the tools they needed to make a meaningful difference in their sex lives—whatever that might look like.

As the Good Vibrations retail model began to spread to cities across the country in the early 1990s, so too did its mission of sex positivity. Good Vibrations and the businesses that followed in its footsteps advanced the idea that sexual pleasure was a birthright and that access to sexual information and products had the potential to make everyone's quality of life better. In time, the philosophy of sex positivity became enshrined in carefully worded mission statements and built into advertising and marketing campaigns in ways that positioned feminist sex-toy stores as much more than crude money-making machines. These were businesses with a larger social purpose and a higher calling, a sex-positive brand community in which the goal of changing people's lives through access to information and frank conversations about sex was as important as, if not more important than, selling products and making a profit.

## Sex Toys for a Passionate World

Long before social entrepreneurship became a buzzword and companies started hiring culture czars to promote their core values, there was Carrie Schrader. While Babeland owners Claire Cavanah and Rachel Venning had worked hard over the years to bring their vision of a fun, feisty, feminist sex shop to life, it was Schrader who transformed the store's existing personality into a company culture that would guide every aspect of the business.

Schrader first heard about Babeland when she was a college student at the University of Washington in Seattle, and had developed a soft spot for the store long before she started working there. It was *the* place, she told me, where she had felt the safest when she was coming out as a lesbian: "I would go there and just read books and look at other lesbians, and be like, 'Oh my

In-store display of the Statue of Liberty holding the Magic Wand in one hand and Babeland's mission statement in the other. Babeland's Lower East Side store, 2001. Photograph by the author.

Exterior shot of Babeland's Seattle store, 1998. Courtesy of Babeland.

God,' and look at other women who were buying sex toys and be like, 'Oh my God.' [Babeland] was pivotal to me."[1]

Schrader grew up working in retail, and if there was one thing she knew how to do, it was sell things. When she first began working on the sales floor at Babeland in 1998, she sold sex toys like she would sell any item, explaining to customers, "This is the product and this is what it does." One day, everything changed for her. A woman who had never had an orgasm came into the store. While Schrader was helping her choose a vibrator, she had a powerful realization: this woman trusted Schrader to give her the information she needed to make a profound change in her life. "I walked into the back room to get this vibrator for her and I was just flooded with the fact that she trusted me to help her and that this information was really going to have an impact on her life. And just by coming into the store she was taking steps to have more aliveness in her life," Schrader recounted.[2]

The power of that interaction literally moved Schrader to tears and from that day forward she approached her job with a newfound sense of purpose and commitment. She came to believe that the interactions Babeland enabled between sales staff and customers could be transformative, and that every time someone walked through the business's doors seeking more pleasure in her or his sex life, it was, Schrader claimed, "one small revolution." Babeland's ability to positively impact people's lives was, she felt, boundless. "I really began to believe that what we create in the store attracts people. The energy that we all hold brings people to us and can effect powerful changes, not only for the people who walk through our doors . . . but when one person leaves the store and feels great and tells a friend, who tells another friend, who tells another friend and then it's not just one life that we are helping, but many, many [lives]."[3]

Babeland traces its retail lineage directly to the collaborative, sex-positive business model pioneered by Joani Blank at Good Vibrations. Friends since right after college, when they had met at a potluck, Cavanah and Venning opened the Seattle store when they were in their midtwenties, after a conversation in Cavanah's bedroom led to an "Aha!" moment. (A previous business idea they had tossed around, a lesbian club called Speculum, had failed to materialize.)

That day, while Venning was avoiding going to class at the nearby University of Washington where she was pursuing an MBA, she noticed a bottle of sexual lubricant on Cavanah's bedside table. "You use Probe?" she asked. The ensuing discussion about the lack of comfortable places in Seattle for women to get quality sex toys ignited their entrepreneurial fire.

"We just went nuts with the spark of it," recalled Cavanah. "It lit up the room and that day [Rachel] called Joani Blank, the founder of Good Vibrations in San Francisco, and said, 'We want to consult with you because we want to open a business like yours.'"[4] As luck and good timing would have it, Blank was headed to Seattle for a meeting of the Society for the Scientific Study of Sexuality and agreed to meet with the pair for a consulting fee of $75. "That was the best $75 we ever spent, bar none," Cavanah later told me.

Blank was encouraging and assured the women that any town, of any size, could support a store like Good Vibrations. Blank told them that it was an "ever-expanding market," Cavanah recalled, because "it was like a consciousness-raising thing."[5] The more people who had positive experiences buying their sex toys from places like Good Vibrations, the more customers were made.

Cavanah, a former antiporn proponent who had once burned her father's *Playboy* before turning to making feminist pornography in college, traveled to San Francisco where she spent a month learning the nuts and bolts of how Good Vibrations ran its business. "My recollection," Cavanah told me, "is that Joani took [the internship] very, very seriously. She decided not only to teach me how to sell the toys like they do, but she thought it was important for me

Welcome to Toys in Babeland. After two years of running the most beautiful sex toy store in the world (do you detect a bias?) at last we have a catalog! When we opened our store two years ago, it was for one reason: we couldn't get good lube at a good price. While our inventory has grown, our original goal—to make it easier for women to get quality toys and reliable sex information—has stayed the same. We are acting on our belief that sexual exploration empowers people. Getting a dildo or a vibrator may not change the world, but acting in the interests of your own desire may change you! The only downside of realizing our dream of producing a catalog is that we will no longer be able to meet each Babeland customer. Please feel free to contact us by fax, mail or e-mail with any suggestions or comments. Drop in if you find yourself in Seattle.

Illustration of Babeland cofounders Rachel Venning and Claire Cavanah in the company's first mail-order catalog, spring 1996. Courtesy of Babeland. Illustration by Ellen Forney.

to sit down with the accountant, see all their books, get a list of suppliers, go to their publishing company . . . go to their warehouse and see their mail-order business . . . see how much money they were losing at the time. It was a thorough apprenticeship. She didn't leave one thing out."[6] But perhaps the most important takeaway for Cavanah was seeing just how open, tolerant, and accepting Good Vibrations employees were toward "every kind of sexuality, every second."

When Cavanah returned to Seattle, she and Venning opened their Capitol Hill storefront on a shoestring, dumpster diving for display fixtures and using a cigar box for cash. "Our sales every day would be between $50 and $200, and we would remember every customer," Venning recalled.[7]

By the time Schrader began working at Babeland several years later, the store had established a reputation for providing quality sex toys and no-nonsense information in a fun, comfortable environment. According to Cavanah, "We thought we would sell a dildo to every lesbian in Seattle and that would be the end of it. We underestimated just how much people wanted these products and the environment that we were selling them in."[8] The business grew steadily, and in 1998 the company expanded its brick-and-mortar retail operations to New York City.

Back in Seattle, Schrader was promoted to Seattle store manager and began to instill her beliefs about the business into the company's organizational structure and retail culture. One night, during an employee meeting, she turned to her staff and said, "We provide a service. It's huge. It's a mission. Let's talk about it. Let's claim it. Let's name it. Let's put it into our consciousness and have an intention around what we do here and then let's make the whole business, and what we do, about this mission."[9] With input from everyone in the company, including Cavanah and Venning, Schrader drafted a mission statement that succinctly described what Babeland was all about: promoting sexual vitality, encouraging personal empowerment, educating the community, and supporting a more passionate world.

When the final version of the mission appeared in the March 20, 2000, *Babelander's Report*, an in-house employee newsletter, Schrader attached the following note: "[The mission] is yours to use whenever you want and we can use it as a company to establish and cultivate our relationship with the public. But the main idea behind it is that we all believe and work from the same intention. Intention is what binds us together, and keeps us moving forward."

Once the mission was in place, the next step was getting everyone in the company to buy into it as a shared enterprise. According to Schrader, it was not a hard sell since these were things employees were already doing on the sales floor every day. But explicitly naming and claiming them as an essential part of the company's identity imbued them with a higher purpose and significance.

## Building a Sex-Positive Brand

From the outset, Babeland's mission statement was important for several reasons. First, it communicated a set of principles and values that everyone connected to the company could rally around with a shared sense of purpose, commitment, and pride. As Babeland store manager Dana Clark put it, "The mission is why I want to be here." Second, the mission represented what one employee described as the "brain" of the business. Much like a compass, it guided every aspect of the company, from hiring and customer service to product selection and advertising. The mission was a touchstone that owners and managers could return to again and again as they made decisions about

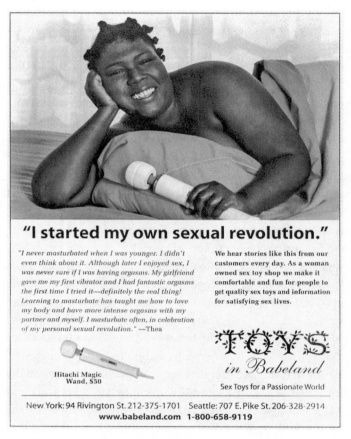

Babeland advertisement highlighting the company's commitment to sex education and personal empowerment. From *Bitch* magazine, summer 2003.

how to grow and channel the company's resources, or whether or not a particular sex toy was in keeping with the business's feminist values. Finally, and perhaps most importantly, the mission functioned as a kind of sacred text that defined and carried the brand, allowing the company's "belief system to be codified and passed along" to customers, offering them the promise of being part of something much bigger and seemingly more meaningful than a simple sales transaction, including their own personal sexual revolution.[10]

Babeland's mission distilled the company's brand identity into an easy-to-digest message. As brand experts will attest, the marketplace is full of commodities that look alike and function in similar ways, from toothpaste and detergent to vibrators and dildos. The major distinction, arguably, between different products and the companies that make and sell them is the stories that become attached to them. It is the practice of branding, what scholar James Twitchell refers to as a "commercialized process of storytelling," that gives people the opportunity to say, "We want to be part of *this* story, not *that* one."[11]

Brands aren't something that we physically touch. Rather, we connect to brands emotionally, a process that can be difficult to capture precisely with words. "By emotional," branding expert Marc Gobé writes, "I mean how a brand engages customers on the level of senses and emotions; how a brand comes to life for people and forges a deeper, lasting connection."[12] Gobé argues that in today's marketplace, shopping is less about purchasing a particular product than about how people experience a brand and the stories that surround it. "Emotional branding is a means of creating a personal dialogue with consumers. Consumers today expect their brands to know them—intimately and individually—with a solid understanding of their needs and cultural orientation."[13]

By developing a brand that emphasized sexual education, empowerment, vitality, and community, Babeland invited customers to be part of what Gobé describes as "new realms" of experience that transcend the products themselves. One Babeland employee described the store as a space that "elicits exploration." People don't just come into Babeland "thinking that they're coming into just another sex shop," she explained. "They are expecting something different." They might not know in advance what that is, or what that might look like, but according to her, "they are ready for it."

Babeland is certainly not the only company striving to create a brand that excites its employees and customers and connects them to a larger vision and purpose. In *Delivering Happiness: A Path to Profits, Passion, and Purpose,* Tony Hsieh, the CEO of online retailer Zappos, a company best known for selling footwear, discusses how he focused the company's brand on providing the best customer service possible and created a company culture to support that goal. According to Hsieh, "a company's culture and a company's brand are really two sides of the same coin. The brand is just a lagging indicator of a company's culture."[14]

Whereas Zappos' vision was all about "delivering happiness" in a shoebox, Babeland's vision was about "delivering sex positivity" to as many people as possible—an outcome that was not necessarily contingent on customers buying anything. When I started working on the sales floor at Babeland in 2001, the sales associate job description said very little about selling things. In fact, a background working in retail was not a prerequisite for being hired. The ability to talk about sex comfortably, on the other hand, was. During my job interview with Dana Clark, then manager of Babeland's Lower East Side store, I was asked to discuss my approach to customer service ("I try to 'read' customers and gauge my interactions accordingly," I explained) and whether I had any discomfort talking about sex (I didn't, although I acknowledged there were certain subjects I knew less about, like cock rings and BDSM). She also asked what I personally wanted to get out of the experience of working at Babeland. Clark used words like "culture" and "community" when talking about the company. The interview was clearly an occasion for her to assess my qualifications, but it was also a chance for her to evaluate how well I fit with the company's culture. As I would later learn from sitting in on job interviews with prospective employees, whether or not someone was perceived as "feeling" the mission played a significant role in who ended up being hired.

The most important part of my job was helping customers feel comfortable in the store and in their own skins. The "nitty gritty of this whole business," Schrader explained in the employee handbook that I received, "is helping people to overcome their shame or fear about sex by leading them to the right toys, books, and videos that will help them do just that."[15] I was expected to be friendly, welcoming, reassuring, compassionate, knowledgeable, and, importantly, nonjudgmental; and while these things are a fairly standard part of any retail job, they take on a particular significance when the work deals with sex.

Working at Babeland was completely different than any retail job I had ever had. In high school I had worked at a clothing store at the mall and had also tried my hand at waitressing (failing miserably). I later spent six months working at Top Shop in London when I was in my early twenties and, years later in the mid-1990s, worked at feminist bookseller Judith's Room in New York City. By the time I began working on the sales floor at Babeland, I was well versed in retail-based customer service. But selling sex toys was not like selling dresses, pizzas, or books. It required a different level of skill, finesse, sensitivity, and emotional labor, because it was impossible to know in advance how comfortable someone might be with either sex toys or their own sexuality. It was a much more intimate and sometimes tricky exchange. I was trained to read a customer's body language when they entered the store. This was especially important if someone seemed shy or nervous. First-time customers were often easy to spot, because they lingered by books and bath items, products that were placed at the front of the store to ease customers into a space that could be intimidating for some. According to Cavanah, "The people that we are inviting in, that we are really organized around, are the novices; the people who would just never imagine themselves going into a sex-toy store. . . . [our goal is] delivering an experience to them that they just couldn't imagine."[16]

## "These Are My People"

I first met Heather, a Babeland customer, on the sales floor when she turned to me and said with gratitude, "Nobody does retail like Babeland does retail." Not long afterward, we met at a café across the street from the store, and Heather expanded on this idea. She had discovered Babeland after seeing its ads in the *Village Voice*, which, she said, always made her laugh. (The ad copy that accompanied an image of the Pocket Rocket vibrator claimed to put "more women into orbit than NASA has in a lifetime.")

Heather made her first trip to Babeland with a girlfriend as part of a "date night." For her, Babeland was the "complete opposite" of what she'd experienced at other sex stores, which she described as uncomfortable and unwelcoming places where sales staff acted "like you were bothering them if you had a question." At Babeland, she felt like she was "hanging out with people more than shopping." The store's welcoming vibe, its approachable and knowledgeable staff, and what she saw as the "passion" of the people who worked there left an impression. She and her girlfriend bought over $100 worth of merchandise that night—"without thinking," she said—and she'd been back a half a dozen times since. "I prefer spending my money where people are actually putting an effort behind what they do. I have that type of loyalty."[17]

As I listened to Heather talk about the things that drew her to Babeland and kept her coming back, it dawned on me that she was articulating an encounter with experiential retailing, a concept that has gained steam over the past few decades. More and more brick-and-mortar retailers are looking to be part of what Columbia University marketing professor Bernd Schmitt refers to as the "experiential economy"—making brands come to life in tangible ways.[18] How a brand comes to life for its customers can mean any number of things, but experiential retailing requires winning the "hearts and minds of consumers" by engaging with them in ways that go beyond just selling them products.

Heather was not the only customer I spoke with who expressed an emotional connection to the Babeland brand. Juawana visited her first sex store as a seventeen-year-old (she sneaked in) for no other reason than that she wanted to see what all the fuss was about. It was an Adult Superstore on Boulder Highway in Las Vegas, not far from where she grew up in Henderson, Nevada. Nobody talked to her and she was too scared to buy anything, so she just walked around the store and browsed. The shop was full of grown men who eyeballed her—probably, she said, because she "was dressed like a seventeen-year-old" and technically shouldn't have been there.[19]

By the time Juawana visited Babeland in Seattle several years later, she had heard of feminist sex shops and had the expectation that they'd be different from places like Adult Superstore. "I remember when I went in that I wanted to support it, because I knew [Babeland] was a feminist business." At the time, however, she didn't have any money to spend on sex toys. The only things she could afford were small, inexpensive items like condoms, lube, or the occasional book. Despite this, she said, "[I] never felt left out . . . because I had access to the mission."

Juawana relocated to Seattle in 2011 and Babeland quickly became part of her feminist community. She felt a sense of kinship with the people who worked there—"These are my people," she told me—and a feeling of "ownership" over the store. There, she could be a feminist, she could be sex-positive, and she could be "totally unashamed" as a sexual person. Babeland fostered a sense of sexual curiosity and community that was not dependent on her ability to buy things, but rather her capacity, as she put it, "to be down with the mission." As she explained, "It really does give you a sense of community being in that store. You walk in and it's so well designed. It's comforting, and it's so hip. You feel like you are buying into feminism—like you are literally buying into your own feminist identity. It feels special."[20]

Babeland employees played an important role in how Juawana experienced the store. "Going in [to Babeland] you know [sales staff] are working there for a reason, because it is mission based. You know they 'get' the mission, because otherwise they wouldn't be working there." Juawana felt she could safely make assumptions about sales staff based on what she knew about the company's mission—that they were feminists and likely to be queer identified. She liked that sales staff were willing to share their opinions about how a product worked and offer recommendations based on firsthand experience. As a result, she trusted their opinions sometimes more than she trusted her own.

> The customer service is so on point, you don't even know it is customer service. [You think] "Oh, this is my friend. Give me some advice about this sex toy." The experience, stripped away, is still a retail experience. You are still buying a product and being sold to . . . but there is a

little added something there. When I leave Target, I don't feel like I contributed to my feminist community. But I feel good shopping at Babeland; it feels like I am "doing good," like [I'm part of] a greater movement to put your money where your politics are. I feel the same when I shop at a vegan grocery store.[21]

Heather's and Juawana's accounts of shopping at Babeland are a marketer's dream. They speak to the company's ability to create a brand experience that transcends products, cultivating in the process a sense of community, kinship, and brand loyalty—just as Schrader had predicted when she made the mission the center of Babeland's retail culture. Putting a finer point on it, Juawana said, "If I had to choose [where I wanted to shop], I'd always choose Babeland because it's much more holistic and robust of an experience."

## Not Just Sales Clerks

The success of Babeland's mission hinges on its sales associates. During her time as the Seattle store manager and, later, as the company's general business manager overseeing operations in both Seattle and New York, Schrader was committed to hiring the right people for the job and making sure that the frontline sales staff felt supported in their work. They were the ones on the sales floor talking to customers and selling products and were therefore in the best position to affect the success of the business. Schrader held regular meetings with employees to get their feedback regarding their employment at Babeland. She encouraged staff to find their spark. "What excites you about working here?" she would ask. "What do you love about your job? If you had a magic dildo to wave around the store, what would you change?"

Schrader believed that happy and fulfilled employees were in a better position not only to advance the company's mission, but also to grow its bottom line. "I really believe that if we—sex educators, management, everyone who is working in the store—are happy to be there, if they are empowered by the mission, it is like energy that attracts people. People come in [to the store] and they want to come back. It just fucking feels good. I started to see that happen in Seattle, and I started to see our sales figures rise."[22]

Schrader worked hard to make Babeland a good place to work. This involved creating systems and spending money. Schrader hired managers, assistant managers, and a bookkeeper; she increased the starting hourly wage for sales associates and created job descriptions, employee handbooks, employee reviews, and guidelines for handling cash—policies and procedures that needed to be in place if the company was going to continue to grow and open new stores. These were also things that helped ensure that employees were treated fairly and knew what was expected of them, as well as what they could expect from management. Schrader saw the mission as a springboard for prosperity. She was convinced that if employees were happy, customers would sense this and would want to be part of the sex-positive experience that Babeland was creating.

During my time at Babeland, employees frequently referred to the idea of living the mission. Rebecca Denk, who became Babeland's general business manager after Schrader left the company in late 2001, explained it this way: "[Sales clerks] at Babeland are not just selling dildos. I think it is a higher calling in a way. I just think that [the mission] is vital to the work we do: exciting customers and finding new customers. It goes beyond just making the sale."[23] According to Jacq Jones, who worked at Babeland before starting her own store, Sugar, in Baltimore, "For most of the people who work at [Babeland], this is not just a job. Choosing to work at Babeland is a statement to the rest of your community about what your values are and what you think is important in your own life."[24]

This view was not limited to just a few Babeland employees. Almost everyone I spoke with at feminist sex shops across the country, from store owners to sales staff, acknowledged that it was the mission—and the fact that a sex-toy business would even have a mission—that attracted them to the idea of working at a feminist sex shop in the first place. They wanted to be part of the story of sex positivity and personal empowerment that businesses like Good Vibrations and Babeland were advancing.

This was certainly true for writer and bisexual activist Amy Andre. Andre moved to San Francisco in 1997 after college and applied for a job at Good Vibrations the very next day. Like many people I interviewed, Andre was a customer at Good Vibrations before she was an employee. She liked what the company represented, including its "philosophy and the feel of what they were doing."[25]

When Andre arrived in San Francisco she thought, "That's the place for me." She had worked as a peer sex educator at Planned Parenthood in high school and had also interned there in college. Good Vibrations seemed like a natural fit. Andre applied for a sex educator/sales assistant position but wasn't hired. She was so determined get a job with the company, however, that she applied for three different positions over the course of a year before finally landing a gig working in the warehouse. Andre figured that if she could just get her foot in the door, other opportunities within the company would likely present themselves. She was right. A few months later she moved into a position in the company's Education Department on its Outreach Team, which involved going out into the community and leading sex education workshops at local universities and high schools. Andre spent the next six years working at Good Vibrations. For her, the company's mission was much more than words on a page; it was a source of daily inspiration: "I came to Good Vibrations just admiring the hell out of the mission. I've never applied for the same jobs over and over again over the course of a year until they finally let me in. And I loved that mission and I lived that mission every day. . . . I absolutely believed in that mission. I believed that every interaction I had with a customer was a transformative experience, for that customer and for myself. I had customers tell me that point blank and that changed my life."[26]

Good Vibrations was also experimenting with giving committed employees like Andre a greater say in how the business would be run—an experiment that would illustrate some of the challenges of pursuing a feminist mission while also trying to make a profit.

Joani Blank's commitment to cooperation and community building eventually led her to sell Good Vibrations to her employees in 1992. The decision to restructure the company as a worker-owned cooperative followed closely on the heels of an internal dispute that erupted in 1990 over whether or not the business should carry the book *Doc and Fluff*, a novel by Pat (Patrick) Califia. At the time, Califia was a mainstay in San Francisco's leather scene and one of only a handful of people who was writing about sex. For many within the company, it was, as one person explained, a "no brainer" that Good Vibrations would carry anything Califia wrote.

Blank, however, felt differently. Although she admitted that she had not read the book, she was concerned when she heard from an acquaintance that it contained depictions of violence. At a staff meeting one day, Blank announced that Good Vibrations would no longer sell *Doc and Fluff*. Employees disagreed, voting to carry the book, but Blank exercised her veto power and blocked the vote. For many employees, it was a defining moment: despite the fact that Good Vibrations had been democratically run for years, Blank, as the business's sole owner, wielded a disproportionate amount of power. How egalitarian could the business's decision-making processes be, employees wondered, as long as Blank could at whim override any staff decision she disagreed with?

The fallout from this incident, which resulted in anger and hurt feelings among many staff members, prompted Blank to consider selling the business to her employees. By this point, Blank was around less and most of the day-to-day operations of the company—staffing the store, filling mail orders, generating marketing and publicity materials, and training sales staff, for example—were being done by about a dozen employees. Selling the business to her employees would formalize many of the democratic processes that were already rather loosely in place. By early 1991, research on different worker ownership models was underway, and discussions were taking place about what this change might look like, both legally and in terms of the IRS, and what it would mean personally for all involved.

What Blank was suggesting was somewhat unprecedented. She wasn't planning on selling the business to her employees and then stepping away from it. Rather, Blank was proposing to become a co-owner with her employees, while simultaneously maintaining involvement in the day-to-day operations of the company. How would this work? What would it look like? Would Blank be just another employee or would she, as the founder, have a special status in the co-operative, including owning more shares?

Early in these discussions, staff members were asked to respond to a questionnaire and reflect on how their jobs might be different if they were owners of the business and not just employees. Some said that they would have a bigger stake in the business, a greater sense of self-determination, more job security, more commitment to the business, and more pride. One person acknowledged that worker ownership was a "great social experiment, a sort of utopian ideal that's about personal responsibility, controlling one's own destiny . . . understanding the whole of the business/system/paradigm and your own place in/effect on it." Another talked about worker ownership in terms of feminist principles: "Our business is about putting feminist theory into practice—radical feminist theory, as I see it—and employee ownership is extremely feminist. Therefore, instituting employee ownership is a logical evolution in the life of our business."

Anne Semans, who began working at Good Vibrations in the mid-1980s, had this to say: "[Worker ownership] means my vote, my opinions, my contributions, my loyalty, and my overtime are worth something. For me the immediate or urgent appeal isn't about money as much as it's about validating my work here, which ultimately enables me to feel more like Joani's colleague rather than her employee. Co-ownership is Joani saying, 'Hey, you've made a difference in this company—helped it grow and stuck it out during the hard times; it's becoming as much a part of you as it has been a part of me.'"

After almost two years of research and planning, which involved meetings with various consultants, accountants, and lawyers, the business officially transitioned to a worker-owned cooperative in 1992.[27] As one original owner, Terri Hague, recalled, "We each bought in [to the business] for a $500 share and each of us had an equal vote and equal say. . . . We literally signed each other's worker/owner papers and passed them around in a circle: 'Yep, you are an owner.'" Hague recalled that the transition to a cooperative model was "very, very exciting, because it was new for all of us."[28]

The company's conversion to a worker-run cooperative was a mix of excitement and possibility as well as challenges and frustrations. The company was expanding its operations and hiring more employees to meet new demands. By fall 1994, the fledgling cooperative had expanded from twelve to forty-five employees and was beginning to experience growing pains as it struggled to figure out how the cooperative structure, including its democratic principles and decision-making processes, might accommodate a growing number of worker-owners — each of whom had a vote in how the business was run. By the late 1990s, the company had grown to over one hundred people, and the challenges of running the business as a worker-owned cooperative only mounted.

In the early years of the co-op it was fairly easy to make decisions. There was a relatively small group of owners and everybody in the company knew one another. But as the business grew, and then grew some more, decision making became increasingly difficult and cumbersome; and, in some instances, interpersonal relationships became strained as people with different goals jockeyed for power. Not all workers were drawn to the business for the same reasons. While many were attracted to the company's sex-positive mission and values, others were enticed by the cooperative structure and the idea of owning their own labor. Over time, resentment grew toward management, who some felt were exercising an unreasonable amount of control. According to one person, the cooperative eventually "chewed up and spit out" a lot of good people — primarily senior staff who became frustrated with what they saw as the burdensome structure of the co-op and the reinvention of the wheel with almost every round of new hires. One of the first people to leave the co-op, in 1994, was Blank, who in memos addressed to the board of directors suggested that with the sale of the company she had perhaps given up too much power. What had sounded wonderful in theory — the existence of a woman-owned and worker-run sex-toy business — proved far more difficult in practice.

Indeed, according to Winks, Blank had not originally wanted to sell the business to her entire staff. Rather, she had wanted to sell the business to about five staff members who had been with the company for a number of years and whose opinions she trusted. The problem, however, was that there were about twelve employees at the time and the company didn't have a model or any guidance for how to "finesse selling a company to half its staff," Winks told me.[29] What do you do with the other half? Since they didn't have answers to these questions, they simply pursued the path they were already on, which consisted of turning the business into a cooperative and selling it to the entire staff.

In time, the cooperative model posed challenges for growing a retail business. According to Semans, "I felt at some point [the business] almost came to a standstill because we got to a certain size and we ended up with this really burdensome co-op structure, which made it very hard to grow. We ended up with all these ideas that wouldn't go anywhere [because] we couldn't get the votes to pass them."[30] The cooperative decision-making process seemed to be the biggest problem. "Where it all bogged down," Winks explained, "was in our not being able to identify what decisions needed to go to the whole staff and what didn't."[31] Was it really necessary, for example, that everyone in the entire company vote on what color carpet would be installed in the Valencia Street store, or what color van the company would purchase?

Winks was also struck by how much more conservative and less adventurous people seemed to become once the company became a co-op. All of a sudden workers realized that certain decisions, such as expanding the company's mail-order operations, might affect the raise they would get the following year. Cumulatively, the effect was paralyzing; as a result, a great deal of time and energy was spent on what Winks described as "internal navel gazing" — tweaking the company's governance system, its management structure, its system for salary setting, human resources, and so forth, as opposed to focusing on outward growth, including opening new stores. Many employees found this immensely frustrating.

But stagnating growth and internal power struggles were not the only issues. The cumbersome cooperative structure also made it increasingly difficult for the business to fulfill its primary mission, which was to get sexual products and information into the hands of as many people as possible. For Winks, who played a pivotal role in opening the second Good Vibrations retail store in Berkeley in 1994, this was hugely disappointing: "The mission of the company is supposed to be to make these resources and information as accessible to as many people as possible. As the cooperative structure grew, and more and more of the energy of the employees in the company went toward internal processes instead of toward our external mission in the world, it was profoundly discouraging to me. I felt like the real duty of the business was almost being overlooked for the sake of interpersonal, personal navel gazing, really. There was a lot of internal wheel spinning."[32]

In 2006, after fourteen years of operating as a worker-owned cooperative, Good Vibrations' grand experiment came to an end when the company once again underwent restructuring, this time resuming a more traditional corporate structure, with former worker-owners transitioning to shareholders. As former Good Vibrations employee Charlie Glickman recalled, "I don't think there was really any one thing [that contributed to the decision], although I think you could generally categorize all the different threads into one, which was that the co-op just wasn't working."[33] The problems the co-op faced were not new, but mirrored what many of those who had worked at Good Vibrations over the years had observed: it was often difficult, if not impossible, to get the votes needed to get anything done. As the company grew in size, almost no one knew all their coworkers, and managers could not manage because they had responsibility without authority. But it was also the case that the cooperative structure, combined with being a sex business, made it difficult for the company to approach banks and other lending organizations for loans. By the mid-2000s, Good Vibrations' need to access capital to stabilize operations and finance expansion plans had become more pressing, and many within the company conceded that a structural change was necessary in order for the business to thrive in a marketplace that was rapidly becoming increasingly competitive, a point I return to in subsequent chapters.

## Creating a Sex-Positive Diaspora

Despite the end of the cooperative experiment, Good Vibrations had played an early and pivotal role in spreading the message of sex positivity far and wide. By the time I began working at Babeland in the early 2000s, Good Vibrations was well known in feminist circles and beyond. The drive to expand the company's mission through marketing and advertising had taken off in the late 1980s when a core group of people, including Semans and Winks, initiated what Semans described as an "aggressive campaign" to expand Blank's original vision beyond the boundaries of San Francisco's Mission District. "We had always felt really strongly about the mission. We had all experienced it personally—a powerful transformation because of learning about your own sexuality," Semans told me.[34]

The commitment on the part of Good Vibrations employees to empower as many people as possible around their sexuality spurred the growth of the company—and the wider market for sex toys—throughout the 1980s and 1990s. People thumbed through Good Vibrations' mail-order catalogs, which went all over the world; they attended in-store after-hours educational programs; and, with the advent of Internet-based retail, they eventually made their way to Good Vibrations' online store. Good Vibrations employee Sarah Kennedy remembered it this way:

> [Good Vibrations'] catalogs went all over the place. Our speakers, our outreach folks went all over the place, and we started having folks come and learn in our stores and then they started their own stores and they went all over the place. I think a lot of what happened with the sex-toy market and sex-toy industry came from the work that Good Vibrations did in the late seventies, eighties, and [early] nineties—Joani's era—to make it so that it was a cool thing, an okay thing, a fun thing. Sex-toy stores were now for women and their lovers and their partners and their friends . . . and I think Good Vibrations put that in place.[35]

The resulting sex-positive diaspora meant that more people in more places had access to sex toys and positive messages about sexuality. Isaiah Benjamin, a trans-identified employee at Babeland, recounted the first time he came into contact with a Good Vibrations catalog as a queer teenager growing up in upstate New York. For someone with little access to information about queer sexuality, the catalog was inspiring: "[The catalog] gave me something to look forward to and it gave me a lot of information and ideas," he said. "Just the way that it was nonjudgmental and out there as an opportunity for people of any gender to buy this stuff and use it without it being some kind of dirty thing. That was powerful for me at that age to see that."[36]

Matie Fricker, the cofounder of Self Serve in Albuquerque, described a similar experience. "Good Vibrations changed my life," she told me in no uncertain terms. It was a place, she said, "where the politics matched the hype."[37]

Retailer Jacq Jones was similarly won over by the experience she had the first time she encountered Babeland in the late 1990s at the Michigan Womyn's Music Festival, where the company was selling sex toys and conducting workshops. She vowed that if she ever lived in a city where Babeland had a store, she wanted to work there. Several years later she moved to New York City, and, according to her, "I basically sat outside of Babeland until they hired me."[38]

Jones came to Babeland with a history of working in human sexuality and reproductive health. She majored in women's studies in college and spent nine years working for Planned Parenthood in different capacities. The opportunity to provide sex education in a pleasure-based environment like Babeland, rather than a clinical setting, appealed to Jones.

Although working at Babeland was Jones's first real experience in retail, her background in counseling served her well. She was able to use the skills she had developed as a counselor to assess customers' comfort levels and adjust her interactions accordingly. She was mindful of the words she used, as well as her body language, and tried to convey to people that whatever they wanted or desired sexually was perfectly fine as long as it was between consenting adults. Jones approached every customer as someone that Babeland was building an ongoing relationship with. "Working at Babeland," she told me, "and working in that environment was, unquestionably, my favorite job ever."[39]

Jones worked at Babeland's Lower East Side store for almost two years in the early 2000s, first as a sales assistant/sex educator and later as an assistant store manager, before moving back to Baltimore. One day, while she was complaining about her job in human services, her wife turned to her and said, "What makes you happy is working in a sex store, so let's do it. Let's open a store." Jones's initial response was, "We can't do that!" But actually, they could. Financially, they were in a good place; they had home equity and savings they could use for start-up money. There was really nothing stopping Jones from pursuing what had long been a dream: opening up a feminist sex shop of her own.[40]

The success of Good Vibrations and Babeland made it possible for Jones to imagine running her own feminist sex-toy business. The first thing she did was look for a lawyer. She wanted to find someone who was preferably queer, but definitely queer-positive, and who had experience working with sex-related businesses. She found someone who fit the bill and, with the help of her lawyer, she incorporated the business and researched local zoning ordinances, making sure that every I was dotted and every T was crossed. She found a retail space in Hampden—a Baltimore neighborhood that Jones described as an "incubator for small businesses"—and joined the Hampden Village Merchants Association. She opened a bank account, got insurance, hired employees, and set up a payroll. She also developed a mission statement: "Sugar is a lesbian-owned, multi-gender operated, for-profit, mission-driven sex-toy store. By providing education and toys in a shame free, sex-positive, fun environment we help people of all genders and orientations experience their own unique sexuality with shameless joy and passion."

The sex-positive focus of Babeland and Sugar united these businesses in a larger, world-changing enterprise, what we might think of as a brand community of progressive sex-toy retailers. It also set these businesses apart from more traditional adult stores, which, according to the dominant narrative, were far more interested in the bottom line than they were in educating and empowering people around their sexuality. Jones explained the importance of Sugar's mission:

> Any business book or theorist will tell you that what a business sells is not really the product. We sell feelings, the experience of being in the store, and information. In order for a business to be successful, you have to know what you are really selling. The mission statement drives what we are really selling. It helps me and the rest of the staff maintain clarity about why we are here every day; it also helps to set us apart from other stores and provides the reason [why] people buy from us, rather than online or from another store. It's important to me since stores like Sugar or Babeland are still a rarity. By providing the mission statement on the website, we help folks have an expectation that we're different and hopefully help them to feel safe coming here—especially if they've had a bad experience at a traditional sex-toy store in the past. It also, frankly, helps set us apart from the bajillion other adult stores in the world.[41]

Here, Jones articulates a process of brand differentiation without ever using the word "branding." She recognizes the need to distinguish Sugar from the "bajillion other" adult businesses in the world, and is keenly aware that what Sugar is selling, and indeed what attracts many people to the store in the first place, goes far beyond the items sitting on the shelves. And while the products themselves are certainly not inconsequential to the sex-positive narrative that Jones is creating, they are not the whole story, either. Sugar is selling feelings, emotions, and a carefully crafted environment in which people are invited to experience their sexuality in new and sometimes quite profound ways. "When people found out the store was opening, they were gleeful," she told me. "When you don't have access to a store like this, it sucks."

As the message of sex positivity spread to cities across the United States, and other countries, too, and more people encountered its positive effects, they were often inspired to join its cause as sex-positive crusaders, either by working at feminist sex-toy stores or opening businesses of their own. For many employees, living the mission and being part of a company they felt so deeply connected to and personally transformed by meant that it was often easy for them to forget they were workers laboring under capitalist conditions, and that part of their job actually involved selling things. In time, the disconnect between money and the mission, which was fueled by the belief that their work was a higher calling, rather than a conventional retail job, would lead to serious problems as many businesses struggled to reconcile their feminist principles with the reality of the marketplace (see chapter 8).

Despite these tensions, a new market was taking shape, and leading the way was a growing network of sex-positive retailers—Good Vibrations, Babeland, Sugar, and others—who were united around a shared vision of sex education and personal empowerment. Their commercial success, however, would ultimately hinge on their ability to develop alternative merchandising and marketing strategies aimed at taking the sleaze out of sex shops in an effort to woo female consumers who, they believed, preferred to shop in more tasteful and welcoming retail environments designed specifically with them in mind.

*four*

# REPACKAGING SEX

———

Social subjects, classified by their classifications,
distinguish themselves by the distinctions they make,
between the beautiful and the ugly, the distinguished and
the vulgar, in which their position in the objective
classifications is expressed or betrayed.

PIERRE BOURDIEU
*Distinction*

A-Action Adult Books sits in the shadow of the Stratosphere hotel-casino just blocks from the wedding chapels, pawn shops, and bail bond businesses that line the north end of Las Vegas Boulevard. A bright yellow awning hanging out front announces "Video Sales and Rentals." On either side of the storefront are two signs with the words "xxx-rated" in big red letters set against images of scantily clad women striking suggestive poses. There is no front door and no windows, only an arrow indicating that the entrance is around the corner on a street that looks more like a deserted alleyway.

Inside the door, a sign over a turnstile indicates that it costs twenty-five cents to enter. When I walked in, in fall 2015, the affable clerk, a white man with gray hair who looked to be in his late fifties, jumped to his feet to let me bypass the turnstile.

"Women don't have to pay," he told me as he ushered me inside.

A-Action Adult—a name likely chosen so it would appear first in the phone book—is like a dinosaur in a time capsule, a version of an adult store that no longer exists in many places. This is a no-frills operation. The computer behind the counter looks like it has been there since the business opened thirty years ago. Signs hand-lettered in black marker, some with misspelled words and unflattering language, are posted throughout the store. One publicizes a

DVD sale: "$5.95 DVDs, now $2.95." Another reads: "Please observe: Time limit 30 minutes when looking at magazines."

The draw for customers who frequent A-Action Adult is not only or necessarily pornography—although there's a great deal of it for sale in the form of DVDs and magazines, both new and vintage; rather, it's the video arcade booths that line the walls at back of the store. Each booth—and there are at least a dozen—is equipped with a glory hole that allows people in adjacent booths to engage in or watch sexual activity.

A-Action is a space for sexual encounters, especially for gay, bisexual, bi-curious, and closeted straight men that use the arcade for anonymous or clandestine liaisons.

Entrance to the arcade requires purchasing a minimum of $4.00 worth of tokens, which buys customers twenty minutes of video. Additional token purchases are required if your stay exceeds two hours. "Anything goes," explained the clerk, as long as it takes place in the privacy of the booths—although no smoking or drugs are allowed, he added. Surveillance cameras and security mirrors mounted on the walls ensure that customers abide by the rules. The only time he's ever had to kick someone out, he told me, was for fighting.

The clerk talked fondly about the business's regulars, including cross-dressing clientele, and told me stories about the different kinds of sexual activity that take place in the booths. Sometimes, this includes the occasional straight couple looking to fulfill a fantasy or pretend they are strangers who meet and have sex in the video booth. He admitted that he's learned a great deal about human sexual behavior since he started working at the store.

A-Action offers a small selection of sex toys, although nothing fancy—mostly inexpensive plastic vibrators and rubber dildos displayed in bulky packaging. The items seem more like an afterthought than an essential part of the business model, a colorful display at the back of the store that patrons pass on their way to the video booths. The inventory doesn't look like it has been updated in years and many products were covered in a thin layer of dust.

This was a business that traded in sexual opportunity, not sexual information. The video booths were the main event, the real selling point, and, most likely, big moneymakers. And while the clerk was chatty and friendly—even describing in unsolicited detail his experience using a penis pump—the business's male customers (and they were all men) gave me quizzical looks, seemingly unsure about what to make of my presence. Who was I and what was my purpose? Was I sexually available? And if not, why was I there?

Interior shots of A-Action Adult Books, Las Vegas, 2015.
Photograph by the author.

Interior shot of A-Action Adult Books, Las Vegas, 2015.
Photograph by the author.

A-Action Adult reminded me of a roadside adult store in Massachusetts that I had visited more than ten years earlier called Adults Only. At the time, I had lamented about the experience to a male friend, complaining that the man sitting behind the counter had ignored me and hadn't bothered to ask if I needed any help or had any questions. Much to my surprise, my friend told me that he had worked briefly at the same store several years earlier.

"I would've done the same thing," he said nonchalantly. "It's nothing personal, but I was there to collect the money, not to give information or provide sex education. My job was to run the cash register."

Had he received any special product training? I asked. He shook his head no. "These products sell themselves," he insisted. "People know if they want something this big"—he held his hands about a foot apart—"or this big," he said, moving them closer. "I was paid minimum wage, which at the time was $5.15 an hour, to deal with customers who were sometimes drunk and often rude. I wasn't paid to help people, or educate them. I was paid to make sure they didn't steal stuff."

A-Action Adult Books and Adults Only are the kind of stores that feminists like Dell Williams and Joani Blank rebelled against when they started their vibrator businesses in the 1970s. They are also examples of a dying breed of sex shop. In many cities, adult bookstores with video arcades and peep booths have been zoned out of existence, while others have reinvented themselves as sexual resource centers in an effort to keep up with changing times and make their stores more welcoming for all kinds of customers, especially women. They have reduced or eliminated their porn inventory in favor of sex toys, painted their stores to make them lighter and brighter, and in many cases hired women to work on the sales floor.

Despite these market shifts, old-school sex shops like A-Action and Adults Only remain key to the ways in which many feminist retailers understand and promote their businesses, offering a necessary counterpoint against which the clean and well-lighted sex shop assumes its cultural meaning and import. Indeed, the Good Vibrations retail model is defined largely by what it is not: It is wholesome and women-friendly, not sleazy and male-oriented; clean, not dirty; and classy, not crass. These discourses of distinction, and the corresponding dimensions of difference that are presumed to exist between what one feminist retailer described as the "gross, male part of the industry" versus the "tiny, burgeoning feminist part," operate quite powerfully in the cultural imaginations of store owners and employees. In conversation after conversation, feminist retailers presented conventional adult stores in an exaggerated and almost caricatured form, positioning them as the cultural low-other against which the supposedly more elevated world of women-friendly sexuality boutiques is defined. As scholars have noted, what is often considered to be socially peripheral—in this case the stereotypically seedy adult store—is frequently "symbolically central" to producing and maintaining social distinctions of various kinds.[1]

The Good Vibrations retail model offers an interesting case study for examining how sexual codes and conventions can be repackaged—and indeed regendered—with an eye toward wooing women. Yet marking the distinctions between crass and class, and sexual sleaze versus safety, is hardly a value-free endeavor. Rather, it is a practice imbued with social judgments that produce, among other things, a commercially viable version of white, middle-class female sexuality that brings with it a tangible set of effects, including wider community acceptance from prospective landlords, neighborhood associations, and zoning boards. Making sex-toy stores "respectable" is thus an intensely social process that is as much about race and class as it is about gender and sexuality.

When it comes to class, however, this concept proves especially difficult to define. Scholars generally agree that class involves more than one's relationship to the means of production. Writing in the 1970s, lesbian feminist Rita Mae Brown noted that "class involves your behavior, your basic assumptions about life . . . how you are taught to behave, what you expect from yourself and from others, your concept of a future, how you understand problems and solve them, how you think, feel, act."[2] Communication scholar Lisa Henderson has more recently asserted that social class refers to "the economic and cultural coproduction of social distinction and hierarchy," pointing to the ways in which class categories work to mark a "cultural universe."[3] We can see these class differences at play as feminist sex-toy stores have laid claim to a degree of marketplace legitimacy and moral authority previously denied their purportedly lowbrow counterparts. Feminist retailers are therefore positioned, and sometimes caught, between new sexual possibilities for women and familiar markers of class distinction, the conventional logic of boutique culture and the counterlogic of sexual access and openness, a commitment to diversity and inclusion and the constraints of gender essentialism in the world of niche marketing.

## Safety versus Sleaze

When Claire Cavanah and Rachel Venning decided to open Babeland in 1993, they knew they wanted to create a business with a boutique feel, a store that would be attractive to women, yet not off-putting to men. Cavanah saw the space as a blank canvas that she and Venning—much like artists—could use to say whatever they wanted. The most important message they wanted to convey, according to Cavanah, "was to invite women in [to the store] to experience these toys in another way."[4] From the warm lighting and the yellow color wash on the walls to the homespun signs and the way products were displayed, Cavanah and Venning tried to create a fun and friendly retail environment that drew upon a different set of visual cues about what a sex-toy store could look like and who it was for.

From the beginning Good Vibrations, too, had tried to create a welcoming and homey environment for customers.

"We tried to make it so that you were inviting people into your living room," former Good Vibrations manager Cathy Winks remarked. "When you read the old articles about the early [Good Vibrations] stores, it was about the armchair and the rug and the plants and how it was so cozy. And that is what we were making a conscious effort to create—a really safe, cozy space for people."[5]

Interior shot of Babeland's Seattle store, 1998. Courtesy of Babeland.

Babeland's rebranded and redesigned Seattle store, 2015. Courtesy of Babeland. Barbie Hull Photography.

Fashioning a sex-toy store to resemble a comfy living room was a radical departure from the stereotype of an adult store as a dimly lit and unwelcoming place. But this was precisely what Good Vibrations founder Joani Blank was trying to do, especially early on. By styling her store in a way that mirrored the layout and design of the home, a sphere traditionally associated with women, Blank was effectively domesticating and, some might argue, sexually sanitizing her vibrator shop by anchoring it in the emotional comfort of a familiar space.

In many respects, what Blank was doing echoed the efforts of pioneering feminist pornographers, such as Candida Royalle, who founded Femme Productions in 1984. Royalle felt that a female point of view was "glaringly absent" from the world of pornography.[6] She was convinced that there was a market for pornography that focused on female pleasure; it just needed to be made. But what might porn for women look like and how might it be different from what already existed?

Royalle ignored many of heterosexual pornography's taken-for-granted conventions, including the ubiquitous money shot—the obligatory image of male ejaculation that confirmed for viewers that actual rather than simulated sex had occurred. Instead, she showcased performers' faces when they climaxed and focused on their sweaty, writhing, and contracting bodies. She also was not especially interested in featuring genital close-ups, another staple of mainstream pornography. She preferred medium and long shots, which presented the pornographic body in new ways. Royalle wanted to portray more sensuality and tenderness, and greater passion and communication, between performers. For her, making porn for women required employing a different visual language for representing sex and pleasure.

Much like feminist pornographers, Blank also took a cultural form historically associated with men—the sex shop—and transformed it into something she hoped would be more female friendly. From the get-go, Blank was determined to avoid the look and trappings of a typical adult bookstore, with its highly sexualized aura and "seamy" appearance, preferring instead to make Good Vibrations as unerotic as possible. She thumbed her nose at selling lingerie because, according to her, it "perpetuated a stereotype of what a sexy woman is"; and she rejected pornography altogether—at least until the late 1980s when Susie Bright convinced her that she should begin carrying a carefully curated selection of erotic videos. (Notably, Royalle's films helped women-friendly sex shops add pornography to their product mix.)

Blank wanted to create a store that was not only warm and welcoming, but communicated a set of messages about women's sexuality that was different from those one would typically find in a traditional adult store. Ultimately, Blank and the retailers who followed in her footsteps deployed an alternative "sexual vernacular"[7]—a different way of representing sex and organizing sexual knowledge that pivoted on highly gendered appeals to what women supposedly wanted when it came to sex and, by extension, sex-toy stores.

Even the layout of most feminist sex-toy stores was designed to encourage sexual curiosity while minimizing feelings of emotional or psychological discomfort. "One of the things that I have noticed," former Babeland employee Alicia Relles said, "is that there's a safety when you walk into Babeland. There is a corner for books and magazines. Half the people go right over there, and there is a safety in that." This was no accident; rather, it was a deliberate strategy that allowed nervous customers to ease themselves into the store by showcasing products that moved from "mild to wild." As Relles explained:

> I like the way that [Babeland] is structured and that there are points in the store that allow people to have different vantage points of things and to distance themselves from objects that may be scary or intimidating. The dildos are presented in a way that is about color and presentation versus that this is actually a dick. The things that are highlighted in the store are very much about color and aesthetics and are not so screamingly phallic. You are not confronted with certain images or, even if you are, it is done in a different way.[8]

For feminist retailers and sales staff, ideas about what constitutes sexual safety and comfort are closely linked to the desire to protect unsuspecting customers, especially women, from people or products that might be "screamingly phallic" or otherwise shocking or scary. These ideas were not only built into the design and layout of stores; they also informed how these businesses thought about customer service. According to Good Vibrations' Charlie Glickman:

> People should feel comfortable [when they come into our store]. I don't know how many times I've seen people walk through the door and suddenly they take a deep breath and relax when they realize it's not a scary place. If you go into your standard porn store, it is bright lights, flashy, and a hard sell. We don't do a hard sell. We ask you if you have any questions and then we leave you alone. If you have a question,

you're welcome to ask us anything . . . and if we don't have the answer, we will try to find someone who does.[9]

The belief that sexuality can be frightening was something these businesses worked hard to counteract in the hope of making their stores as accessible as possible to people that might otherwise never go into a sex-toy store. "This is very important to us," Good Vibrations' Carol Queen explained, "because it means that more and more people who haven't had access to comfortable or correct information will get it from us."[10] Feminist retailers wanted to send the message to customers that sex-toy stores did not have to be, as Grand Opening's Kim Airs put it, "uncomfortable, shameful, or dirty to get something that you want."[11]

Although most retailers, regardless of the products they sell, endeavor to create environments where people feel comfortable, this idea assumed added symbolic weight for feminist sex-toy stores, because these businesses deal specifically with sex. By striving to make their stores welcoming and safe, feminist retailers were attempting to establish a different set of retail norms and merchandising strategies than what customers would likely encounter if they were to visit a more traditional adult business, such as A-Action Adult Books. These revamped norms were also a conscious effort to challenge ideas about sex negativity—and women's sexual availability to men—which feminist retailers believed permeated both the adult industry and the wider culture. Queen explained:

> I assume that you've been in some traditional adult bookstore–type sex spaces, and there is just something about the way that they are put together that doesn't seem . . . friendly. You sure can tell why all these guys stuck their noses in Good Vibrations and said, "I don't really like those places myself." Of course they don't! They are not really very likable as sex spaces and, in some ways, the ways that they are unlikable sort of support cultural sex negativity. Why would you want to shop for this kind of stuff in a clean and nice environment? Who would think in those terms? *Well, women thought in those terms.* That's who![12]

## Wooing the Marin Housewife

Creating a comfortable and safe retail environment is a defining feature of the Good Vibrations retail model and reflected the type of audience that Good

Vibrations was initially hoping to attract: the sexually reserved yet curious woman who might have never imagined venturing into one of "those places."

While Good Vibrations wanted to be a store that, according to Queen, "could be safe enough for anybody"—including women and men of diverse backgrounds, gender presentations, and sexual orientations—who they especially wanted to be safe for was a particular subset of women. Many employees I spoke with who worked at Good Vibrations in the 1990s invoked the stereotype of the Marin housewife to describe their target demographic. Marin County is located in the North San Francisco Bay Area. According to recent U.S. Census data, 72 percent of its population is white and the median household income is just under $91,000, making it one of the wealthiest counties in the United States. Residents are known to be both politically progressive and affluent.

The description of the Marin housewife paints a picture of the idealized Good Vibrations customer that is rooted in a very specific constellation of gender, race, and socioeconomic stereotypes. According to former Good Vibrations employee Roma Estevez, the Marin housewife is a middle- to upper-middle-class, presumably white, suburban woman who is "not very sexually adventurous; who maybe doesn't have an orgasm or who doesn't reliably have an orgasm; who doesn't talk about sex with her friends or husband or mom; who is straight, of course; and who is interested [in sex] but really needs a lot of encouragement and hand-holding."[13]

During the years that she worked as the manager of Good Vibrations, Cathy Winks often reminded her staff that they needed to think of the Good Vibrations customer as the suburban lady who heard from a friend at church that there was a sex-toy store in the city that was "really nice for women." "What is going to make this woman feel safe walking into a sex-toy store for the very first time?" Winks frequently asked her staff. "What kind of music will be playing? How will people be dressed? How will this customer be treated?" Winks encouraged sales staff to be attentive to these details in order to ensure that the store continued to be a comfortable and safe space for even the most shy or sexually inhibited woman.[14]

Anne Semans also emphasized this point. "There was a real tendency," she told me, "to forget that suburban housewives made up 80 percent of our mail-order [business] and that we couldn't just assume that everyone was going to be comfortable with a certain terminology or a certain attitude or cleverness."[15]

Good Vibrations' retail strategy rested on the belief that these white, sub-urban (and supposedly heterosexual) housewives needed more hand-holding and encouragement around their sexuality than other women. If these women could feel safe in a vibrator store, then presumably anyone could. Thus, the business's emphasis on sexual safety and comfort assumed a highly gendered, class-specific, and racially coded dimension that served as a powerful organizing principle for what it meant to be a different kind of sex shop.

The representational strategies and aesthetic norms that have evolved alongside the Good Vibrations retail model not only function to distance feminist sex-toy stores from more traditional adult businesses; they are also a by-product of highly gendered and class-specific discourses regarding cultural tastes, those stated preferences that, according to French sociologist Pierre Bourdieu, "are the practical affirmation of an inevitable difference."[16] Laura Weide, who had stints working at both Good Vibrations and Babeland in the 1990s and early 2000s, acknowledged that the "alternative aesthetic" that many feminist sex-toy stores adopted "sort of assumes a gendered contrast."[17] Women-friendly sex-toy stores often rely on elements of style and "tasteful" displays, such as painting the walls lavender, hanging original art, using warm lighting and colorful signage, and having comfy chairs and couches to give their businesses a nonthreatening and more feminine and homey touch. At one point, Early to Bed in Chicago even displayed playful needlepoint art—an activity traditionally associated with women—that featured sex toys and sexy slogans. Within these retail contexts, then, ideas about female sexuality have become virtually indistinguishable from the allegedly safe and nonthreatening codes of middle-class sexual decorum and respectability.

Respectability is an ideologically dense concept, one that's infused with a number of often unspoken value judgments and moral prescriptions. Sociologist Beverley Skeggs argues that respectability invariably contains opinions about class, race, gender, and sexuality. Respectability, she explains, is a key element in defining what it means to belong and to be seen as worthy. However, not all groups have equal access to the mechanisms needed to generate and display respectability. To be viewed as respectable is thus to embody moral authority.[18]

For feminist sex-toy shops, being respectable also involves marking the differences between clean and dirty. This distinction is on the one hand symbolic: Prurient, titillating, and hypersexual representations of sexuality are frequently rejected in favor of what is thought to be more wholesome, woman-friendly, and ostensibly tame versions. But the difference between clean and dirty sex shops is also quite literal. When I asked retailer Jacq Jones from Sugar how she created a safe space for women at her store in Baltimore, she said this:

> For me, it means first of all clean. I cannot tell you how much of a difference it makes, because literally all of the stores in Baltimore that sell sex toys other than us, every time I have been in them . . . they are quite literally, at minimum, dusty if not dirty. That sends a very clear message about what you are doing . . . and I hear back from a lot of our customers. One of the ways they describe it, the language they use frequently is, "It's so nice to be in a place where I don't feel like my feet are sticking to the floor."[19]

For Jones, creating a safe and comfortable retail environment, especially for women, requires that she literally keep a clean shop, one that is dust and dirt free, tidy, and frequently mopped. Having a clean store is an important part of setting a different tone and communicating a different set of messages about the kind of sexualized space she wants Sugar to be.

More complicated to disentangle, yet equally important, however, is what the so-called dirty adult store represents symbolically. Sex-positive retailers seek to intervene in a culture where sex is frequently positioned as dirty—especially in its commodified forms where sex intersects with the exchange of money (e.g., prostitution, pornography, the purchase of sexual products). Given the power of this cultural belief system, these retailers have a vested interest, both politically and commercially, in challenging the idea that sex—and by extension their businesses—are inherently dirty. This involves not only painting a stark contrast between their "fun, feisty, and feminist" businesses and "sleazy" adult stores, but presenting a somewhat sanitized version of who their businesses are designed to appeal to and why.

The notion of the dirty adult store is anchored in a very particular construction of male sexuality in which men are perceived as needing specific kinds of sexual stimuli, experiences, and environments to turn them on. "I think the typical adult stores aimed at men promote the idea of dirty," Ellen Barnard, the owner of A Woman's Touch in Madison, Wisconsin, told me, "because they know that for some men that is the trigger. That is the thing that makes them so excited. We didn't do that. We said, 'No, actually, [sex] is not dirty, it is wonderful.'"[20]

Men, it would seem from this stereotype, need a certain amount of sleaze in order for sex to be sexy. Women, on the other hand, are presumed to want something different: a more sanitized and wholesome version of sexuality. Both characterizations, however, are severely limiting.

In her research on British retailer Ann Summers's home sex-toy parties, sociologist Merl Storr reminds us that discourses are not simply statements of individuals' ideas or preferences; rather, they are "sets of beliefs and assumptions which shape the way social groups understand the world."[21] Discourses are never neutral, but are "intimately connected" to power relations, becoming themselves sites of struggle over the meaning of, for example, male and female sexuality and the bounds of socially acceptable consumption. To be attentive to discourses, then, is to be attentive to power.[22]

The discourses of distinction that are routinely mobilized by feminist retailers, such as clean versus dirty and sexual safety versus sleaze, not only produce a particular kind retail environment but also construct an image of an idealized sexual consumer that is perhaps not as encompassing of racial and class diversity as these businesses might hope. Amy Andre emphasized this point when discussing what she saw as the "hyper-attention paid to cleanliness" at Good Vibrations:

> We kept emphasizing the clean and brightly lit store, and I think [these things] have very definite class and race implications that were never explicitly stated; but I think it was a way of saying, "You won't encounter black men or poor men here. You won't encounter people here who are physically having a sexual experience in this location. You are not going to have to go to North Beach and be around strippers, and maybe be mistaken for a stripper or a prostitute. Nobody is going to think you are the bad girl in this place or that you are a sex worker because you are entering a toy store." I think there was a lot that wasn't being said when we were communicating to customers.[23]

These silences—what was not being communicated, especially in regard to race and class—constitute a structuring absence, reinforcing often unspoken judgments and stereotypes that elevate certain consumer desires (and desiring subjects) above others, drawing boundaries in the process around sexual belonging and exclusion, male and female sexuality, and good versus bad sex.

Taking the sleaze out of sex shops, and making sexual consumption a respectable activity, was more than just a symbolic gesture; it also brought a tangible set of rewards to feminist retailers. Their ability to distinguish their businesses from their allegedly seamier counterparts—and the people who supposedly frequent such places—has helped legitimize their stores in the eyes of anxious landlords and neighborhood associations concerned about the implications of having one of "those businesses" and the elements they purportedly attract—"dirty old men," poorer clientele, sex workers, and drug dealers—in their buildings and neighborhoods.

Retailer Aileen Journey told me that she learned to be "pretty vague" when she was looking for a commercial space in Northampton, Massachusetts, for Intimacies in the late 1990s, because she did not want her business to be associated with the stereotypical adult store. "If I say 'sex store,' people immediately think of a dirty, sleazy [place] and I didn't want them to get the wrong idea."[24] Searah Deysach, from Early to Bed in Chicago, echoed this: "I don't think I said the word 'sex' ever [when I was looking for a space] and I focused so much on the fact that it was designed for women, because I don't think that people see women as a threat, really, pretty much ever. And I think if someone says, 'sex-toy store,' they think immediately of whatever kind of riff-raff . . . but if it is an 'erotic boutique' or whatever stupid name I had come up with, they see it as something that is softer and more couples-oriented."[25]

Jacq Jones had a similar experience when she was opening Sugar in Baltimore. According to her, there was a bit of a "hullabaloo" with the local community council about her store, because many council members didn't have a reference point for the type of business she was opening. At their meeting, Jones distributed Sugar's mission statement, described the store, and detailed who would make up its customer base. She also referenced Good Vibrations and Babeland, which, according to her, went a long way toward allaying the community council's concerns; not only were some of the council members familiar with those businesses, but they understood the fundamental differences between an educationally oriented sex-toy store and a stereotypically sleazy one and, presumably, the different clienteles these businesses supposedly attracted.

Such distinctions are not simply a linguistic sleight of hand but have real effects when it comes to leasing commercial spaces and reassuring nervous community members that these are not dodgy or dangerous enterprises, but instead, as Jones put it, "a place that [is] going to be a safe space for women."[26] Feminist retailers have thus created a new normal. In today's sexual marketplace, "women" has become a code word for a safe and respectable model of sex-toy retailing; in turn, safety and respectability have become synonymous with a commercially viable version of white, middle-class, female sexuality. This has allowed feminist retailers to carve out not only a profitable market niche but a degree of moral authority in a commercial realm traditionally characterized by sexual stigma, shame, and ill repute.

## Class versus Crass

During my research at Babeland in the early 2000s, I met a twenty-something African American woman who was visiting the store for the first time. After browsing for a few minutes, she took me aside and told me that for months she had been having coffee with her coworkers at the café across the street and had always assumed Babeland was a shoe store. She was about to leave her job in the neighborhood and decided to pay a visit to the store that she'd been looking at from afar for all these months. She was shocked—and to some degree pleasantly surprised, she revealed—to discover that Babeland was a sex-toy store. "I had absolutely no idea," she said. From the outside, the store appeared to be a small boutique specializing in designer shoes. "What about the dildos on the shelves?" I asked. "I thought they were shoes," she laughed. That this woman, and occasionally other customers, mistook Babeland for a shoe store (or a jewelry store or hair salon) suggested that Cavanah and Venning had succeeded in creating a sex-toy store that looked like a specialty boutique that could presumably be selling anything.

The language of boutique culture is laden with assumptions about aesthetic sophistication and fashionable retailing. Feminist proprietors, sales staff, and customers frequently—and often without reflection—used the terms "classy" or "upscale" to describe what they saw as the biggest differences between women-friendly sex-toy stores and their less glamorous counterparts, what one writer described as "seamy peep-show sex shops."[27] "[Babeland] has that boutique feel, where it doesn't feel dirty or secretive," said one employee. "I enjoyed your store," a woman wrote in an e-mail to Babeland, "because it wasn't trashy at all." Ideas about classy retailing have found material expression in the visual merchandising and in-store displays used by these stores, becoming yet another way these businesses differentiate themselves from run-of-the-mill adult stores. As Good Vibrations' Estevez explained: "Good Vibrations shoots for a more classy feeling in the store and in the personality of the catalogs and the website. I think originally that was probably a really good idea and a really good stance to take to differentiate us from the sleazy sex-toy shop that had a lot of metal in it and a lot of cheesy packages. So, I think originally it was really smart and it really worked."[28]

Taking products out of bulky packaging with images of female porn stars on the front is one way that feminist retailers try to create a more comfortable and "classy" retail vibe. Even though sex-toy packaging has become sleeker and more sophisticated in recent years, with an eye toward nonhuman forms and bold, colorful branding, feminist retailers maintain that displaying items outside of their packaging, or repackaging products in nondescript wrapping, can go a long way toward changing the kinds of messages their businesses communicate about sex and gender. When I worked at Babeland, customers would sometimes flinch at the point of purchase when their vibrator was handed to them in a box that featured a woman in a sexually suggestive pose—which was not how the item was displayed on the shelf. "I wouldn't have bought this if I had first seen the box," was a response I frequently heard from both women and men who seemed to prefer their merchandise packaged in less overtly sexualized ways.

For feminist sex-toy retailers, displaying merchandise outside of its soft-core packaging was a conscious rejection of what many viewed as an extremely limited version of female beauty and desirability. "We are not playing into that fantasy," Babeland's Cavanah explained to me. "So then, half [the customers] don't know where they are. What is it if it's not a vapid woman fantasy? What is it? Well, it's a vibrator and it's supposed to feel good! It's much more the practicality of it than the fantasy of it."[29]

Displaying tester models that customers can pick up and turn on not only helps to change the look and feel of these stores, but it's a merchandising strategy that invites people to interact directly with products, creating, ideally, a different level of comfort. Customers can hold items in their hands, feel the material products are made from, and test the strength of an item's vibration against their wrist or shoulder. Feminist retailers believe that the tactile experience of touching and handling a vibrator or dildo not only helps customers figure out what to buy but can also go a long way toward normalizing objects that might be intimidating to some shoppers. "Mail order is great, and the catalog and website is great, but the really transformative effect that Good Vibrations can have on people's lives comes from walking into a physical space and going, 'Wow, I'm being confronted with this transgressive material and shivery, shaky things and if I just breathe deeply and sit with it, it's not so scary,'" says Winks.[30] Intimacies' Aileen Journey agreed: "When you have [items] that people can take into their hands, it makes such a difference. ... People start to feel like this stuff is okay."[31]

For those customers who might already be familiar with the aesthetic codes and conventions that operate in more traditional adult stores—dim lighting, or lighting that is shockingly bright, lots of print and video pornography, and plastic novelty items in bulky packaging accompanied by signs that say, "Do Not Open!"—encountering a sex-toy store with attractive displays and playful signage can be confusing and even a little disorienting. And it wasn't just the one woman I met; Cavanah described many occasions when customers came into Babeland and, according to her, "They didn't know where they were: 'Is this a hair salon? Is this a coffee shop? Where am I?' People were having an entirely different experience than they thought they would."[32]

Writer and cultural critic Laura Kipnis has skillfully discussed the connection between sexuality, aesthetics, and class signifiers. In the essay "Disgust and Desire: *Hustler* Magazine," Kipnis argues that Larry Flynt and *Hustler* disrupted the taken-for-granted codes and conventions associated with men's magazines such as *Playboy* and *Penthouse*—publications that reflected a sexual sensibility largely defined through middle-class standards of decorum, civility, sophistication, and taste.[33] *Hustler*, according to Kipnis, defiantly addressed itself to a working-class audience and was "determined to violate all the taboos observed by its more classy men's-rag brethren."[34] *Hustler* introduced penises—a sight verboten in other men's magazines—and included images of pregnant women, fat women, middle-aged women, and amputees that were intended to shock as well as titillate. According to Kipnis, the improper and even gross sexual body presented in *Hustler* assumed its social and political significance in contrast to the proper, polite, and contained female body depicted in *Playboy* and *Penthouse*. In violating the representational conventions of men's magazines, *Hustler* transgressed the socially acceptable limits of sexual tastefulness. Kipnis's discussion is a reminder that what is considered sexually gross and repulsive or tasteful and acceptable are matters of class distinction that delineate the boundaries of inclusion and rejection.

Kipnis's analysis of *Hustler* and its more tasteful—and therefore more socially acceptable—counterparts offers an instructive parallel for thinking about the kinds of distinctions that feminist sex-toy retailers and, increasingly, manufacturers actively produce to differentiate their businesses from more conventional and presumably less women-friendly companies that trade in a raunchier and often X-rated style.

Candida Royalle, who created a popular line of vibrators in the late 1990s, Natural Contours, in addition to running her video company, articulated one of the strongest expressions—and indeed naturalizations—of the relationship between gender, class, and aesthetic sophistication in describing the appeal of her products to women:

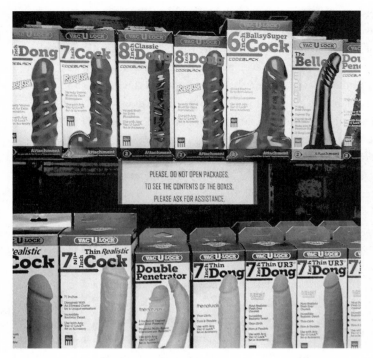

Dildo display with a prominent Do Not Open sign. Studio 21 in Addison, Illinois, 2015. Photograph by the author.

Dildo display at Babeland's Seattle store, 2015. Courtesy of Babeland. Barbie Hull Photography.

I always say that women love sex. They just want it done well. They want to look at it done well. One of the biggest words that women would use when they would write me letters thanking me for my work is the word "class." They would say, "Thank you. Finally, something with class." Women don't want low-class stuff that makes them feel even more ashamed of their sexuality and of themselves for looking at it. And I think it is the same thing with these [vibrators]. They wanted something with class. And that is, I think, how you get to women. You give them something with class, with quality, with some kind of artistry, and they will respond much better than the same old, cheesy kind of approach you can take with men.[35]

In Royalle's opinion, bringing markers of quality and artistry to the sexual marketplace through product design, packaging, and display is not only "how you get to women," but it is also how you rescue sex, porn, and sex toys from their stereotypically crass and lowbrow status. For Royalle, this larger project of "sexual uplift" is intimately connected to advancing the mission of sex positivity: "Women have such a legacy of shame about our sexuality. And by doing it this way there is nothing dirty or shameful about these products. It is not going to make you feel dirty or shameful and in fact it will reinforce feelings of positive self-acceptance of their sexuality. I think that has been very important and that is what [women] have needed."[36]

Royalle's theory, while certainly compelling, reflects an extremely fixed and limited version of what women supposedly want when it comes to sex and sex toys—views that have broad implications for shaping consumer demands. Although these ideas certainly hold true for some women, including those who have written to Royalle expressing their gratitude, it would be a mistake to assume that she speaks for, or that her products speak to, all women. The "truth" that Royalle presents about female sexuality is at best a partial truth, one that she was able to parlay, with great success, into her business ventures. Yet there are a number of women for whom ideas about sexual comfort, safety, and respectability translate into a kind of sexual sterility that is anything but sexy or appealing. Even someone like Winks, who spent ten years working at Good Vibrations, admitted that she found Good Vibrations to be decidedly unsexy the first time she visited the store as a customer in the early 1980s. "I get the safe atmosphere that they are trying to create," she commented, "but it is almost oppressively countererotic, which is how I experienced it on my first visit there."[37]

There are plenty of women who actively embrace the sense of cultural transgression, taboo, and anonymity they experience when they venture into a store that has not attempted to sanitize sex or mimic the retail aesthetics of the Gap or an Apple Store. One white, middle-class lesbian I spoke with during the course of my research told me that she enjoyed shopping at more conventional adult stores with her girlfriend, because women-friendly sex stores "could be selling anything." For her, the gendered recoding of these spaces effectively desexualized them to the extent that "they could be a jewelry store"—and were thus, for her, rather boring.

The same was true for thirty-something Juawana, a white, college-educated feminist who noted that while Babeland is unequivocally her "favorite sex store," she also enjoys the experience of visiting more conventional adult stores, like the Adult Superstore in Las Vegas. "I enjoy the gritty experience. That's part of the fun—being in a dark and dingy, not actually dangerous but kind of sketchy place."[38] The issue for her wasn't the look and feel of traditional adult stores, but rather that these businesses rarely carried the quality products she wanted to buy. Thus, the codes of feminine respectability and classy retailing that Good Vibrations and Babeland cultivate to distinguish themselves from traditional sex-toy stores—distinctions that clearly have appeal for many people—do not always lend themselves to the kinds of sexually transgressive or inclusive experiences that some women desire; and as Juawana suggests, for some shoppers the appeal of female-friendly sex shops might be less about how they look and feel, and much more about the types of products they carry (see chapter 5).

## Zoning Sexual Respectability

When Good Vibrations was on the verge of opening its second retail location in Berkeley, California, in 1994, an unexpected stumbling block arose: the store's permit was rescinded less than a week before its scheduled opening. According to newspaper accounts, a resident had complained to Berkeley City Council officials that Good Vibrations had been issued a permit as a gift shop and bookstore rather than an adult business, the latter of which would have resulted in a number of restrictions, making it impossible for the business to operate in its chosen location.[39]

Employees and supporters of Good Vibrations rallied, signing petitions, sending e-mails, and making phone calls to city officials. They argued that

Good Vibrations was not a dirty bookstore that appealed to "prurient interests"—referring to the language used in the Berkeley ordinance; rather, it was a sexuality resource center with an educational mission and, as such, a valued and respected business. One letter sent to city councilwoman Carla Woodworth stated, "Good Vibrations is not a smut store frequented by creepy guys in raincoats. It is tasteful and provides needed information on AIDS and other pressing sexuality issues."

The store's permit was eventually reinstated, but only after Good Vibrations marshaled the symbolic resources and community support it needed to convince city officials that it did not fit the stereotype of a sleazy adult business. It also had to demonstrate that the majority of its product mix was not sexual in nature, but instead consisted of educational materials and gift items. In the end, Good Vibrations' ability to differentiate itself from what Carol Queen described as the "more lurid [retail] environments or less educationally oriented or [less] clean and well lit" establishments provided it with a degree of moral authority not necessarily available to its less reputable counterparts.[40]

The Good Vibrations incident illustrates how the discourses of distinction—classy versus crass and tasteful versus tacky—that feminist retailers regularly mobilize when discussing their businesses are not simply descriptive terms, but generative ones that produce social hierarchies of cultural value, legitimizing certain businesses while delegitimizing others. The effects of this are numerous, ranging from which businesses are approached by journalists to provide expert voices in media stories about sexuality and health, to which are welcome in their local Chamber of Commerce; but perhaps most illustrative of the increased social status conferred on many women-friendly sex-toy businesses—although certainly not all—is the degree to which they are able to successfully navigate otherwise restrictive zoning ordinances.

In recent decades, cities have increasingly used zoning ordinances as mechanisms to regulate adult-oriented businesses while simultaneously upholding the First Amendment protections that such businesses are guaranteed under the U.S. Constitution. In other words, cities cannot prohibit sexually oriented businesses just because concerned citizens and public officials do not like their content. What they can do, however, is generate content-neutral ordinances designed to lessen the secondary effects thought to be associated with these businesses, such as blight, increased crime—especially prostitution—and lower property values. Oftentimes, this means that adult businesses—regardless of their missions or intended audiences—are relegated to isolated industrial zones on the outskirts of a city, far from schools, churches, other adult businesses, and, significantly, well-heeled shopping districts and their customers.[41]

That is what almost happened to Self Serve in Albuquerque. Owners Molly Adler and Matie Fricker encountered unexpected zoning issues when they were looking for a commercial space for Self Serve in 2006. Due to a change in zoning laws that they hadn't anticipated, they suddenly found themselves zoned out of Albuquerque's more established shopping districts, including Nob Hill, the neighborhood they ideally wanted to be in. Complying with the zoning ordinance meant one of two things: they could open their business in a desolate industrial area, or they could keep the store's inventory to 25 percent or less adult merchandise. In this case, the classification of "adult" included anything that was designed to stimulate the genitals or specific anatomical areas, including the buttocks and nipples. The designation also included items that depicted images of genitals, such as pornography and even some sexual health books.

Adler and Fricker didn't want their business to be located in a remote industrial area for a number of reasons, including the fact that they didn't want to push sex, and by extension their store, to the cultural margins in what essentially amounted to a commercial quarantine. This was the exact opposite of what they wanted their store to communicate to customers, which was, "This is a nice place for you to go," Fricker explained.[42] And as a brand-new business with no prior ties to Albuquerque, they had neither the financial resources nor the established community connections to fight the zoning law. This meant that in order for Self Serve to have a storefront address in a more established shopping district, Adler and Fricker needed to figure out how to run a sex shop with less than 25 percent of the shelf space devoted to adult products. To abide by the letter of the law, they measured every square inch of their retail space, including the shelves, and created a grid that allowed them to meet the exact specifications of the zoning regulations.

Doing so involved a little creativity and some judgment calls. They determined, for example, that BDSM products did not count as adult merchandise, because floggers and blindfolds were not designed to stimulate genitals; however, they decided to play it safe and categorize harnesses as adult because they were used in the service of sexual activity. They generated a spreadsheet and kept detailed records of every adult versus nonadult product they carried, including the amount of shelf space they occupied. This meant that every time they wanted to carry a new adult product, like the latest, greatest vibrator, they

Self Serve Sexuality Resource Center in Albuquerque, New Mexico, 2007.
Photograph by Tina Larkin.

needed to balance it out with three times the amount of nonadult inventory. So they beefed up their body care section and decided to sell chocolate, which ended up working out well, Fricker explained, because "chocolate is sexy and chocolate makes you feel good." But the ordinance certainly posed challenges for the business, including financial ones. "About 80 percent of our money comes from 20 percent of our products," Adler noted.[43]

Eleven months after Self Serve opened, two representatives from the city paid the store a visit, claiming that they had received a complaint that Self Serve was violating the city's zoning ordinance. It was Adler and Fricker's worst fear materialized. These were people with the power to shut their fledgling business down. "I was so scared. I was terrified," Fricker recounted. "I very nicely explained that while they might think [there's a violation], we actually really respect the zoning code, built our store around it, really want to be good neighbors. We really do understand and respect that these are the constraints."[44]

Fricker walked around the store with the officials and explained what was on the shelves and why certain merchandise was categorized the way it was. Then she waited. Two days later, she received a phone call informing her that the store was "zoning compliant." Several years later, when another set of representatives from the city visited the store, Fricker knew the drill and the outcome was the same.

Zoning ordinances are yet another battleground for feminist sex-toy stores, which are certainly not immune from the perception that adult businesses lack redeeming cultural value. The stereotype of adult businesses as polluting agents that bring with them unwanted and contaminating secondary effects—including crime and "creepy guys in raincoats"—and therefore need to be isolated from the general population, as well as other nonadult businesses, is a reality that businesses like Good Vibrations and Self Serve must contend with when they talk to potential landlords, local community groups, and zoning boards. In some cases, it can even affect their ability to get insurance, because their businesses are considered too risky.

For Good Vibrations and the companies that have followed in its footsteps, challenging negative stereotypes has involved producing distinctions of various kinds in an effort to differentiate their wholesome, educationally focused, female-friendly businesses from the stereotype of the sleazy adult store. This has helped them grow their businesses among a particular subset of female consumers who have not always felt welcome in more traditional sex shops; it has also helped them gain a degree of marketplace legitimacy and moral authority historically denied their purportedly lowbrow counterparts. Yet securing their status as respectable retailers requires ongoing symbolic and ideological work that depends as much on what is not being communicated about race and class as it does on what is being said about gender and sexuality. It is a process that also, and perhaps unwittingly, produces certain beliefs about male and female sexuality, and good versus bad consumer desires, that organize these businesses in absolutely fundamental ways, including which products they carry and why.

*five*

# THE POLITICS
# OF PRODUCTS

———

If I prefer quality in the clothes I wear, the furniture I buy, in the things
that I get for myself in the life that I lead, [then] why should there be
any difference in the products that I buy for my sexual pleasure?

CANDIDA ROYALLE

Dressed casually in jeans and a T-shirt, Tyler Merriman sat at a desk in her fastidiously tidy Seattle office. A white, boyish-looking lesbian in her mid-twenties, with short brown hair and thick black glasses, Merriman looked like someone who would feel right at home in any one of Seattle's hipster hangouts. On a shelf next to her desk sat a stack of heavy, glossy catalogs from sex-toy manufacturers Doc Johnson and Cal Exotics; on the floor was a large cardboard box from a distributor filled with brightly colored vibrators, butt plugs, and anal beads awaiting evaluation—the likes of which Merriman received on a weekly basis.

The product buyer for Babeland, Merriman decided which merchandise would make it onto the store's shelves. She took her job seriously, considering a variety of factors—how well an item reflected the company's sex-positive mission, and whether she thought it would appeal to Babeland's customers and make money. It was a delicate balancing act that required her to be well versed in the sexual politics of product selection.

Often, Merriman explained as we sat in her office on a cold and rainy Seattle afternoon in early 2002, decisions about what merchandise to stock—or not, as the case may be—were fairly straightforward. "We're not going to carry pocket pussies or blow-up dolls because they don't fit with our mission," she told me. "We're obviously not antipornography feminists, but we sort of be-

Display of male masturbation devices at the Lion's Den
in Las Vegas, 2016. Photograph by the author.

lieve that there is a part of sex toys, or the way that sex toys are made, that have
some negative things to say about women."[1]

That sex toys and related products convey a powerful set of ideas about sex
and gender was an idea articulated by almost every feminist retailer, buyer,
and marketer I spoke with. Merriman was a product gatekeeper, and I saw
what this involved when she pointed to a packet of intimate wipes sitting on a
shelf. "These would probably sell in many, many other sex-toy stores, but we
won't sell them," she explained, because "it's [a product] that's clearly about
making women's genitals, their pussies, smell like vanilla. And that is not how
women's pussies smell; and again, it plays into women's sexual insecurities
about the way they smell. I don't think women need any more pressure to
make their pussies smell differently than they do. I don't want to be part of it
and I don't think Babeland wants to be part of it."[2]

The practice of reviewing, testing, and vetting products is, for Babeland and
other feminist sex-toy shops, not only about assessing the durability, func-
tionality, and safety of particular items, but also about ensuring that products
reflect the company's core values. Selecting which products to carry is therefore not just a pragmatic decision but a political one, too. "Whoever is the

buyer at Babeland is going to have to understand what kind of things match us and what doesn't," cofounder Rachel Venning emphasized.[3]

Paying close attention to the products they sell is yet another way that feminist sex-toy stores differentiate themselves from more conventional adult retailers. However, in an industry not typically known for making quality items that are long-lasting, well designed, and aesthetically pleasing—at least not until recently—it can be a challenge for store buyers to find what one proprietor described as those "hidden gems" in a sea of mass-produced and cheaply made products that often promote ideas about gender and sexuality that are antithetical to these stores' missions.

Searah Deysach from Early to Bed in Chicago knows this all too well. Deysach stopped carrying products made by one mainstream sex-toy manufacturer as a result of the company's repeated use of sexist, racist, and transphobic language in their marketing and on their packaging. "The company as a whole was so gross," she told me. "I just don't want to support them at all with my trans-loving, feminist money." In another instance, Deysach decided to not carry harnesses from a company that appeared to be stealing designs from a smaller business that she loved and supported. She also opted out of stocking a vibrating cock ring called the Rude Rabbit, because the rabbit looked mad, and when it vibrated, its eyes glowed red, which according to her made it look "particularly demonic." "I just don't want angry-looking toys here. We try to make sex fun and happy. Not mad and mean."[4]

For Deysach and other sex-positive retailers, the products they sell are the material expression of their feminist values and sex-positive principles. If a retailer decides that a specific item—or the company that makes it—doesn't mirror these things, it will likely never find a home on their shelves. Making these decisions, however, often involves a willingness to forgo profits that might otherwise result if retailers offered people a quick fix to a perceived sexual problem or played on their sexual anxieties. Making money in the sex-toy business, Deysach explains, often involves selling things like numbing creams, anal bleaches, and "fake pussies"—none of which she's willing to carry. "I feel it's our job as sex educators to tell people why the tongue vibrator not only doesn't work but why it's problematic; or why anal desensitizing lube is bad for you; or why [vaginal] 'tightening cream' is the most antifeminist thing that anybody ever invented," she says.[5]

Being a sex-toy retailer with standards is not, Deysach concedes, a method to get rich fast—or really, at all. "If I sold poppers [a recreational drug used to enhance sexual performance] and penis enlargers, I could buy myself a Cadillac."[6]

Early to Bed founder Searah Deysach. Courtesy of Searah Deysach.

From engaging in discussions about whether or not to carry pornography—material long associated with conventional adult stores—to sourcing quality merchandise made from body-safe ingredients, to selling products produced by small mom-and-pop manufacturers known for treating their employees well and compensating them fairly, feminist sex-toy retailers employ numerous criteria when deciding what to sell and which companies to do business with. While these decisions vary from company to company, feminist retailers spend a great deal of time, energy, and care evaluating—and often debating—which items will make it onto their shelves and what this merchandise communicates not only about sex and gender but also, importantly, about their businesses.

## Porn with a Mission

When Joani Blank started Good Vibrations in 1977, she had very strong opinions about the kinds of products she wanted to carry and those she wanted to avoid. For her, creating a female-friendly sex shop meant having a product mix that was different from what customers were likely to find at more traditional adult stores geared toward men. In addition to refusing to sell lingerie,

Good Vibrations window display, 2016. Photograph by
the author.

Blank also rejected "stupid novelties" and gag gifts like gummy candy penises
or soap on a rope shaped like a penis. ("I don't think soap on a rope has ever
improved anyone's sex life," she told me.)[7] And for years, she carried only
a few inexpensive dildos, preferring to keep them out of sight, because she
didn't want to deal with the "creepy men" who would sometimes wander into
the store and ask to see them.

Former Good Vibrations employee Anne Semans had her own theory about
what was driving Blank's choices:

> My theory on Joani's early [product] selection was that it was very
> much motivated by getting women to learn about their bodies and
> their clits, really, so the vibrator was the thing to turn women on to, so
> to speak. I think that then dildos were associated more with the sort of
> traditional or typical adult men's stores, or [were something] you could
> find really easily in another adult store. And I think that those things
> really were not a priority for her and so dildos fell into that category and
> later, similarly, it was [porn] videos. And it was really customers who
> would come in and say, "Why don't you carry videos?" Or "Why don't

you have more of these dildos?," which caused whoever was working there at the time to go, "Oh, maybe we can expand our selection."[8]

Over time, and as Blank hired new staff, the store's product mix slowly started to expand. People like Susie Bright, Cathy Winks, and Semans, for example, made the case that Good Vibrations needed to move beyond selling just those products that Blank was personally most comfortable with. They encouraged her to carry silicone dildos, bondage gear, and safer sex supplies, the latter of which Blank had initially avoided because she felt that the cultural discourse about safe sex reinforced sex negativity. Employees also made the case that Good Vibrations needed to add more toys for people with penises, including cock rings and male masturbation sleeves like the Flesh Light. There was a sense among Good Vibrations staff that if the business was truly committed to being a safe space where people of all genders and sexual orientations could buy a variety of products, then it needed to stand by this claim and expand its product mix accordingly.

An example of this was the business's decision in the late 1980s to begin carrying erotic videos, which marked a major turning point for the company. Pornography was not originally part of Good Vibrations' product mix, not because Blank was antiporn per se, but because personally she wasn't into it — "It just wasn't my world," she explained — and she assumed this was the case for other women, too. She felt that pornography was a sex shop cliché, and worried that carrying it would undermine the alternative retail vibe she had worked so hard to cultivate. It was also the mid-1970s, a time when the feminist porn wars were gaining steam nationally and pornography made specifically for women was not yet a reality. Blank's attitude toward sexually explicit films slowly began to change when she hired Susie Bright to work on the sales floor at Good Vibrations in the early 1980s.

As I discussed in chapter 2, Bright's enthusiasm for Good Vibrations' educationally focused mission thoroughly matched Blank's; and by the mid-1980s, in addition to managing Good Vibrations and working as a writer and editor at On Our Backs, Bright had also begun to pen a regular column on pornography for Penthouse Forum, earning her the nickname "the Pauline Kael of porn." According to Carol Queen, Bright became so closely linked to the world of pornography — "becoming one of the earliest porn theorists," she reasoned — that she was soon traveling to college campuses across the country to screen her porn education slide show, "How to Read a Dirty Movie."

Bright's interest in and knowledge about the world of pornography and erotic films soon found its way to Good Vibrations. "VHS was exploding," Bright told me. "Movies are like stories. They are just like books. It's education; it's entertainment. I thought of Good Vibrations as being part of the cultural conversation and expansion around sex, so not having movies was sort of like saying we don't use forks."[9]

Bright, however, first had to convince Blank that putting together an erotic video library was not antithetical to the store's women-centered and educationally oriented mission. She did this, she told me, not by generating an argument about potential sales or profitability—which in time became significant—but by convincing Blank in political terms that it was valuable for Good Vibrations' customers to have access to the fantasy world that pornography offered. "I felt this was a fascinating world, and I was sick of women being kept out. I wanted everyone to know what I knew. And I knew that everybody wanted to peek."[10]

Bright and Blank shared some of the same reservations about starting a video library and discussed how they might remedy these concerns in an effort to make the collection as accessible to as many people as possible, while at the same time not losing sight of the business's mission. For one, Blank hated the word "pornography" because of the "baggage it carried," and refused to use the word, preferring instead the label "sexually explicit." But she also loathed what she described as the "lurid" video box covers. As Bright recounted:

> [Joani] was like, "You know what I hate? Those awful box covers." And I was like, "I know. They suck." They are misleading and cheesy and just the kind of thing to make our customers run screaming into the night. I said that we just won't have them. We will write our own descriptions for movies, and we will take the black VHS tape and just put it in a blank box. This way, everybody will be watching things based on what we say about it, and they won't see this stupid, pouty girl in a bikini with her tongue sticking out that has no relationship to what the movie is about. That was her biggest concern. She didn't know anything about the content of porn and what it was like. It was also a concern of mine, because I felt like those covers were misleading, and part of the crap production values that made so many women turn away from porn.[11]

In 1989 Good Vibrations began carrying a small selection of explicit erotic videos, which Bright had carefully screened and selected to ensure that the business was carrying the best of what the porn world had to offer. Bright looked for films that focused on authentic depictions of female pleasure, where women genuinely looked like they were enjoying themselves and didn't appear to be faking orgasms. She also looked for movies that were free from gender and racial stereotypes. Former Good Vibrations staff member Roma Estevez, who was one of the people who took over the porn buying and reviewing responsibilities after Bright left the company, recounted that period of time: "The video collection was controversial at first, but Susie slowly began to convince reluctant customers of the benefits of erotic film. In Susie's mind, porn was a vehicle, much like erotic literature or paintings, which, like sex toys, could enhance one's sexual experiences. Soon, her collection of favorites became acceptable to customers, and then, very popular. Good Vibrations was a very different place to rent pornography. Certainly there were other venues in the city to rent such films, but they lacked the charm and the 'clean, well-lighted' atmosphere that was Good Vibrations."[12]

Finding videos that fit the general criteria used by Bright was no easy job for those who followed in her footsteps. Estevez, for example, quickly discovered that she had to watch a lot of films in order to find fifty to seventy-five titles a year that were worth including in the store's collection. And since the quality of most porn films at the time was low, it became, in her words, a "daunting task." A movie might have a hot sex scene, but a sexist or racist title would take it out of contention. Estevez realized that she was not going to please everyone and that she would occasionally have to defend her decisions to angry customers or coworkers who objected to a particular movie. She did her best to find videos that fit the business's sex-positive, women-friendly ethos and, at the same time, might appeal to both the porn connoisseur and the average husband-and-wife team who wanted to watch porn together. For her, this also meant avoiding any films with any "hint of violence" because "it just wasn't worth the ensuing conflict."

One internal debate involving pornography took place in 1992, several years after Good Vibrations started its video library. Tensions flared following the news that Carol Queen and Blank had met with San Francisco–based Fatale Video, a lesbian porn production company that was interested in making a film about the "girls of Good Vibrations." In a memo to staff detailing the meeting, Queen noted that the opportunity could wind up being a "grand plug" for the company. What did everyone think?

Opposition to the idea was swift and heated. As one staff member wrote in response, "We have always worked hard to be 'respectable.' This would be an abrupt departure from our current path. . . . I for one do not want to be a 'girl of GV' in this sense of the word. We strive for a safe space for customers and employees. Encouraging such an image would be disrespectful to both and would shatter the 'strictly business' veneer that protects us."

"This idea seems so incredibly ludicrous!" another person replied. "It's against our philosophy. I don't want to encourage/promote sexy store clerks, the store as a place for sex and fantasy. . . . I like the idea of GV and video production. But [Fatale]? No thanks!"

Having a video library was one thing, but the idea of making a movie that portrayed the "sexy girls" of Good Vibrations was quite another. Employees were not opposed to the idea of Good Vibrations producing sexually explicit videos; but this particular proposal blurred too many boundaries that staff members had worked so hard to establish over the years, including the idea that there was a difference between making sexual products available and making oneself sexually available, supporting people's sexual fantasies and being the object of those fantasies. The job of those who worked at Good Vibrations involved sex, but it was not sex work—at least not in any traditional sense. Thus, maintaining the perception of professional propriety on the sex shop floor was, for many staff, simply nonnegotiable. Queen relayed the consensus position in her reply to Fatale:

> It was clear to Joani and me from our discussion with you that your proposed video project sought to playfully honor Good Vibes as a sex-positive community institution. Still, most of us seem to have great trepidation—if not wholly negative feelings—about being depicted in a porn movie. I don't only mean that people do not want to be in the video—they feel that the existence of a video further sexualizing the business is the last thing they want. At the meeting where this was discussed one woman said, "We've worked so hard to maintain a wholesome image." Everyone who answers the phone and greets the public expressed concerns about the assumptions that would be made about us and the business as a result of using Good Vibes (or something like it) as a site for erotized fantasy and sex play.

Sex positivity is not, as this example suggests, a sexual free-for-all where anything goes, at any time; rather, it is a sexual belief system that feminist retailers must constantly negotiate as they attempt to make decisions about what they think is best for their businesses, employees, and customers. There is no unanimous opinion about what kinds of products are women-friendly or what it means to be a safe space. These are all matters of discussion, debate, and, at times, intense disagreement.

Despite occasional skirmishes among staff about the video collection, all kinds of people rented and purchased porn from Good Vibrations, and the business quickly became a hub of distribution for films that were not readily available at many other video stores, including feminist pornography. As Cathy Winks explained in the introduction to *The Good Vibrations Guide: Adult Videos*, "It didn't take long for us to realize that we were providing a completely unique service for a grateful and enthusiastic audience. Good Vibrations was in the right place at the right time to represent the erotic tastes of consumers largely ignored by the mainstream adult industry: women, male/ female couples and lesbians. Whether our customers were novices with next to no prior exposure to porn, or experienced 'connoisseurs,' they appreciated our efforts to sift through the thousands of erotic videos released every year in search of the cream of the crop."[13]

The video library was still relatively new when Queen began working at Good Vibrations in 1990. The collection was, according to her, "eclectic." It included almost all the women-produced porn that existed at the time, including films by Candida Royalle and Fatale Video. It also included classic films from porn's golden age, such as *Behind the Green Door* and *The Opening of Misty Beethoven*, and some of Bright's personal underground favorites like *Smoker*. "It remained the case, however," said Queen, "that we were limited in terms of what we could offer based on what was being made by most porn production companies."[14]

Good Vibrations eventually decided to throw its hat into the ring and began making the kind of porn its staff and customers wanted to see. In 2001, it started a video production arm called Sexpositive Productions (SPP). Although conversations about the company making its own brand of pornography had percolated for years, by the late 1990s a small group of employees initiated a serious effort to get a video production team off the ground. Queen was part of these efforts, and according to her, "Sexpositive Productions was a way for us, as a company, to address the fact that we saw far too few good porn movies featuring bisexual characters and plots, big women performers, diversity, and various kinds of [explicit education]—all things that customers constantly asked us for. . . . We wanted to address these absences . . . and find new—better, more respectful, more realistic—ways to represent otherwise under represented groups of people."[15]

Sexpositive Productions sought to disrupt the white, heterosexual male gaze, challenge dominant notions of beauty and desirability, and offer viewers nonfetishizing depictions of the diverse ways that people experienced their sexuality. Between 2001 and 2003, Good Vibrations' video production department, led by Sarah Kennedy, produced five films: *Please Don't Stop: Lesbian Tips for Giving and Getting It*, which featured an all-women-of-color cast; *Slide Bi Me*, a bisexual romp that was nominated for a Gay AVN award; *Whipsmart: A Good Vibrations Guide to Beginning SM for Couples*; *Voluptuous Vixens*, showcasing curvy women; and *G Marks the Spot*, an educational video about G-spot stimulation and ejaculation.

Making porn that reflected the company's larger sex-positive mission was not the only thing driving SPP. Many Good Vibrations employees believed that producing porn would generate big revenue, which they could then use to fund the kinds of educational outreach and community-based programming that weren't necessarily profitable, but nonetheless remained central to the business's core mission. "Porn funded. I really love that idea. . . . It seemed like a natural progression to world domination," Estevez told me.[16]

The life span of SPP was short, however. Rave reviews for its movies notwithstanding, Good Vibrations' foray into porn production proved too costly to sustain. By the time SPP finally got off the ground, years after staff had first discussed the possibility of a video production department, the marketplace had shifted and other companies had begun to make the kind of feminist, queer, and alt porn that Good Vibrations had long wanted to make. But more than this, Queen explained, the "economics of this was never right."[17] Alternative porn like the kind SPP was producing was expensive to make and did not have the mass appeal that many other kinds of pornography had. Thus, selling the volume needed to make money was an ongoing challenge. In addition, the rise of Internet pornography, which offered viewers access to all kinds of sexual flavors and kinks with an easy click of the mouse, also cut into the company's sales.

Through SPP and Good Releasing, another production department it started in 2009, Good Vibrations took pornography and made it its own, showing that the company did not have to wait for others to produce the kind of sexually explicit films its customers—and its employees—wanted to see. Good Vibrations had the means and the vision to fill what it saw as the representational gaps in the marketplace. In doing so, it repositioned pornography as yet another tool for sexual enhancement and education. As Queen noted, "When we regard porn as an entertainment medium and expect the best of it, some of that porn gets better and better."[18]

## When Art Meets Eroticism

It was a long cab ride to Hunters Point, a gritty, urban-industrial area in the southeastern part of San Francisco. It was early summer 2002 and I was on my way to Vixen Creations, a lesbian-owned and -operated silicone dildo manufacturing company, to interview its founder—and Good Vibrations alum— Marilyn Bishara.

Bishara, a former New York City cab driver with a gravelly voice and an easy smile, was working as a computer programmer at Good Vibrations in the early 1990s when she noticed that the company had ongoing issues getting silicone dildos delivered on time. Silicone is an ideal material for sex toys, because it's nontoxic, nonporous and therefore more hygienic, and warms to the touch. At the time, there were only a few small companies making silicone products— it's a tricky and expensive material to work with—and the fact that merchandise was always on back order was costing Good Vibrations money.

Bishara had previously worked for outdoor apparel and gear company The North Face and knew a thing or two about manufacturing, including the need to reliably deliver a consistent product. She also felt she had a good understanding of the kinds of products Good Vibrations customers wanted—toys that were colorful and pretty to look at—so she hatched a plan: she would go into business for herself and make the silicone products that Good Vibrations was not able to dependably stock.

Bishara began experimenting with silicone and mold making, and within a few months she was making dildos in her kitchen. It was a small, do-it-yourself operation. "I used to make the dildos and then take them out and wash them in my kitchen sink, package them on my bed sometimes, in my bedroom," she told me. "Some would get returned because they had cat hair in the package or something. I didn't have a shop; I would say, 'Okay, I have an order and now we have to fill it.' And Good Vibrations, of course, was my first customer."[19]

Bishara used her credit cards for start-up money and eventually moved from her kitchen into a small, 500-square-foot location in San Francisco. In the beginning, she had one employee who made the molds, poured the silicone, and packaged all the orders. As the number of orders began to climb, Bishara hired more employees and eventually relocated to a 5,000-square-foot studio space in Hunters Point. It was here, on a sunny day in June, that the cab driver stopped and let me out in front of a large, repurposed factory building.

Vixen Creations was part workplace, part clubhouse, and part artist's studio. Shelves held dildos and butt plugs organized by style and color next to long, wooden tables lined with rows of rubber molds. Every dildo and butt plug was hand poured and pulled, a process that was both time consuming and labor intensive. (Pulling a dildo requires some elbow grease. You peel the base away from the mold and grip it tightly with one hand, while pulling and twisting the top of the mold with your other hand until the form is released, often with a loud "pop!" After items are pulled, stray pieces of silicone around the edges are trimmed before they are packaged and shipped.)

"We try to incorporate function and style and a certain amount of beauty [into our designs]," Bishara told me. "I believe that there is a segment of the population—and it is a pretty high number—that want the best. They just want to know that they are buying something that is going to last [and] will spend a little bit more money for their sex toys."[20]

Like so many of the entrepreneurs I interviewed, Bishara was acting on a hunch that there was a need for a particular service or product that was not being met by the mainstream adult industry. "Once you start working in a place like Good Vibrations," former Good Vibrations employee Cathy Winks explained, "you realize that this isn't rocket science. It is perfectly simple to be providing something that is not being provided by the mainstream culture, and we [at Good Vibrations] know that there are people who are interested and need it and want it. There you go: videos, dildos, sex books."[21]

Vixen was one of the first companies to enter what would eventually become the luxury sex-toy market, helping to create consumer demand for products that were well designed, aesthetically pleasing, and made to last. One of its first employees, Marlene Hoeber, had an undergraduate degree in sculpture and turned to artist Constantin Brancusi for design inspiration. Vixen experimented with form, function, and color and, according to Babeland's Claire Cavanah, just "blew everybody out of the water." Before Vixen, the silicone market consisted largely of what Hoeber described as "three scoops of lavender ice cream"—nonrealistic, wavy dildos in pastel colors, or their more whimsical counterparts, dildos that resembled ears of corn, dolphins, and goddesses.[22] It was a market ripe for innovation. Bishara solicited feedback from retailers and listened to what customers said they wanted. Vixen created silicone dildos with a gentle curve to hit the G-spot, a double-headed dildo, and the Gee Whiz, an attachment that fit on the head of a Hitachi Magic Wand for G-spot stimulation that Bishara described as the "Cadillac of [vibrator] attachments."

Although it may sound so obvious to think about sex-toy design in relation to the body's anatomy and contours, this wasn't typically done until companies like Vixen entered the game. One example was the Tristan butt plug, created with design input from the product's namesake, sex educator and author Tristan Taormino. As Taormino toured the country in the late 1990s promoting *The Ultimate Guide to Anal Sex for Women*, she encountered people who complained that traditional butt plugs, shaped like a slim teardrop with a slender base, had a tendency to fall out. Could she make a better butt plug based on the design feedback she was getting from fans and, if so, what would it look like?

Taormino reached out to Vixen and told them she was interested in working with them to design a new and improved butt plug. She flew out to San Francisco and toured the company's facility, learning what was and was not possible given its pour-and-pull manufacturing technique. She showed them sketches—a design with a longer neck, a bulbous head, and a rectangular base with a cutout resembling a bowtie that could fit comfortably between the cheeks. Vixen made a series of prototypes and, with Taormino's help, they tweaked the design, modifying the head and neck until they got the shape and contours just right. "For me," Taormino explained, "it was really about trying to solve a problem [rather than make money]. . . . Vixen was this queer-owned company. I want[ed] to work with them and support them."[23]

Not every Vixen product was viable from an economic standpoint. Vixen stopped manufacturing silicone anal beads, despite their popularity, because the process of making them was so tricky and expensive. The beads required a specific type of string that silicone would stick to; knots had to be tied at different intervals along the string and lined up perfectly with small holes in one half of the mold before injecting silicone to form the beads. It took two hours to make one pair of anal beads, and Vixen was charging only $11.00 for them. "It was killing me," Bishara said. "I had to hire people just to make them, because I had promised them to people and I was losing money on them. It was just a nightmare."[24]

Profit was not the only—or main—variable in socially conscious sex-toy retailing and manufacturing. For Bishara, other things mattered more. She enjoyed being her own boss and made it a priority to treat her employees well—which by many accounts she did. She provided benefits, paid time off, and fed her employees a free, hot lunch every day, which they ate family style around a table. (The day I visited, there was warm peach cobbler for dessert.) She bought a company car that one former employee said was "pretty much on permanent loan" to her two lead employees. "I think if you are good to your employees, you are going to have a good product and a happy company, and it's going to free flow, especially over time," Bishara said.

By the early 1990s, female entrepreneurs and consumers were placing new demands on the adult novelty industry, and Vixen was one of the first companies to respond, defying the long-standing industry practice of churning out cheaply made products that were never intended to last. During the time she worked at Good Vibrations in the 1980s, for example, Susie Bright recalled thinking, "Why do [sex-toy manufacturers] make this garbage? Don't they understand that when women buy a vibrator, for them it is like buying a washing machine? It is supposed to work. It's not supposed to conk out the first second. [Women] expect it to be like an appliance."[25]

But for decades, according to Metis Black, the founder and president of sex-toy manufacturer Tantus, the mainstream sex-toy industry revolved around the idea of planned obsolescence:

> [Retailers] would stock the same items over and over again because the model [of retailing] was based on a guy buying a product, taking it to his hotel room, using it while he was on the road with whomever, and then throwing it away; so the fact that it wasn't going to last very long wasn't important. What was important was that it cost $20 and it was going to be there for the here and now. And the next time, that person is going to buy the same item for $20 because it worked for them before.[26]

As the women's market grew and retailers like Good Vibrations began offering warranties and sending defective merchandise back to manufacturers, making it clear they were not going to stand behind shoddy products, companies had to "try a little harder to make something that would last a little longer, have a better motor, look prettier, [and] have more appealing packaging," according to Good Vibrations' Winks. For decades, Winks explained, the adult novelty business "didn't put any more care into the products that they were making than Cracker Jack toys . . . because they figured that people were too ashamed and embarrassed about what they were buying and would be more inclined to just blame themselves if the toys didn't work than to blame the manufacturer."[27]

In time, manufacturers and retailers realized they were dealing with a more sophisticated consumer class, a group that Greg DeLong, the founder of NJoy, described as "intelligent perverts with disposable incomes"—people who had no problem spending money on their pleasure. The timing was right in 2005 when DeLong and his then business partner Chris Clement started NJoy, a company that makes sleek, stainless steel sex toys. A mechanical engineer with a degree from Tufts University, DeLong had used sex toys—even making his own—and realized that most were "cheap, plastic junk." "It just occurred to me having been in product development and knowing something about branding, that neither existed in the sex-toy industry in the late 1990s."[28] As he saw it, the market, which had been primed by companies like Vixen, Tantus, Fun Factory, and others, was just begging for a "new paradigm" of quality and design.

DeLong is a hands-on business owner, overseeing design, development, and quality control at his company's headquarters in Massachusetts (although NJoy's products are manufactured in China). He sketches sex-toy designs on cocktail napkins, designs 3D models using the latest engineering software, repolishes products by hand, and has even reglued boxes to ensure that the highest quality items reach his customers. He proudly boasts that in the first five years of the company's life, only five products were ever returned due to quality concerns.

Fundamental to NJoy's philosophy are "omnisexual products" that can be used by anyone of any sexual orientation. When he designed the Pure Wand, his first and arguably most popular design, DeLong wanted to make a product that could reach both the prostate and the G-spot. The design process, as he described it, was "very intuitive." He knew he wanted to make a pretty shape, and that it needed to be curved, so it would be easy to hold. "If you could've seen me," he laughed, "I was cutting out these paper designs and reaching around my back to see if it could get to the places I wanted to reach."[29]

As far as DeLong is concerned, he makes consumer products, not just adult novelties. When I asked him to explain the difference, he said, "A consumer product is something that will enhance someone's life, something that a person will take pride in"—much like a new car, or a designer handbag. Although there's obviously a big difference between a designer bag and a dildo, the emphasis on lifestyle branding was, for him, comparable.

The recent focus on luxury and lifestyle branding means that some sex toys are now big-ticket items that can range in price from $100 to $400 and upward. (It is now possible to purchase a gold-plated vibrator that retails for more than $3,000.) This has given some price-conscious retailers reason to pause. The Tool Shed's Laura Haave refuses to carry certain products just because they are trendy.

We are an old school brick-and-mortar store. I am here for Milwaukee 100 percent. So there might be something that everyone in New York City and San Francisco loves. Fuck you, East Coasters. You know what I mean? It's too fucking expensive for Milwaukee. We are a blue-collar

NJoy founder Greg DeLong. Photograph by Jeff Consiglio.

town. We are in the Midwest. I am not going to carry a $200 vibrator that is a weird shape that no one is asking for. But I will do legwork to carry things that people come in and say, "I want this. I have to go to another state to get it, but I'd rather get it from you." If people ask for it, then they value it. But I am not going to bring in the latest trendy thing because everyone has it.[30]

While the growth of the luxury market has made it more likely that images of pretty-looking sex toys that resemble sculptures will be featured in women's lifestyle magazines and proudly displayed on their owners' bedside tables, this market shift also poses challenges to retailers like Haave who are committed to offering quality products at a price point the average consumer can afford. According to Haave, "What we carry is much more of a social and political issue than who we employ."[31]

## Nontoxic Toys and Sustainable Sex

It all started with a shipment of sweaty sex toys. It was a hot and humid day in August 2003 and Jennifer Pritchett and her then business partner were days away from opening Minneapolis's first feminist sex shop, Smitten Kitten. They had sunk all their money into their first shipment of products, but as they excitedly opened the boxes of toys, packing peanuts flying everywhere, they knew immediately that something was wrong. The toys were leaching an oily substance. It was coming off the products, out of the clamshell packaging, through Styrofoam packing peanuts, leaving big greasy spots on the cardboard box. What, they wondered, was wrong?

They rinsed off the toys, patted them dry, and set them on towels in the middle of the store to see what would happen. After a minute, the toys once again began sweating, and the air was filled with a noxious odor that gave them a headache. At this point, they panicked. "All of the dildos and vibrators were just a wreck," Pritchett recalled.[32]

Pritchett called their distributor and he told them not to worry, that it happened all the time. The items probably melted in the truck, he explained, saying, "It's just what happens with these toys." Pritchett sent the products back. New ones were shipped immediately and the store opened as planned, but something just didn't feel right to her.

The business partners then called Metis Black from Tantus, and that was the first time they heard the word "phthalates" (pronounced *tha-lates*).

For years, sex-toy retailers used to joke about the "mystery rubber jelly" that many vibrators and dildos were made from—materials that often smelled funny and would frequently degrade. While these products were relatively inexpensive and therefore sold well, not much was known about the materials used to make them or their potential health risks.

As it turned out, there were reasons for concern. In 2006 the Danish Environmental Protection Agency released a research report that verified what many people had long suspected: it was likely that the majority of sex toys on the market, most of which were manufactured in China, contained toxic chemicals, including phthalates, a family of industrial chemicals known as plasticizers that are used to make hard plastics soft and pliable.[33] Phthalates are found in a variety of products, from children's toys to shower curtains to medical devices. The problem with phthalates is that they break down over time and release harmful gases, which cause toys to discolor, get sticky, and have an unpleasant taste and odor; and more and more studies indicate they may cause reproductive defects and hormonal disruptions, especially in infant males. In 2008 Congress approved a nationwide ban on phthalates in children's toys.

But in 2003, when Smitten Kitten opened for business, few in the adult industry were talking publicly about phthalates, let alone waving a big red flag. According to Pritchett, that's when Smitten Kitten's mission changed from being just another sex-positive, educationally focused feminist sex shop to becoming a business committed to environmental justice and personal health. Pritchett, who has a graduate degree in women's and gender studies, contacted customers to let them know that they had sold them some things that they previously thought were good for them but now believed were bad and if they brought the items back, they would replace them with silicone options. She immediately revamped the store's inventory and got rid of vinyl and jelly products in favor of body-safe items made from silicone, ceramic, glass, and hard plastic. "That almost put us out of business," Pritchett said, "but we didn't open this business to participate in an industry that wasn't good for people."[34]

In 2005 Pritchett founded the Coalition against Toxic Toys, a nonprofit organization intended to educate consumers and raise awareness about the kinds of materials used to manufacture sex toys. "Our philosophy," says Pritchett, "is that if we know how dangerous these chemicals are for children and dogs, we don't want contact with them, either." A year later, she sent ten of the top-selling products in the industry to an independent lab in California that does consumer product testing, so the items could be analyzed. The lab's findings

Smitten Kitten owner Jennifer Pritchett. Courtesy of Smitten Kitten.
Photograph by Jenn Bauer.

closely mirrored the results of the Danish study. Some of the most popular sex toys on the market included chemicals such as phthalates, polyvinyl chloride (PVC), and polystyrene, which were known to cause cancer and birth defects and interfere with hormones.

There are no FDA regulations or established industry standards for sex toys, in part because items are marketed and sold as adult novelties or gag gifts rather than functional items that people actually use. Yet as consumers have learned more about the materials in their sex toys, due largely to the educational efforts of companies like Smitten Kitten, they are demanding better, healthier, and more eco-friendly products.

Smitten Kitten's efforts have been redoubled by those of other progressive feminist retailers like Self Serve in Albuquerque, which launched Phthalate Awareness Month in 2008 to raise public awareness about the plastic softeners. Self Serve is one of an increasing number of businesses opting to sell only phthalate-free and nontoxic sex toys made from platinum-grade silicone, glass, wood, and stainless steel, making body-safe and eco-friendly options an important part of their brand identities. These efforts are beginning to trickle up to larger manufacturers and retailers, and new, proudly green sex-toy companies, such as Earth Erotics—with the tagline "Doing It Green"—are staking a claim to their place in the adult industry.

Alliyah Mirza founded Earth Erotics in 2006 after reading an article about toxic sex toys and the lack of industry standards. Mirza realized "that there was a market here for something green." Earth Erotics sells a range of green products—handcrafted glass dildos, certified organic lubricants, and platinum-grade silicone vibrators—and offers a version of home sex-toy parties showcasing earth-friendly items. Mirza carefully screens every product her company sells and carries nothing manufactured in China. "I won't carry products where the manufacturer can't or won't tell me what it is made from. I need to be able to stand by the products I sell," she told me.[35]

The greening of the sex-toy industry has also brought greater attention to issues of responsible manufacturing and the problem of packaging and waste. Ellen Barnard, co-owner of A Woman's Touch in Madison, looks for products made by smaller manufacturers, preferably ones whose production facilities or studios she can actually visit. She concedes that it is difficult to completely avoid products made in China since so much sex-toy manufacturing is done there, although whenever possible, she stocks items made by companies that are responsibly sourcing the material they use. "We are pretty fussy about what [items] we will carry," she told me.[36]

Standards regarding eco-friendly products and manufacturing practices differ from company to company. Metis Black from Tantus explained what sustainability means for her. "We are committed to making products that are good for the body and good for the earth and that means the production process itself has to be green." Tantus manufactures its products in the United States and uses platinum-grade silicone in its designs. The company also uses FDA-approved mineral spirits to clean its machines in an effort to avoid leaving toxic residue on its nontoxic toys. "We try to be as green as we possibly can, from start to finish," Black said.[37]

According to Black, the sexual marketplace is still largely an uneducated one in which a handful of manufacturers, retailers, sex educators, and bloggers have worked together to educate consumers about the potential risks of toxic toys and the benefits of sustainable sex. Indeed, these values are now an explicit part of how Tantus markets its products, underscoring the company's commitment to sexual health promotion. According to Good Vibrations' Carol Queen: "People who think nothing of scrutinizing the health implications of what they put in their mouths often seem to forget about the other parts of their bodies associated with pleasure. But when we bring the question up, most people do care very much about how healthful materials are."[38] In an effort to address the growing awareness around sustainable sex, Good Vibrations coined (and trademarked) the term "ecorotic" to signal the availability of more healthy and earth-friendly products for sex.

Although it is possible to walk into almost any adult store today and find sex toys labeled phthalate-free, latex-free, cadmium-free, hypoallergenic, and "safe and pure," among other eco-friendly terms, not all sex toys are created equal, and it remains the case that the sex-toy industry lacks regulations and consumer watchdog groups. This means that manufacturers eager to jump on the green bandwagon can theoretically put whatever language they want on their packaging if they think it will help sell products. Mirza from Earth Erotics refers to this as "greenwashing"—the tendency for companies to stamp their products green when really they are not.[39] Thus, consumers who want to be eco-sexy and sustainable are largely left to educate themselves about the kinds of products they are purchasing and the companies they are doing business with. As Queen notes, "We can minimize our overall 'sexual footprint' by buying higher quality and longer lasting, not toss-away imports, when we're able to."[40]

Feminist sex-toy shops like Smitten Kitten, Self Serve, and A Woman's Touch, and sex-toy manufacturers like Vixen and Tantus, have been catalysts

Tantus's marketing materials highlight the company's commitment to promoting sexual health. Courtesy of Tantus.

for change in the sex-toy industry. They have helped cultivate a consumer class that expects more not only from their retail experiences but from the products they purchase. As Pritchett explained, Smitten Kitten's entrepreneurial mission is to "prove in this industry that good business is good business" and that it is possible to run an ethical company and sell quality toys that don't break the first time you use them. "If we change the industry so there is more quality and choice for everyone," she told me, "then anywhere [customers] go, even a truck stop porno shop, they [will] have access to quality toys."[41]

# six

# SEXPERTS
# AND SEX TALK

———

When women talk about sex,
it changes the culture.

CAROL QUEEN
in "A Toy Is Not a Toy"


It was after hours at Self Serve, a sexuality boutique and resource center located on historic Route 66 in Albuquerque, New Mexico, and seven of us were sitting on chairs arranged in a small circle in the middle of the store. We were not there just to buy sex toys; on that warm June evening in 2008 we were about to learn how to have strap-on sex.

"We are doing something revolutionary here tonight," store cofounder Matie Fricker said to the group as she kicked off the workshop. "There are only a few stores like us in the country and a few places where you can get this kind of information. Many different kinds of people are strapping it on. We know this because of the work we do. We see these people come in shopping for dildos and harnesses, and we answer their questions on a regular basis."

"Are there specific things you'd like us to cover tonight?" Molly Adler, the other half of the store's ownership team, asked.

"Techniques," replied one person.

"Lube," said another.

"Different products that can be used for different occasions," someone added.

"You mean like an anniversary dildo?" Fricker said with a smile.

Over the next two hours Fricker and Adler detailed the anatomy and physiology of anal pleasure and strap-on sex. They debunked common myths, including the idea that men who enjoy anal stimulation must be gay, and emphasized that good sex is like anything else; it has a learning curve, so you

Self Serve founders Matie Fricker (L) and Molly Adler in their Albuquerque store, 2007. Photograph by Tina Larkin.

shouldn't expect perfection the first time you try a new sexual activity or position. They discussed the fit and adjustability of different harnesses, the difference between silicone and rubber jelly dildos, and how best to care for and clean your sex toys. Every now and then, they pointed to books and DVDs sitting on the store's shelves—*How to Fuck in High Heels*, the *Bend Over Boyfriend* series, and *The Ultimate Guide to Anal Sex for Women*—describing them as useful resources that showcased different kinds of people strapping it on.

After the workshop, and over a pint of beer at a local bar, Adler and Fricker talked about their vision for Self Serve. The two met in the early 2000s while working at Boston-based retailer Grand Opening (the business that Kim Airs, who had interned at Good Vibrations, founded in 1993). The inspiration to open a sex-toy shop together came to them one night while talking about work over a bottle of wine.

It was an idea that came from "a place of love," Fricker said.

"A place of passion," Adler chimed in.

While the pair was still living in Boston, they enrolled in a class at the Center for Women and Enterprise, a not-for-profit organization that helps women start and grow successful businesses. As part of the course, they researched the sex-toy industry and reached out to feminist retailers with similar business models, including Early to Bed in Chicago and Smitten Kitten in Minneapolis—two of the only businesses willing to share information with them. ("Just fucking do it!" Early to Bed's Searah Deysach said with encouragement.)

Adler and Fricker took the class seriously and by the time it ended, they had won top prize for their business proposal, a recognition that buoyed their confidence that they had a plan they could successfully execute. They raised $85,000 in start-up money through loans from family and friends and shopped around for a city that would be both livable and receptive to the kind of queer-friendly and trans-inclusive sex shop they envisioned. Albuquerque, with its lively cultural scene and progressive politics, fit the bill, and in January 2007, Self Serve opened its doors for business.

For them, they explained, Self Serve is all about giving people the tools they need to feel more comfortable in their own skins and to claim their desires. The duo strives to create an open and welcoming environment where people can ask questions and get information regardless of their level of experience. Every day, according to Adler, "we are helping people become comfortable with wherever they are at, if they are straight or divorced or in a sexless marriage. We are trying to get them to a happier place."[1] This happens by way of the one-on-one interactions and conversations that take place on the sales floor; it also happens in the after-hours sex education workshops, such as the one I attended, and through the sale of various how-to guides and educational videos. Like other feminist-identified sex-toy stores, Self Serve is not only in the business of giving customers permission to say yes to sex, it's also encouraging and in fact educating them to be informed and savvy consumers. Here, sexual desires collide with consumer desires, producing a retail-based version of sexuality education aimed at generating a new-and-improved sexual you.

## Retail-Based Sex Ed

Sex education continues to be a source of controversy and debate in the United States, both in terms of what is taught and the age at which certain information is introduced. More than twenty-five years ago, social psychologist Michelle Fine discussed the "missing discourse of female desire" in school-based sexuality curricula, an absence, she argued, that negatively affected the development of young women's and men's sexual subjectivities.[2] In standard sex education curricula in the 1980s, young women were not learning to see themselves as autonomous and desiring sexual subjects; rather, they were being taught that they were sexually vulnerable in the face of disease, pregnancy, and a so-called bad reputation. The language of desire in the context of formal sexuality education, Fine wrote at the time, "remains a whisper."[3] Such silences risked impeding the sexual development of young people by making it difficult for candid conversations about sexuality to take place between educators and adolescents. "A genuine discourse of desire would invite adolescents to explore what feels good and bad, desirable and undesirable, grounded in experiences, needs, and limits," thus better equipping them with the necessary skills to negotiate the complexities of consent and coercion, pleasure and danger.[4]

These kinds of sexual silences and evasions only intensified as abstinence-only education programs spread to schools and classrooms across the country beginning in the 1980s, replacing medically accurate information about sex with fearmongering and misinformation as a matter of policy. A comprehensive review published in the *Journal of Youth and Adolescence* regarding the kinds of information missing from sex education curricula indicates that between 1998 and 2009, federal funding for sexuality education focused "almost exclusively on ineffective and scientifically inaccurate abstinence-only-until-marriage programs" to the tune of almost $2 billion.[5] Abstinence-only-until-marriage programs imposed a strict set of criteria regarding what could and could not be taught, contributing to an information gap that left many young people floundering in a state of sexual quasi-illiteracy. But more than this, evaluations of the efficacy of abstinence-only programs suggested that they frequently failed to delay the initiation of sex.[6] Although there's been a shift in recent years toward evidence-based sexuality education programs—those programs shown to impact teen pregnancy rates and teen sexual activity—academic experts argue that the focus on pregnancy and disease prevention continues to ignore other important aspects of young people's sexual development and health, including the impact of poverty and economic inequality on health and well-being, LGBT issues, and the role of gender socialization in maintaining power imbalances.[7] Physicians and public health experts, moreover, also suggest that it is time to rethink how sexual information is presented to adolescents and teenagers in the age of social and digital media.[8] They argue that sexuality education should evolve to meet young people where they are, which is increasingly on social media platforms such as Snapchat, Twitter, Tumblr, and Facebook, and websites like YouTube.

With many people making it to adulthood knowing very little about their own sexuality, sex-positive feminist retailers have stepped into the breach—not only providing adults with accurate sexual information, but promoting messages about pleasure, desire, consent, and agency. Since the mid-1970s, these businesses have been at the forefront of carving out a much-needed cultural space for adult sexuality education. In fact, research conducted by investigators at Indiana University's Center for Sexual Health Promotion found that adult stores offer teachable moments for sexuality education and health promotion.[9] According to the study's authors, "it is apparent that consumers of adult retail stores are asking questions that provide a unique opportunity for the dissemination of sexuality education to adults."[10] These findings empirically support, with tables and figures, what many sex-positive retailers have believed for years: The interactions between customers and sex store employees present occasions for pleasure-based sexuality education that extend far beyond dispensing product information.

Retail-based sex education is a boon, not only for customers but also for these businesses' bottom line. In response to the above-mentioned study, Metis Black from sex-toy company Tantus noted that "common sense and store receipts have proven that sales increase when clerks have education to give good customer support."[11] In other words, sex education doubles as a highly effective sales tool. It is a lesson that many retailers have taken to heart. Indeed, with the growth of the feminist sex-toy store movement has come the rise of the retail-based "sexpert." Although there is no established definition, the term "sexpert" commonly refers to individuals who are largely self-taught and who acquire their expertise — which can vary greatly — not through accredited academic programs but through books or hands-on experience, including working on the sex shop floor.[12]

Sex educator and former Babeland employee Jamye Waxman examined this growing focus on retail-based adult sexuality education in a 2008 cover story for adult industry trade magazine *AVN Novelty Business*. In an article titled "The New Sex Educators," Waxman discussed the rising trend of sexperts who are not only dropping knowledge on the sex shop floor, but who are conducting workshops, writing books, and producing (or starring in) explicit sex education films. "Today," Waxman wrote, "more students are ditching the classroom and seeking out nontraditional educators. . . . These adult students are looking to the pros to teach them how to have better sex."[13]

Good Vibrations was one of the first businesses to put retail-based sex education on the map and popularize the quest for greater sexual know-how. From the start, founder Joani Blank recognized the potential for Good Vibrations to function as what Susie Bright would later describe as a "sex education kiosk," a place where people could get their vibrators *and* helpful information about sex.[14] Blank knew from her previous work as a sex educator and therapist that many people lacked basic knowledge about how their bodies worked, so giving them information about where the clitoris was, or clueing them in to the fact that penises do not always get or maintain erections could go a long way toward dispelling myths and boosting people's sexual confidence.

For Blank, none of this was rocket science. "I couldn't ignore what I knew," she told me.[15] If sex education had a positive effect in a sex therapy setting, it stood to reason that it could have an equally positive effect in the context of a vibrator shop, while also reaching a demographic of consumers that would not necessarily make the trip to a therapist's office or health care clinic. Blank realized early on that running an educationally focused sex-toy store had the potential to democratize access to sexual information in a culture that was severely sexually anemic.

As Good Vibrations grew over the years, Blank hired employees who either brought with them or developed on the job the "sexpertise" they needed to answer the many different questions customers had about sex. One of the first people to embrace the moniker sexpert was Susie Bright. Bright was given the nickname Susie Sexpert by a lover or a friend — she doesn't remember which — when she started working on the sales floor at Good Vibrations in the early 1980s. The nickname was so catchy that it didn't take long before it went viral among her friends. When Bright helped start *On Our Backs* magazine in 1984, along with Nan Kinney, Debi Sundahl, and Honey Lee Cottrell, and wrote the first "Toys for Us" column, which chronicled the world of lesbian sex, she felt the monthly item should have an "advice to the lovelorn" name like Dear Abby or Miss Manners, she told me. ("That was me being cheeky about the tendency of mid-century women's magazines [to offer] advice, with an 'expert moniker' pen name. I wasn't in the least trying to hide my identity.")[16] The name Susie Sexpert took off, and with it, the idea of the sexpert as someone who possessed a great deal of sexual knowledge and expertise that she or he was willing to share with others.

Given Good Vibrations' well-known educational focus, it was perhaps no surprise that the company eventually began to refer to its sales staff as "sex educators." This shift happened shortly after the business became a worker-owned cooperative in 1992, when it changed the title of those hired to work on the sales floor from sales associates to sex educator/sales associates, or SESAS for short. By 2000, employees at Babeland were also being referred to as "sex educators." As former Seattle Babeland store manager Lizz Randall recalled, "After writing over and over again 'sales associates,' it was just like, 'Wait a second. We are not hiring sales associates. What people do is sex education.

That is what everybody is doing on the sales floor every day."[17] Author Tristan Taormino, who had a stint working at Babeland in New York in the late 1990s, agreed. "People who work at Babeland are not just sales clerks who sell dildos. They are actually sex educators, and it's a really important job. I talk to people and answer their questions, and give them sex advice every single day and they go home and use it."[18]

Alicia Relles, who worked at Babeland for many years in several different capacities, recalled the conversations that took place within the company around the title change:

> We all kind of felt that we were doing so much more than working in a retail position. I was like, "I feel like I'm a therapist half the time," so "educator" was a great term to come into place, and I think it was really empowering to differentiate what we were doing. It was empowering to have that word attached to what we were doing at the store, because, I think, again, a lot of us were struck with the feeling of, "Are we just retail workers here?" But we're not, because we are contributing so much more of our time and ourselves and our hearts than just ringing [sales] up on a computer.[19]

Many employees welcomed the change. The term "sales associate," according to some, felt "belittling" or "weird" given just how much specialized knowledge their jobs entailed. The title "sex educator" made the information focus of these businesses explicit to both sales staff and customers, becoming one more way that feminist retailers and employees set themselves apart from conventional adult stores. For many employees, especially those with college or advanced degrees, the title conferred an expert status that mattered to them. It was a tacit acknowledgment of their educational capital and professional worth, and a statement to others that this was no ordinary retail job and they were not typical retail workers. For some, being able to write "sex educator" on their résumés, rather than "sales associate," was a mark of distinction that carried significant symbolic weight; it also meant they were often paid more than other retail workers, because, as one store owner explained, "What we ask of people is way more than sitting at the counter ringing people up. . . . I set it up as if I was hiring a social worker."[20]

Not everyone was entirely comfortable with the shift to sex educator. Although Babeland cofounder Claire Cavanah felt the name was dignifying, she also admitted that she was initially uncomfortable with it, because it "completely denied that we were selling stuff."[21] Former Good Vibrations employee

Janell Davis shared this concern. Although she liked the term, she also thought it enabled some Good Vibrations employees to sidestep the fact that what they were doing was still a retail job:

> In some respects, we were still doing regular retail work in a lot of ways. There was part of me that was like, "Well, this is just trying to glamorize the fact that it is an unusual retail job, but it is still a retail job. Even if you call me a sex educator/sales associate, it is still retail." So, for me, there was a part of it where I was like, "Okay, how semantic do you want to get about it?" But for the most part, I was grateful for the name and thought that it was really helpful and gave us some respect in that so much of what we did had nothing to do with even selling any merchandise."[22]

Another concern that arose for some employees was liability. Retail-based sex educators were not professional clinicians, like Masters and Johnson; nor were they sex therapists like the popular Dr. Ruth. Some Good Vibrations staff wondered if the company could be sued if the advice given by a designated staff sex educator, particularly someone who lacked academic credentials or professional licensure, resulted in a less-than-desirable or a harmful outcome. In a memo that circulated around the time the title of SESA went into effect, Carol Queen reassured Good Vibrations staff that the term "sex educator" had no legal status, licensing, or requirements. Indeed, "there should be no reason for us to avoid calling ourselves sex educators." Sex education, she emphasized, is a "prominent chunk of what we do in our jobs."

By the early 1990s, Good Vibrations had begun to give the company's long-standing educational focus additional form and structure that went beyond just a change in title. In 1992, Queen was tapped to become the company's inaugural director of continuing education. Hired at Good Vibrations in 1990, Queen had by that point worked for more than a decade as a "sex educator without portfolio," as she put it.[23] She was in the process of completing a PhD in sexology from the Institute for Advanced Study of Human Sexuality and had also spent two years on the training staff at San Francisco Sex Information. Combined, these things made her the logical choice to keep Good Vibrations employees "as well informed about sexual matters as possible."[24] As Queen wrote in an item for the company's newsletter: "For lots of people, it seems, staff at Good Vibrations and our mail-order workers are the people they turn to when they have questions about sex, and we take our customers' trust very seriously."[25]

Good Vibrations staff sexologist Carol Queen, 1996. Photograph by
Phyllis Christopher, www.phyllischristopher.com.

Good Vibrations' continuing education program was one way to ensure
that sales staff would have the most up-to-date information possible to share
with customers, enabling them, ideally, to keep their fingers "on the sexual
pulse of America," as former employee Roma Estevez put it.[26] Each month,
Good Vibrations staff got together with Queen or an invited expert to discuss
a particular facet of human sexuality, from sexuality and aging to sex and disability, or to learn more details about the ever-expanding inventory of products the company sold. One month, for example, Susie Bright was invited to
discuss the store's erotic video collection, including what she looked for when
making selections and how to respond to customers who were occasionally
disgruntled or unhappy with video content for one reason or another. Another month was devoted to books. These sessions often included discussions
about how sales staff could respectfully respond to customer complaints about
content they did not like or products that did not fit with their expectations
of what a sexually progressive, feminist-identified company like Good Vibrations should carry.

For the most part, Good Vibrations employees were enthusiastic about the continuing education events, but this wasn't always the case. Internal memos indicate that certain topics and sessions made some employees uncomfortable, exposing in the process fissures and limits around sexual openness and tolerance and the kind of information some staff felt was relevant to the company's needs. In a note to staff that followed on the heels of a continuing education presentation about sadomasochism, Queen apologized to those who were uncomfortable with the demonstration. Queen thought she had indicated that the presenter was bringing a slave/copresenter. "However, a few of you said you were taken by surprise, so perhaps I neglected to do this. I take your criticisms to heart and I'm quite upset that this didn't play well to people."[27]

In addition to the monthly continuing education programs, Good Vibrations was also beginning to move away from a more casual, oral tradition of training new sales associates, in which everyone learned from each other and read books from a required reading list. As the company grew in size, it became necessary to create a standardized sex education training program to ensure both quality and consistency in the information SESAs were providing to customers. To address this need, the company instituted a series of classes that all newly hired SESAs were required to take. Charlie Glickman, who earned his PhD in adult sexuality education from the Union Institute while working at Good Vibrations, developed the curriculum for the SESA training.

The SESA training program, at least initially, consisted of eight modules, each of which was about three hours long. Topics were wide ranging and included discussions about sexual anatomy, vibrators and dildos, anal sex and anal toys, BDSM products, lube, latex and safer sex, male gender socialization, and cock and ball toys. An entire unit was devoted to the company's erotic video library. In this session, Glickman screened a two-hour compilation of short clips from various films, so staff could get a sense of the different videos the company carried and how they could talk about the collection with customers. Glickman also emphasized tactile learning. He would take every condom the company sold out of its packaging so sales staff could feel the thickness of different brands. He did the same thing with sexual lubricants, encouraging SESAs to rub a drop between their fingers so they could feel the texture and viscosity of water-based versus silicone lubricants, and thus talk more knowledgably about these products with customers.

Good Vibrations employees received more training about human sexuality than most doctors, and a core part of what they learned involved the concept of sex positivity. The SESAs were taught that being sex positive was not the same thing as being enthusiastic about sex or having a lot of it; nor was it simply the equivalent of identifying as queer, or kinky, or polyamorous. Rather, a sex-positive person appreciates that human sexuality is endlessly diverse—there is no right way to have sex and no singular definition of normal. The SESAs were trained to be open-minded and nonjudgmental, and to look beyond their own experiences when talking to customers. What a SESA might personally like when it came to a particular sex toy, brand of lube, sexual position, or relationship style might not be what worked for someone else. Whether they were helping a straight man buy his first butt plug, talking to a queer kinkster about her interest in blood play, or validating someone's choice to be celibate, SESAs were taught that every interaction, with every person who came into the store or called the company's call center in the pre-Internet era, deserved the same degree of empathy, compassion, and respect.[28]

Noticeably absent, at least initially, was a training unit on sales techniques. Glickman explained that this was because the company's customer service needs varied greatly across different parts of the business. The San Francisco store had a different "retail vibe" than the Berkeley store, which opened in 1994; and the stores were different creatures than the mail-order operation, which involved telephone conversations with customers rather than face-to-face interactions. For these reasons, Glickman felt it was difficult to create a uniform customer service training program that could be applied evenly across the board. His priority, he explained, was to make sure SESAs were as knowledgeable as they could be about human sexuality and the products the company sold, and that they could talk about these things in a deeply informed and nonjudgmental way. The emphasis for him was information, not sales.

The establishment of Good Vibrations' continuing education program and, in time, the creation of a formalized SESA training program and a stand-alone Education Department reflected the company's long-standing commitment to providing customers with the best, most up-to-date information about sex that they could. It also demonstrated the store's willingness to put its money where its mission was by investing time and resources in human capital. Good Vibrations realized early on that a well-trained and knowledgeable sales staff that could talk comfortably about a wide range of sexual topics was not only the backbone of the company's mission but an essential part of growing both its brand identity and its bottom line—an idea that increasingly found expression in the company's marketing and promotion materials.

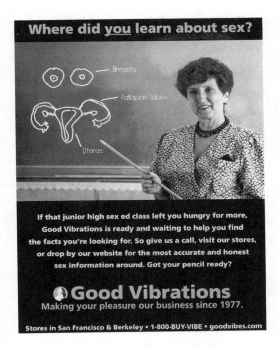

Good Vibrations' emphasis on sex education often doubled as a marketing strategy. From *On Our Backs*, August–September 2001.

## "Talking about Sex Is Our Craft"

While Good Vibrations was developing a more formalized training program for its SESAS, other feminist retailers were advancing their educational missions by creating opportunities where people could talk openly about sex. Many of these conversations were taking place informally on the sex shop floor, but they also happened in other venues: in-store workshops, college classrooms, community spaces, and even in the pages of magazines.

During a Sex Toys 101 workshop that took place in 2001 at a bookstore and community space located just blocks away from Babeland's Lower East Side location, cofounder Claire Cavanah articulated what she saw as the fundamental link between selling sex toys and talking about sex. As Cavanah explained to the group of young women who had gathered for the workshop: "We are women-owned and almost 100 percent women-run and the main thing we do is hook people up with the right sex information. And that comes from selling toys. Selling sex toys keeps our doors open, but the toys also start conversations about sex, which we really believe is the most important thing you can do to broaden your sexual horizons. . . . I think talking about sex and vibrators to women is a feminist act because we are trying to empower women around their sexuality."[29]

For the remainder of the workshop I watched as Cavanah, along with Babeland store manager Dana Clark, talked about sexual anatomy, sex toys, and gender socialization. They exchanged playful banter, answered questions, and encouraged the young women in the audience to talk about the kinds of messages they had received about sex and masturbation. One woman said that she felt fortunate to grow up at a time when workshops such as this existed. "Girls will talk a lot about sex," she said, "but they won't talk about masturbation, so when I get onto a sex topic I usually try to incorporate masturbation into that. And it works, because people will start to talk about it."

This was exactly what Good Vibrations founder Joani Blank hoped would happen when she started her business. Blank felt that talking about sex should be as casual as talking about the weather; she also thought that as a culture our worst "sexual dysfunction" was our inability to talk about "the nitty-gritty details" of sex. People might talk about a one-night stand with friends, or boast about a lover's sexual prowess, but rarely did they discuss how they masturbated, what sexual positions they enjoyed, or how sex actually felt. Putting individuals in an environment like Good Vibrations, she once told me, "where talking about sex is like, 'Oh, this is what we do here. We talk about sex. Big deal,' is therapeutic." She further explained, "I used to say that our worst sexual problem, and I don't care how good your sex life is, but in this country and perhaps in other cultures, too, the worst sexual problem we have—our worst sexual dysfunction, I used to call it—was our inability to talk about sex. So that's what I was selling: it was encouraging and supporting people in their ability to talk about sex, and that didn't always involve selling them a product."[30]

It was not just any way of talking about sex that businesses like Good Vibrations and Babeland promoted. Rather, it was a specific genre of sexual speech, one that was meant to inform rather than titillate or seduce. For these businesses, talk about sex was conducted with a deliberately matter-of-fact style so that if someone came into the store with a question about the G-spot or prostate stimulation, she would not have to worry that her request for information would be viewed as either sexually inappropriate or a come-on. Babeland cofounder Rachel Venning described this genre of speech as "sex education talk":

It's not just that we sell sex toys, but it's the way we talk about sex that makes us so unique, which is why we get to be in magazines and stuff like that, and normal adult stores don't. I think that's really at the heart of what makes us different. . . . It's like sex education talk. There is a little cadre of sex educators and some sex workers and sex-toy sellers who can talk about sex in a way that is informed with lots of accurate information and yet it is presented in an accessible way that relates to people and their sex lives without being super dry. . . . I think we give people a lot of permission to talk about sex, to think about sex.[31]

This idea was so central to Babeland's commercial identity that Venning once asserted, "Talking about sex is our craft." She generated this theory one summer while attending the Michigan Womyn's Music Festival after someone challenged her about why Babeland was selling its manufactured wares in an area designated for craftswomen. Venning paused for a moment and said, "Well, our craft is that we talk about sex and we get people to talk about sex."

"I thought that was really brilliant," Cavanah later told me when recounting the story. "That's truly what we do. And that [sex talk] is not for sale, but whatever it is, people still want to buy the stuff and I think that's because we talk about sex the way we do and we create an environment where people can talk to each other."[32]

The opportunity to talk about sex and pleasure in an environment that supported positive sexuality was one of the biggest reasons employees cited in explaining why they wanted to work at Babeland or a similar store. Many had previously worked as counselors or case managers at places like Planned Parenthood, HIV/AIDS education programs, rape crisis centers, abortion clinics, sex information hotlines, and community-based health programs and were, frankly, burned out from talking to people who were often in crisis around some aspect of their sexuality. Babeland's Lizz Randall explained that she had really wanted to work someplace where people were "celebrating sex, and they weren't forced to go there, and they didn't necessarily need money to get in the door." There are very few places, she acknowledged, where you can get paid to do pleasure-based sex education.[33]

Staff sex educators at Babeland and elsewhere operate on the assumption that an added value is assigned to the frank and accessible way they talk about sex, which attracts customers and keeps them coming back. "People love shopping at Babeland," said Felice Shays, "because we welcome them with . . . all of their questions, and we have smart answers for them and we don't bull-shit them if we don't know the answers." For Shays and others, the version of sex education talk that Babeland promotes is understood as a valuable commodity with its own intrinsic worth. Its value is derived largely from the fact that positive, nonjudgmental, and educationally oriented talk about sex, especially about women's pleasure and LGBT identities, is such a scarce commodity in our culture. In fact, there are very few places where people can go to talk openly about sex and know that it's okay; they are not going to be made to feel ashamed for asking questions or having an interest in learning more about their sexuality. According to Babeland's Venning, "We try to have sex educators that work in the store know what's going on [in terms of sex] so there's an actual value to offer people. There is some reason for them to ask us questions, because we might actually have some advice based on knowledge."[34]

Good Vibrations' Queen recalled times when women would come into the store, especially during the company's early years, and just be "blown away by how matter-of-fact it was." Talking openly and frankly about sex, without having to be concerned about what kind of message they might be sending to whomever they were talking to, wasn't something that most women were accustomed to doing. "Sex may be many things, but it generally wasn't matter-of-fact. To be that way, we [at Good Vibrations] came to understand—and Joani probably understood from the get go—was a form of activism."[35]

But it was more than just a form of activism; it was also a retail strategy that helped expand the commercial appeal of Good Vibrations beyond sex toys alone. "We understand that the more sex can be comfortably talked about in the culture, obviously the more economic space we potentially have and businesses like us have," said Queen. "And that, we think, is a good thing."[36]

The idea that feminist sex-toy stores are making a scarce and therefore valuable resource available by facilitating open and honest conversations about sex was one way that some employees also made sense of occasional price hikes. According to Babeland sex educator Christine Rinki, "We were talking about pricing once and I was thinking, 'You know, we could charge more.' I had really been resistant to all the price hikes, but [I thought] we can do this because what people are getting with their products is a lot of information and this whole process. So, you can go somewhere and spend $12 and just have this vibrating machine, or you can come to us and get all of this, the whole interaction that surrounds it . . . and you can pay $20 for it and that's okay."[37]

Not all shoppers, however, are in search of a holistic experience when looking to buy a new dildo; and while many Babeland customers expressed their gratitude for having a place where they could get information—"There's no place else I can go to ask this question," customers often commented—it was also the case that others simply wanted to make their purchases and leave with minimal interaction and no obligation to talk about their sex lives. Babeland's Isaiah Benjamin told me that many trans-identified people he knew felt more comfortable shopping for sex toys on West Fourth Street in New York City's West Village, where more conventional adult stores like the Pink Pussycat are located. For them, the appeal was precisely that employees don't engage in conversations with shoppers. "They don't try to help you. They don't ask you questions," he explained. "They will sell anything to anyone without giving you information about it."[38] In this scenario, there is no expectation, and therefore no pressure, for customers to self-disclose about their sexual identities, histories, or desires. Customers can walk into these stores, buy what they need, and leave with minimal to no interaction. The lack of engagement offers a buffer zone of security and a sense of anonymity among people who, in many cases, are already culturally marginalized or judged because of their sexual orientation or gender identity. For some customers the opportunity to not talk about sex, but still get the items they want, can be an exercise in sexual freedom and autonomy.

Although store owners and employees readily acknowledged that some shoppers have no desire to share intimate details about their sex lives, a set of standards and norms were being produced whereby these businesses became places where customers were expected to talk about their sexuality and, as one employee put it, "confess in varying ways." Indeed, staff sex educators were trained to solicit and encourage such confessions, producing occasions for what French philosopher Michel Foucault has described as an "incitement to speak about [sex] and to do so more and more."[39] Scholars after Foucault have argued that "speaking sex" is less a transgressive celebration and more an incitement to further discipline. However, my research shows that talking openly about sex is, for many people, a path to real sexual empowerment.

Feminist retailers are committed to facilitating occasions where sex can be comfortably talked about, because they have bought into the idea that doing so makes everyone's quality of life better. Searah Deysach, from Early to Bed in Chicago, emphasized this point: "One of the things we are here to do is educate, to normalize. People come in and say, 'I don't feel comfortable asking this question,' or 'This is a really weird question.'" An important part of what Deysach does on a regular basis is to reassure customers that there's nothing they could ask her that she hasn't heard before. It only seems strange because "it's probably something they've never talked to anyone about before," she said.[40]

Talking about sex in a ho-hum, matter-of-fact way is something employees actively model for customers. "There is not a sign up that says, 'You can ask us anything,'" Blank told me. "We model that [for customers]."⁴¹ Glickman re-iterated this point, saying,

> We live in a world where most people don't know how to talk about sex
> in a way that's nonsexual. How many people talk about the nitty-gritty
> details of their sex lives with somebody who is not a lover, if even then?
> One of the things that we at Good Vibrations model is how to talk about
> [sex]. I had a customer come in once and it was clear that he was looking
> for a vibrator that he could use on his girlfriend's clit while he used his
> fingers inside of her and he didn't have the words to describe it. He was
> motioning with his hand—a kind of G-spot motion—and all he could
> say was, "You know, what I'm doing." He didn't have the language for it.
> And we really try to model [for customers] what that language is.⁴²

Although talking openly about sex is actively encouraged, it is not the case
that anything goes. Employees safeguard the boundaries between what they
consider appropriate and inappropriate sexual speech and behavior in an
effort to ensure that the store remains what they imagine to be a comfortable
space for even the most sexually inhibited and shy customer and, by extension,
for themselves as workers.

There's a general understanding among employees that customers can ask
them anything about sex toys or human sexuality as long as it's done in a manner that is respectful and maintains a sense of appropriate boundaries. It was
quite rare at Babeland, at least during the time I worked there, to encounter
a customer who was looking for sex, or who wanted someone to help him or
her "get off." Babeland got the occasional prank phone call, and sometimes
customers hit on sales staff, but overall employees didn't encounter a lot of
"wankers," as they were commonly referred to. When I asked one of my coworkers why she thought this was, she speculated that it might be because the
taboos around sex and sexuality that encourage and help foster sexual ha-
rassment don't exist at Babeland the way they do in other settings, making it
harder, as she put it, to "play that game." In other words, Babeland's sexual
openness can be disarming, neutralizing the potential for people to exploit
the shock value of sex.

This doesn't mean that customers have never tried to be shocking or out-
rageous; it just means the behavior typically fell flat because it failed provoke
the kind of responses they were looking for. Babeland's Dan Athineos told
me a story about a man and woman who came into the store one day to carry
out a domination and submission scene—although this was not immediately

obvious to her. The woman directed the man to try on a harness. Athineos showed him where the bathroom was and told him that the harness needed to go over his clothes. A few minutes later, the woman asked Athineos to come over. The man was standing at the bathroom door wearing nothing but the harness and a pair of high heels and suggestively touching his nipples. "Does this look okay?" he asked her in a little-boy voice. "There are clubs for this," she replied and walked away. In this instance, it wasn't the scene itself that was the problem as much as where the couple had chosen to enact it. In using the store as a backdrop, they had transgressed the unwritten code of conduct that customers (and staff) are expected to adhere to in order to ensure that the store remains the kind of welcoming and comfortable space the owners want it to be. The general rule of thumb, at least from what I observed, was that if a customer was behaving in a way that made Babeland employees feel uncomfortable, with their ostensibly thick sex-positive skins, it was likely to make the average customer uncomfortable, too.

Staff sex educators are trained to elicit and normalize conversations about sex, but the products themselves also facilitate the talking-sex part of the mission. Vibrators and butt plugs double as props and conversation starters that allow customers to ask questions about their bodies and talk about subjects — prostate stimulation, strap-on sex, BDSM — that in other contexts might be seen as either inappropriate or taboo. Randall from Babeland explained it this way:

> I almost feel like if we didn't have to sell a product and just gave advice that would be great, too. It's almost like the sex toys front us to be able to get our mission out there, because what we really want to do is give information and, at a base level, help women, and now everybody, explore [their sexuality]. We want to promote vitality. And why do we want to do that? Because we think it's important and that it directly affects basically the state of the world. If we don't sell sex toys or sell some product, how are we going to do that except to have our own agenda and do guerrilla tactics? In a lot of ways, having a retail business means we're allowed [to talk about sex]. Somehow we are legitimate now because we are selling a product.[43]

The idea that selling sex toys legitimizes conversations about sex by giving them a transactional form and function is an interesting theory that complicates any clear-cut understanding about which commodity — sex toys or sex talk — is actually at the heart of the commercial exchange. But more than this, it suggests that the logic of consumer capitalism enables and sustains the talking-sex part of the mission. As one person explained, "If you are going to put money down to buy this thing, that [transaction] gives you a sense of entitlement to ask questions." Former Good Vibrations employee Janell Davis explained:

> I think you could be selling oranges in the store and people would come in just to talk to us about their sexuality and the oranges would be sort of irrelevant. Sometimes I feel like what we end up selling them has nothing to do with what they were coming in for. They just wanted to be able to say, "I have never had an orgasm. I am really afraid." Just to be able to have somebody say, "Oh, okay. What can I do to help you?" Sometimes I felt that the merchandise was almost irrelevant.[44]

Conversations about sex fuel the educational missions of these businesses and define their commercial identities so thoroughly that for some employees the merchandise often recedes into the background, becoming, in some cases, an afterthought. "Sometimes I forget about the toys, which sounds kind of awful," one Babeland employee admitted. "I guess I'm more focused when I talk to people about what the toys do, so we start talking about anatomy, comfort, partners, and all of those things, rather than being like, 'Well, this product is great because of this.' The interaction is more about their needs and wants, which has to do, I think, with [providing] general sexual information."

Good Vibrations' Amy Andre saw this as a problem. Andre eventually took over running the SESA training program that Glickman had developed and was tasked with making it bigger and more standardized than it already was. A priority for her was to integrate sales techniques into the program, because up until then, she said, "We didn't have company dialogue about sales techniques."[45]

At the time Andre became the SESA training coordinator, she was also serving on Good Vibrations' board of directors, so she had intimate knowledge of the company's budget and its financial needs. For her, it was a "no-brainer" to focus on sales. "It was kind of shocking to me that this hadn't happened before and the reactions I got were also shocking and very daunting." Andre's rationale for teaching employees about sales techniques was simple: yes, part of a SESA's job is sex education, but you're also selling things and you need to know how to do this. "That's the backbone of what we do: sell things," she told me. "And if we don't sell things, then we cannot educate people because we won't have a company for people to come to for education."[46]

Andre encountered what she described as "enormous resistance," mostly from the SESAs themselves. The resistance took two different forms. One was, "Leave us alone. We already know what we're doing." The other form of opposition was, "I came here to be a sex educator. I don't want to do sales." Andre was struck by the fact that across the company employees readily, and even eagerly, acknowledged that learning how to be a good sex educator was an ongoing process; and yet many of the same people, some of whom had no retail background whatsoever, felt that they already knew everything they needed to know about selling things. The pushback Andre received was pronounced and frustrating.

> I think that people thought the idea of having a sales technique or a sales strategy was a way of manipulating the customer. And there was also this idea that the ideal was to give a lot of education. . . . Any guidance beyond something that directly answered the exact question that the customer verbalized was capitalist and corrupt and antithetical to the mission of Good Vibrations. I couldn't disagree more. It is capitalist, but I don't necessarily think that's a bad thing. We have a store; it's a business. It's embedded within a capitalist structure. I felt that if people didn't want to engage in business practices then they shouldn't be owners of a multimillion-dollar business.[47]

Sex education was not separate from sales, Andre argued, but was itself a sales technique; it was a platform for talking about and selling sex toys that could be channeled to benefit both the customers and the company's bottom line. And yet there was a tendency among sales staff, across a number of different feminist sex-toy businesses, to think about sex education as being distinct from and unconnected to sales. This viewpoint was prevalent and entrenched, and it would eventually take the threat of financial disaster to change the way many store owners and employees thought about the relationship between profitability and social change (see chapter 8).

## A Sex-Positive Ecosystem

In the opening sequence of the instructional sex video *The Ultimate Guide to Anal Sex for Women*, Tristan Taormino, author of the best-selling book by the same name, is seen pitching her how-to film to John Stagliano, the head of the Evil Angel porn empire. Sitting suggestively on the edge of Stagliano's cluttered desk, Taormino enthusiastically sells her vision. "It's not going to be like those boring instructional sex videos that are on the market," she tells him. "I want it to be hot. Really hot, so that women will run out and want to have anal sex."[48]

In the next scene, Taormino is standing next to a large anatomical chart, an array of sex toys displayed on the table in front of her. Taormino is positioned as a sex educator and expert and on this occasion her students are an experienced group of anal all-stars—porn performers who are known for their strong "backdoor" performances. She begins the on-camera lesson by asking the group to discuss the various taboos and myths that might contribute to negative attitudes about anal sex. She then uses their responses as a way to demystify anal sex for viewers at home who may be curious but inexperienced. Taormino is informative but not overly clinical. She uses words like "pubococcygeus muscles" and yet still manages to crack jokes with ease.

Taormino's video illustrates how the direct and informational style of sex talk taking place on the retail floor both led to and reinforced other forms of sex education. Over the years, Good Vibrations and Babeland became incubators for sex-positive educators, ideas, and projects that then went out in the world to reach a wider audience than just those people who were coming into the stores. For Taormino, working on the sales floor at Babeland in the late 1990s was an opportunity to tap into the sexual psyche of the average American sexual consumer. As Taormino writes in the introduction to her book *Down and Dirty Sex Secrets*, "Every day I worked [at Babeland], dozens of ordinary folks walked through the door looking for what we had inside. Their searches almost always began with a question. Most of them were complete strangers, and yet they told me things that were extremely personal and deeply intimate. Their revelations were sometimes moving, sometimes surprising and always fascinating."[49]

A benefit of working at a place like Babeland was that Taormino had direct contact with customers. She was able to hear straight from them, unfiltered, which aspects of human sexuality piqued their curiosity. By the time Taormino started working at Babeland, she had already written *The Ultimate Guide to Anal Sex for Women* and had toured the country promoting it. "I knew this was a book that I needed to write, and that it would appeal to men and women. I knew that I wasn't the only one who was desperately searching for good information on anal sex," she told me in an interview. She also realized that the book's subject—anal sex—"did not exactly lend itself to the traditional book reading" at a place like Barnes and Noble. "Most bookstores weren't clamoring to create a huge poster of the cover, put it in the window, and announce a book signing by me. It was no *Chicken Soup for Your Ass*, even if I thought it was."[50] Instead, Taormino had to find other ways to promote the book, and feminist sex-toy stores seemed like a logical place to find a receptive audience.

So Taormino hit the road and began teaching workshops on anal sex at sex-toy stores across the country. During her book tour, people began asking when she was going to turn *The Ultimate Guide to Anal Sex for Women* into an instructional sex video. The following year, in 1999, she teamed up with Stagliano and Evil Angel to produce her first adult film.

Using pornography as a medium for sex education is certainly not a new idea. Robert Eberwein's comprehensive history of sex education in film and video demonstrates that since the early part of the twentieth century, the technology of moving images has been used as a tool for dispensing information about sex, from films about venereal disease in the early twentieth century, to safer sex education films in the 1980s, to Betty Dodson's videos about female masturbation and sexual pleasure in the 1990s.[51]

It is likely that Taormino would have eventually turned *The Ultimate Guide to Anal Sex for Women* into a sexually explicit instructional video without the encouragement of fans. But the positive feedback she received from people who attended her workshops—her potential audience, in fact—was a barometer that allowed her to gauge the level of interest for the film, even before the project was off the ground. According to Taormino, "People were asking me about a video—and I've always been a big cheerleader for porn. I had been doing a lot of different sex workshops, and working at Babeland, and I felt like I wanted to make this video. My purpose with the video—which I say in it—is that I not only want to teach people how to have safe, pleasurable anal sex, but I want to inspire them to run out and do it."[52]

Taormino's experience promoting her book and making her first movie is instructive for what it suggests not only about the larger context of sex-positive feminist cultural production, but also about the importance of the customer feedback loop. Working at Babeland and conducting workshops across the country allowed her to take the sexual pulse of a subset of consumers. What she learned served as inspiration for future books and films that were tailored, to some degree, to the kinds of things that Taormino's target audience expressed as gaps in the sexual marketplace.

Shar Rednour and Jackie Strano had a similar experience with their first film, *Bend Over Boyfriend*, which they coproduced with Fatale Video.[53] Rednour had previously worked as the managing editor of *On Our Backs* and on several different shoots for Fatale Video; Strano, meanwhile, was working on the sales floor at Good Vibrations. By the late 1990s, the two realized that interest in anal sex was growing, particularly among women who wanted to anally penetrate their male partners. "Everybody I knew, all the straight girls and all the bi girls, [wanted to do it,] and everybody [was] coming into the store wanting strap-on dildos and wanting to know how to do it to their boyfriend or husband. It just seemed like all of a sudden people were talking about it," Strano recounted.[54] The couple, who had long wanted to make porn for lesbians, knew that this was the film they needed to make. As Rednour recalled, "No educational film existed that tackled this subject. Plus, we really liked the idea of lesbians teaching heterosexual men about receiving penetration. We also knew that if we started with this film, it would sell and we could use the money we made from queering straight sex to fund our dyke porn empire."[55]

Rednour and Strano were confident that if women were coming into Good Vibrations in San Francisco—an admittedly skewed sample, they realized—with an interest in learning more about "pegging," then it was only a matter of time before women across the country would ask how they, too, could be in the sexual driver's seat. As Rednour explained, "We knew if there were twenty people that we had waited on [at Good Vibrations], then that was the crest of the wave that was going to be coming if you just gave it a little bit of a push."[56]

The duo believed that porn had the potential to help people of all sexual orientations and gender identities have better, hotter, more intimate, and more satisfying sex lives. The mission they crafted for their production company, SIR Video—which stood for Sex, Indulgence, and Rock-n-Roll—was to "change the way people fuck," and this included creating porn that was entertaining, especially for women. They also knew from working at women-centered enterprises like *On Our Backs* and Good Vibrations that entertaining women sexually often involved first educating them that they had a fundamental right to enjoy sex in whatever form it might take, be it a piece of erotic writing, a vibrator, or pornography. They took this lesson to heart when making their films.

Rednour and Strano looked for investors who were willing to fund *Bend Over Boyfriend* and were "rejected and laughed at" everywhere they turned, because no one believed that an educational film about straight men "getting it in the rear" would sell.[57] They eventually teamed up with Fatale, which had secured a loan from Good Vibrations founder Joani Blank, who always seemed to have a knack for knowing what the next big thing would be. *Bend Over Boyfriend*, Rednour colorfully remembered, "sold like sweet tea in August. Like hotdogs at the pennant. Like Magic Wands at a Betty Dodson convention."[58] The film was so popular that the duplicator had difficulty keeping up with demand.

*Bend Over Boyfriend* features Carol Queen and Robert Morgan as the video's anal educators. "We are here to teach you how to do it right and also

*Bend Over Boyfriend* creators Shar Rednour and Jackie Strano on the cover of *On Our Backs*, June–July 2000.

help you understand that any fantasies that you have had about sharing this kind of intimate play can come true in a safe and fun manner," Queen says, as she looks directly into the camera. In frank, accessible, and matter-of-fact language intended to instruct and inform, Queen and Morgan work to dispel a myriad of common myths and misperceptions about anal sex, and offer encouragement and practical advice to viewers interested in expanding their sexual repertoires through anal play.

The educational components of *Bend Over Boyfriend* work on multiple levels. Not only does the film instruct those watching at home how to have safe and enjoyable anal sex — lube is a must, Queen and Morgan emphasize — but it also models for viewers how to watch an instructional sex video and put whatever tips and advice they may get into practice. This is done by featuring two different couples sitting in front of their respective television sets — popcorn and remote controls in hand — watching *Bend Over Boyfriend* and, eventually, getting down to business.

*Bend Over Boyfriend* and *The Ultimate Guide to Anal Sex for Women* belong to a larger sex-positive ecosystem in which all the various parts — sex education books, videos, and conversations on the sex shop floor — mutually reinforce and sustain each other. Just as the videos came out of the directors' experiences working at feminist sex-toy stores, they also direct viewers back to these businesses, encouraging them to purchase the various products sold there.

One of the most interesting aspects of *Bend Over Boyfriend* is the way it coaches viewers to be well-informed and savvy sexual consumers. Messages about consumption are not buried in the film but are explicitly rendered. At one point, for example, Queen finishes a detailed discussion about the different kinds of sex toys someone might use for anal sex—from silicone butt plugs to leather harnesses—and instructs those watching at home to "grab your credit card, go shopping, and meet me back here." In this moment, a very clear relationship is established between sex education and sexual consumption and the wider sex-positive ecosystem that *Bend Over Boyfriend* is part of.

Integrating messages about consumption into the narrative fabric of *Bend Over Boyfriend* was not accidental; rather, it was a tacit acknowledgment on the part of the filmmakers that the movie was indebted to and a part of a much larger ecosystem of sex-positive cultural producers, from dildo manufacturers like Vixen Creations, whose products are featured in the film, to retailers such as Good Vibrations. Here, the circuit of feminist cultural production and information provision comes full circle: consumers wanted information about a sexual subject not readily available to them; SIR wanted to make films that could deliver information about sex in an entertaining way; and stores such as Good Vibrations were looking for exactly the kind of feminist and queer-oriented pornography that Rednour and Strano were making, in large part because customers were asking for it. The resulting sex-positive ecosystem links these different feminist enterprises together—how-to guides, pornography, sex toys, and sex-toy stores—through a shared vision of changing the way the culture thinks and talks about sex. This interconnected and mutually reinforcing system was on full display during the strap-on sex workshop at Self Serve that I describe at the start of this chapter, when store owners Matie Fricker and Molly Adler pointed to copies of *The Ultimate Guide to Anal Sex for Women* and *Bend Over Boyfriend* on the shelves, citing them as valuable sexuality resources. Indeed, this ecosystem is not ancillary to the growth of the women's market for sex toys and pornography, but a fundamental part of shaping the broader educational context that supports sex-positive feminist retailing as a commercial enterprise, a political intervention, and a much-needed platform for accurate information and matter-of-fact talk about sex in a culture where open conversations about pleasure, desire, and consent continue to be muted.

# seven

# SELLING IDENTITY

——

For me, feminism was the first political identity that opened
the door to seeing other political realities. I really subscribed,
and still do, to the idea that the personal is political. That [informs]
everything I do: from how I fuck to who I fuck to how I sell
sex toys. Everything I do is colored by understanding myself as
part of a huge fabric of politics and identity.

FELICE SHAYS
Babeland

It wasn't the glowing fan mail that Babeland was accustomed to receiving.
The letter was from a repeat customer, a woman who wrote to say that she
had always appreciated that Babeland was, in her words, a "womyn-centered,
lesbian-owned and operated business." However, during her last visit, she explained, a young man had approached her and asked if she needed help. "I
[was] shocked, and still am shocked, that a man is working at your store,"
she wrote. "Despite the fact that he appears to be gay, I feel that he could not
possibly know how I, a lesbian-identified womyn, need to be helped in a store
such as yours. It goes without saying that he doesn't know what it is to be a
womyn, nor a lesbian, never mind what it is to be a sexual lesbian womyn. He
simply could not assist me in the way that I need[ed] to be helped."[1]

It was 1999, and the man in question was actually a twenty-something,
boyish-looking lesbian. Not only had the customer misrecognized the gender
identity and sexual orientation of the employee, but because of this misread-
ing she had concluded that the salesperson lacked the necessary qualifications,
and indeed the experiential knowledge, to provide her with the kind of customer service she felt she needed.

What was interesting about this woman's letter was not only its account
of gender misrecognition and its subsequent effects, but the extent to which

issues of shared identification and experience clearly mattered to her. These things were so important that she took time to write the company a letter expressing her displeasure. To encounter someone she assumed to be a man working on the sales floor at Babeland had upended her understanding of the business as a "womyn-centered, lesbian-owned and operated" store and everything this chain of signifiers represented.

Identity is a common touchstone in our political vocabulary, a word that puts "the ideas of 'being' or subjectivity and experience in the centre stage of politics," according to feminist theorist Himani Bannerji.[2] Discourses of identity and belonging figure prominently in the world of feminist sex-toy shops, making these businesses an interesting example of what Bannerji refers to as "identity projects."

Indeed, it is difficult, if not impossible, to understand the history of feminist sex-toy stores without wading into the murky water of identity politics; and yet the language of identity, and of feminism and queer politics more specifically, is rife with unstable categories that can, and often do, change over time. There is no singular or fixed definition of feminism that informs feminist sex-toy stores. Rather, individual store owners and employees typically determine what feminism or queerness means for a particular business. Where this gets especially tricky is when they are drawing upon familiar markers of identity while simultaneously working to dismantle binary ways of thinking about gender and sexuality. In other words, the logic of the marketplace can also create a tension between a business's political ideals and its commercial imperatives. What does it mean, for example, to run an explicitly feminist sex-toy shop when the average consumer might understand feminism as antisex or antimale? How do you appeal to male customers, when "women-run" is sometimes interpreted as "women-only"? In short, what do commercialized versions of identity politics look like in the context of feminist sex-toy stores and how effective are they when it comes to advancing their educationally focused missions?

## Feminism: Its Possibilities and Discontents

If you had walked into Eve's Garden's first retail showroom in the mid-1970s, you wouldn't have seen any men milling around looking at sex toys. Dell Williams, like many feminists at the time, believed that women needed places and institutions to call their own. When she founded Eve's Garden, she instituted a women-only policy. As Williams wrote in her memoir, "The ban had to do with creating a comfortable place for women to explore their own sexuality, and in 1974, this necessarily meant gender privacy."[3] She eventually relaxed this policy and began welcoming men, but only during certain hours and only if accompanied by a woman.

From the start, the idea of being a welcoming place for women was the central organizing principle of Eve's Garden. In fact, for decades the company used the same tagline it did when the business started: "We grow pleasurable things for women." Despite suggestions from friends and colleagues over the years that she change the slogan to something more gender neutral, such as "We grow pleasurable things for people," in order to appeal to a larger customer demographic, Williams refused. "Women are still struggling a lot more than men in terms of defining themselves as sexual beings," she explained to me in 2001. "I still think it probably makes certain women more comfortable knowing that [the store] is designed for women."[4]

Eve's Garden can be situated squarely within the political ideology of 1970s cultural feminism. According to historian Alice Echols, cultural feminism "held out the possibility that women could build a culture, a space, uncontaminated by patriarchy."[5] At its core, it valorized women's biological differences from men and called for the creation of a gynocentric society characterized by a universal sisterhood and, very often, separatism.

The idea of shared sisterhood was a powerful feminist rallying cry. However, the emphasis that cultural feminism placed on women's differences from men — physically, economically, emotionally, and culturally — frequently came at the cost of ignoring important differences among women based on race, ethnicity, social class, and sexual orientation. The description "for women" often served as shorthand for white, middle-class women, the very feminists who emerged as — and who in many cases continue to be — prominent movement leaders, magazine editors, public figures, and business owners. Feminists of color and their allies actively challenged racism within the mainstream women's movement and rejected a version of feminism that failed to acknowledge, as Chicana feminist Norma Alarcón has noted, that one "becomes a woman" in ways that are "much more complex than in simple opposition to men."[6] By the early 1980s, a number of groundbreaking books and anthologies had emerged — Barbara Smith's *Home Girls: A Black Feminist Anthology*; Angela Davis's *Women, Race and Class*; Cherríe Moraga and Gloria Anzaldúa's *This Bridge Called My Back* — that underscored the complexity of women's experiences and the centrality of intersectionality to both feminist theory and politics. And yet it remained the case that some women (and men)

Good Vibrations staff photo, circa 1989. Anne Semans, top row third from right; Joani Blank, middle; Cathy Winks, bottom right. Courtesy of Joani Blank.

continued to see feminism as a white women's movement and feminist sex shops as spaces primarily for white, middle-class female shoppers.

This is not to say that issues of inclusivity and diversity didn't matter to white feminist store owners and employees; they most certainly did. But if you look at the old photos of Good Vibrations staff from the 1980s, everyone is white and female. Thus, it is perhaps not surprising that some customers got the impression that Good Vibrations was a white women's store. It took a conscious effort on the part of Good Vibrations staff to alter this perception, so that by the time Andy Duran, who is queer, brown, and trans-identified, began working at Good Vibrations in 2005, he was "happy and relieved" to join what he saw as a "very diverse" sales staff. But this change did not happen overnight. As Good Vibrations hired more people throughout the 1990s—its ranks growing from ten employees in 1990 to more than a hundred by the end of the decade—the company instituted a Multicultural Committee and took steps to diversify the business's marketing materials, its outreach efforts, its product mix, and, importantly, its staff and customers along the lines of gender, race, and ethnicity. As one former Good Vibrations employee recalled, "There were many, many difficult conversations about whether or not the store was for women, whether it wanted to continue to be for women, and

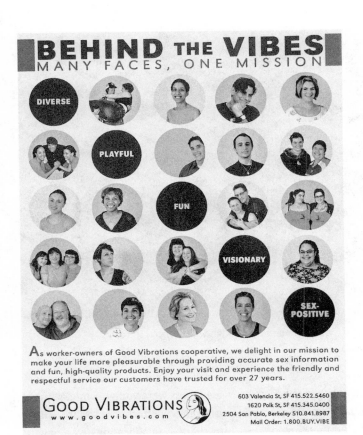

Good Vibrations advertisement from 2004 showcasing its increasingly diverse staff.

what 'for women' meant. All of that stuff was huge and really painful when I was working there."[7]

These discussions were especially difficult, a number of people recollected, in regard to race. As Amy Andre, who spent more than six years working in Good Vibrations' Education Department in the late 1990s and early 2000s, recalled, "There was a lot of racism that wasn't discussed; and there was racism that was talked about in problematic ways and in ways that really didn't get us anywhere. As for myself, as an African American woman in that environment, I felt challenged by race and racism on a daily basis and it made for a very frustrating situation for me."[8]

Andre felt there was a missing dialogue within the company around the fact that most of its employees were young, white, predominantly queer women,

Feelmore founder Nenna Joiner in her Oakland, California, store.
Courtesy of Neena Joiner.

and that the majority of the business's customers were young, white, straight women. Why might an older African American woman choose to shop somewhere else, including the very sex shops that Good Vibrations was created to counteract? How might the company change its marketing and outreach efforts in order to reach customers that, for whatever reasons, were not coming into the store?

These were exactly the type of questions that Oakland entrepreneur Nenna Joiner addressed when she opened the city's first woman-run sex-toy store, Feelmore, in 2011.

When Las Vegas native Joiner moved to the Bay Area in the late 1990s, she was in her early twenties. Her aunt, who had worked for the San Francisco AIDS Project, gave her a copy of *The Good Vibrations Guide to Sex* and suggested that she pay a visit to Good Vibrations' Berkeley store. "I went down there and loved it," Joiner told me. "But . . . every time I went there, I wouldn't see anything that really represented me. All the empowered images were of white women. Being a black female, I wondered, 'Where are we?'"[9]

Joiner realized there was a need in the African American community for more diverse sexual images and resources, so she decided to start a business that could deliver what she thought was missing from other women-run sex shops and the adult industry more generally. "People always ask, 'Why a sex store?'" Joiner said. "I just thought Oakland was really lacking. I could've taken my money and done other things with it, but I saw a need. Sometimes I think you really need to look around your community and see what the true need is."[10]

Joiner developed a business plan, painstakingly researched Oakland's zoning ordinances, and began looking for a commercial space, a process that from start to finish took about five years. She found that banks were unwilling to lend money to an adult-oriented business because it was perceived as too risky, and many landlords were wary of leasing her a space because they did not want to be associated with the stigma of an adult store. But Joiner persevered; and while she waited for the various pieces of her business plan to fall into place, she went through the sixty-hour intensive sexuality educator training at San Francisco Sex Information and began producing pornography aimed at queer women of color. She also met Joani Blank, who became a friend and mentor, even loaning her the last bit of money she needed to open the store.

Located in a former wig shop just down the block from Oakland's historic Fox Theater, Feelmore is part art gallery, part adult store, and part community resource center. Joiner told the interior designer she worked with that she wanted the store to feel like a jazz lounge: cool, comfortable, and classy.[11] There is erotic art on the walls, colorful vibrators on the shelves, and hard-to-find collectibles and memorabilia, from old *Playboy* magazines and framed vintage ads for condom machines to rare books and vinyl LPs that reflect the ethnic and racial diversity of Oakland.

For Joiner, "inclusiveness" is more than just a buzzword; it is the organizing principle of her business. And yet building a brand that moves beyond the either-or categories that define much of the adult entertainment industry— male and female, black and white, gay and straight—requires an extremely mindful and tailored approach. "You don't just throw lube and dildos at this community, especially for communities that have never seen that," Joiner told me. "The goal of [Feelmore] is to make everyone feel safe, regardless of what you look like or who you are."[12]

Joiner tries to reach people wherever they are—and this does not always involve leading with sex. It might mean selling people on the vintage aspects of the store or creating a sense of nostalgia by playing music by jazz singer Sarah Vaughan in the background. She has hosted comedy nights at Feelmore and has held in-store workshops featuring a psychologist and a financial planner. "How can you think about sex if you've just lost your job and you are financially stressed?" she told me.

Joiner is always thinking about how to get to the people who need information the most. The average male customer who comes into Feelmore to buy condoms already understands what they are for. What about the person who doesn't? Reaching those people often means going out into the community and talking directly to underrepresented groups—clients at a methadone clinic or an AIDS organization, for example—about everything from love and codependency to consensual touch. This type of outreach might not translate directly into sales, but it is important to Joiner to be a visible face of black business ownership, so she makes a point to go wherever she is invited whenever she can. In terms of products, Joiner carries more than just one token item that is supposed to stand in for and represent diversity. She makes a concerted effort to stock items that customers cannot easily find in other sex stores, including dildos and packers (which are used to create a bulge in one's crotch area that resembles a penis) that are chocolate and caramel colored.[13]

Joiner does not consider Feelmore to be an explicitly feminist sex shop. Feminism, she tells me, was not part of her cultural vernacular growing up. "I didn't even know what feminism was until I started shooting porn."[14] And yet her vision for Feelmore—to encourage people to feel more, love more, live more—mirrors the sex-positive feminist retail missions of businesses like Good Vibrations and Babeland. At the same time, Joiner is very consciously "trying to go someplace else," as she puts it, to bring a different kind of retail vision to life and reach a market that is underserved. She described the process as an "organic" one that is less about feminism and more about "doing the right thing."

Joiner's way of looking at the world as an African American lesbian business owner positions her outside the white hegemony that defines, and very often limits, how race and inclusivity are discussed within the world of sex-toy stores. For Joiner, considerations of race, ethnicity, and social class are not afterthoughts, but define her business model. "It is so important, not just for my community, but Oakland at large, to have [a sex shop] that represents us in a positive way. Being black and brown, those are my primary constituents."[15] And yet Joiner knows all too well that in order to stay afloat financially she must reach an audience that is wider than just the African American community. "The people who are buying my products," she noted, "don't necessarily look like me."

At Babeland, while owners Claire Cavanah and Rachel Venning acknowledged cultural feminism's limitations, they also found the unifying banner of "women's experience" to be useful in building their business. In a world still characterized by male privilege and sexist domination, they felt that "women," as an identity category, remained relevant—even if it did not fully convey the complexities of today's gender politics.

During a 2002 roundtable discussion that I conducted with Cavanah and four staff sex educators from Babeland New York—a group that was predominantly white and queer and that ranged in age from early twenties to early forties—Cavanah acknowledged that there was some "residual cultural feminism" embedded in the version of feminism that is part of Babeland's core identity. "I'm not ashamed of this," she said, adding, "I think we can work toward the world we want to have, and we can and ought to be able to define ourselves, change our definitions, agree on new definitions, [and] work toward utopia, but as long as we are in the world that we are in, saying that men are this way and women are this way is something of a shortcut."[16]

"How does gender fluidity fit into that?" a staff sex educator asked.

"It is both," Cavanah replied. "We created this world that is very feminist—the world is Babeland. Clearly it is a fantasy—that's why there is a bondage forest and anal island; but I like to think of it as a world where the terms are up for grabs. You can come to work one day as a girl and the next day as a boy, and change the day after that. I think that the fact that it is based around 'women as women' is very important and sets the stage for the kind of freedom that ensues."

"Whoa! 'Women as women' is such a complicated phrase," another staff sex educator chimed in.

"I know. I know, but I refuse to be ashamed," Cavanah reiterated. "Women at the center. That is really what it is. These terms are slippery and language is not that accurate, really." She continued, "'Based around women' is a practical gesture. There are women in the world and there is a condition that I understand to be common among women—I am going to get killed for this one—and we have built Babeland as a sort of corrective to it. I need people to take one term, which is feminism, and walk into my feminist world."[17]

In describing the feminist world of Babeland that she and Venning have created, Cavanah articulates a kind of strategic essentialism in which holding the category of women as a common denominator is understood as a political necessity. On the one hand, Cavanah recognizes that gender is fluid—someone might come to work one day as a girl, another day as a boy, and then change again after that; and indeed there have been instances at Babeland when employees have done just that. And yet Cavanah is also unwilling to relinquish an understanding of gender—and indeed of feminism—that foregrounds women's common condition as a result of living in a sexist world. It is a tension that is not lost on Cavanah:

> It is just a contradiction that has to be. I have been trying to say this all day and that is that women's condition is real; it is also culturally produced and we acknowledge that, too. "Woman" is understood in all sorts of different ways through time and in different cultures; and now its meaning is really up for grabs and I think that is to our credit. The day that women aren't singled out as less powerful . . . there are all kinds of things that are thought about women that we are trying to correct at Babeland and the day that this is not true, then fine. Then we won't be organized around women, but until then we will be and that is going to be my whole life.[18]

The ways in which feminism and the language of identity are invoked and negotiated, constantly, are important precisely because they establish the ground on which these feminist sex-toy stores operate as both commercial enterprises and political projects. Many interviewees acknowledged that feminism occupied such a fundamental part of these businesses that it was like the air they breathed. Babeland employee Paula Gilovich, for example, argued that "just by being alive [Babeland] is doing its feminist part to change the world."[19] Good Vibrations' Roma Estevez described the company as an example of "feminism in action." Her former coworker Janell Davis claimed that being surrounded by feminism at Good Vibrations was like being a "fish in the water." "It was so there," she recalled, "that I don't remember a whole lot of conversation about feminism other than to say that people felt it was really important."[20]

For Babeland's Lizz Randall, it was what feminism had to say about women's sexual agency, autonomy, and desire that was of particular interest: "I feel like we are doing some kind of feminist sexuality in some ways, or helping women get to the point where they can say, 'I like to fuck.' Women using their desire and speaking their desire to me is where I like to tie in the feminism. . . . When I ask people in [job] interviews if they are feminists, they still revert back to 'I did not read all of that stuff, so no.' They think I am testing them. Feminism is still academic for people."[21]

Feminism, at least for Randall, is not an academic exercise but a political belief system that is enacted through, and embodied in, women's ability to un-apologetically name and pursue their sexual desires. Randall readily admits, however, that she has not always embraced the term "feminist" as a way to describe herself or her politics. During our interview she talked about feeling alienated from feminism when she first learned about it in college. "I was one of those people who went through that kind of evolution when you learn about feminism in university and I was like, 'That is not for me.'" She continued,

[Feminism] was presented as middle- to upper-class white women talking in very academic terms, and I was like, "Holy shit. I don't understand, or this isn't me." [It was] when they were still leaving out queers and it wasn't sex-positive feminism, so I was one of those people who was like, "I am not a feminist. I am not going to be that if that means this, this, and that." I have sort of had a turnaround in the past year or so in taking back that word and realizing that feminism doesn't [only] mean all of these academic writers who wrote about feminism. For me it is more about Amber Hollibaugh [a working-class, sex-positive, lesbian feminist activist and author] than it is about all the other names.[22]

Randall was not the only sex shop worker who described conflicting feel-ings about feminism. A number of people I spoke to used words like "strange" and "suspect" when talking about their relationship to feminism. Babeland's Felice Shays, an avowed feminist, went so far as to say that for some people the word "feminist" is "as nasty as saying 'communist.'"[23] Others, however, expressed uncertainty about what, exactly, feminism means anymore. Archer Parr, a trans-identified employee at Babeland, said this:

Feminism is something that I have studied since I was in my twenties, and the more I know about it the less I am able to define it or find the parameters of what is feminist or not. To me, post-structuralism and feminism . . . I cannot separate them anymore. There are so many overlaps for me that I am not ever sure what feminism means necessarily. I certainly think so far as feminism purports to have at its center women's lives—however you define women—that Babeland fulfills that and is very feminist in that sense. I think in some ways, Babeland has one foot in the past and one foot in the future. There is sort of a nod to, "Yes, we are a women-owned, women-run sex-toy store. On the other hand, we are not sure that matters." It seems like a nod to a very recent feminist past where subject position matters, but also a nod to a different moment in time. [Babeland has] several trans employees, so what does it mean to be a woman-owned sex-toy store if gender is really fluid?[24]

The description that Babeland has "one foot in the past and one in the future" nicely captures the ways in which the theoretical and political terrain of feminism has shifted over the past few decades, resulting in what some interviewees described as a generational divide over what counts as feminism in an era when familiar identity categories such as male and female have been destabilized and reconfigured. A queer-identified employee at Good Vibrations who had recently graduated from Oberlin College told me that for her, feminism brings with it a "problem of gender binarism" that is rooted in an earlier generation's ideas about identity politics. Her own hesitancy around embracing feminism stemmed from what she described as its "separatist" tendencies, which she viewed as antithetical to a more inclusive and "queer" understanding of gender.

"For my generation," she said, "that [brand of feminism] can be really disempowering. Gender is not a woman-man thing; sex is not a woman-man thing. Sex can be queer and that is much more empowering than second-wave feminism." The downfall of feminism, she continued, is that "it doesn't want to be challenged." For her, second-wave feminism was a political relic that was out of step with contemporary gender and sexual politics.

The limits of feminism — and perhaps identity politics more generally — are the result of what some of my interviewees viewed as feminism's inability to recognize and incorporate a range of differences into its blueprint for social change. "I don't say I am a feminist," trans-identified Saul Silva remarked during the Babeland roundtable discussion, "because I don't know what that definition means to different people." For younger people like Silva, queer theory and intersectionality have shifted the terms of feminist debate, creating uncertainty for them about who is actually included under feminism's political umbrella and who is left out.[25]

Some business owners, however, have worked hard to "[stay] ahead of the curve," as Early to Bed's Searah Deysach put it, when it comes to promoting a version of retail feminism that values inclusivity. In 2001, when Deysach opened Early to Bed in Chicago, having a sex shop for women was really "of the time." But over time — and it happened rather quickly, she acknowledged — her store morphed from being a sex shop for women into a store for everyone. The first stage of this shift was realizing that cisgender (nontrans) men also wanted to shop in a store like hers, so she began carrying more sex toys for people with penises. By the mid-2000s, she noticed what she described as a "trans-boom" in the culture at large and really began to think about what it meant for her to say she owned a women's sex shop. She adjusted the language she used to be more gender-inclusive. What used to be a section of "toys for men" became "toys for penises"; and she began carrying an expansive selection of gender expression gear, such as chest binders, packing underwear, and stand-to-pee devices, in an effort to better serve the needs of transgender customers. At the same time, Deysach stills feels there is value in recognizing that "people who are raised as girls and women have a different relationship to their bodies and sex than men do in our culture."[26]

Matie Fricker and Molly Adler, the queer-identified founders of Self Serve in Albuquerque, also see inclusivity as a fundamental feminist principle, one they have worked hard to incorporate into their business practices. As Adler explained, "I have a trans partner and we always want to have a critical eye toward trans inclusion, and breaking down gender to some extent. So while we definitely think of Self Serve as a feminist business, that definition for me, or that language for me, has changed in [the time] we have been open. We want to make sure that we include men, include trans people, people of all ages, people who are single, divorced, widowed."[27]

For Fricker and Adler, the idea of radical feminist inclusivity finds expression in the items they sell and the language they use to talk about sex and gender. "We have to stick with ethical, inclusive language that doesn't pigeonhole who someone is or what products they should use," explained Adler.[28] At Self Serve, you will not find any lesbian sex toys, for example; rather, there are items that can be used by anyone, regardless of their sexual orientation, gender identity, or relationship status. When Fricker and Adler teach workshops, they regularly refer to people with "lady parts" and "male parts" instead of using the categories women and men, in an effort to challenge the idea that there is a necessary correspondence between bodies, identities, and sexual practices.

"We want to have a space that is happy and safe for lesbians or feminists or second-wave feminists, but at the same time, we are not going to exclude transgender people or gender-queer people or something that [represents] a different generation," Adler said.[29]

Many retailers acknowledged that running an explicitly feminist sex-toy store could pose marketing and public relations challenges, precisely because there was no guarantee that the version of feminism they promoted would be either intelligible or inviting to all customers. Babeland cofounder Rachel Venning explained the problem this way: "The problem with feminism is that the antifeminist elements in our culture have done a good job of making feminism a very suspect word to a lot of people, so it can be a kind of off-switch to say 'feminism,' which is probably why [Babeland] doesn't say 'feminist' in the mission, because it is a trigger, I think." She continued, "Even though I consider myself to be a feminist, and I consider Babeland to be a feminist business, I have found that 'feminism' is a word that a lot of people don't feel part of."[30]

Venning's assessment of feminism as something that many people don't feel part of was a perception shared by several retailers who politely distanced themselves, and by extension their businesses, from the label altogether. The stereotype of feminists as angry, humorless, politically out of step, and anti-sex was reason enough for them to forgo the term altogether. When I asked retailer Kim Airs, for example, whether she considered Grand Opening in Boston, which she founded in 1993, to be a feminist store, she shook her head and said, "no."

> I don't, but everybody else does. I don't, because I just happen to be
> a woman selling the stuff the way I want it to be sold. So, if that is a
> feminist statement, so be it. If I was a guy and I realized that there
> wasn't a nice place to sell sex toys, I would have still opened it up. I just
> happened to be a woman. That's the luck of the draw. So, I don't see it
> as a big feminist statement. I just see it as making things accessible in a
> comfortable environment. Things that are traditionally not presented
> that way.[31]

While the majority of my interviewees embraced feminism—regardless of how they defined it—others expressed ambivalence about the term because they viewed it as potentially exclusionary or outmoded, or simply too hard to market successfully. And despite the desire to be radically inclusive across gender, race, sexual orientation, and class differences, gender continues to be the primary organizing principle for many feminist retailers and the language they are most comfortable speaking when they talk about their businesses.

From Bic pens for women to the niche marketing of pornography—for example, teens, Asians, lesbians, and more—the broader retail market beyond sex toys relies on separating products into neat and tidy boxes, which can upend efforts by sex-positive retailers to push beyond the limits of binary gender divisions, as well as other rigid identity categories. Successful marketing depends on using commonly accepted terms to classify products in ways that will be recognizable to established distribution channels and consumers, and easily searchable through Google. Thus, feminist retailers and staff must navigate commercial imperatives that are not always in sync with their progressive ideals or more inclusive versions of feminism and queer politics.

## The Question of Men

The first time that Robert Lawrence, Carol Queen's longtime partner, went into Good Vibrations on a day when Joani Blank wasn't working, he did so with some trepidation. It was the early 1980s, and Good Vibrations, much like Eve's Garden, had developed a reputation as a women's store. But he was a man on a mission. Good Vibrations was selling a custom-made, single-strap harness made by Kathy Andrews, the founder of Stormy Leather, an item that he was eager to buy.

"Joani said it's okay for me to be here today," he said to the young woman behind the counter. He pointed to the harness hanging on the wall, and told the clerk he wanted to buy it.

"We don't sell things to men," she replied.

"Well, Joani said I could buy it. Can I try it on?"

"We don't let men use the tryout room."

Lawrence wanted the harness badly—the style was hard to come by and it came with a lifetime guarantee—and was willing to jump through whatever hoops he needed to get it, but the encounter left a bad taste in his mouth. And while he understood the reasons why Good Vibrations wanted to be a safe space for women, the fact that he was perceived as "invading the space with [his] maleness," as he described it, left him wondering: How will this business survive?[32]

By the early 1990s, the question of how, and even if, Good Vibrations should market to men was one that employees were openly discussing and debating. Good Vibrations had by this point developed a reputation not only as a women's store but a lesbian sex-toy store. Staff sexologist and longtime employee Carol Queen explained that there were several likely reasons for this. The label "women-owned" was often interpreted as "women-only," which was seen by some as a code word for "lesbian."[33] Additionally, Good Vibrations was located in the heart of the Mission District, a San Francisco neighborhood with a high concentration of lesbian residents. And finally, many of the women who shopped and worked at Good Vibrations identified as lesbians, including Susie Bright, who, by the mid-1980s, had gained a national reputation as a lesbian writer and sexpert. While Good Vibrations' reputation as a lesbian store was a source of pride for many employees, it also presented marketing and perception challenges.

The issue was not only whether Good Vibrations should actively court male consumers, but whether or not the company should hire men. Queen was on the hiring committee when the first man applied for a position at Good Vibrations in the early 1990s. "It was just *such* a big step," she explained, "and many people in the company were not ready to take it."

> I think what was going through people's minds in those days was that so many of our customers at the store are women-identified that it will freak them out to see a man [working at the store]. And this was a gay man. I don't think it is at all surprising that the first men who got hired at Good Vibrations were gay men, or that the first men who applied and wanted to be hired were gay men. This guy would not have come off as a guy who was looming around in a women's sex space, looking for action. It wouldn't have felt like that at all, but there was a perception — probably partly a correct perception — that so many of our regular customers might find it a concern and that was what derailed this man's application. I don't think it was the thought that he wasn't able to do this kind of work. He was a well-educated guy around sexuality, but it just wasn't the time yet.[34]

In the early 2000s, a similar set of conversations took place at Babeland. Even then, a decade later and among employees at a different company, it was a topic that many people had very strong feelings about. "I almost bulleted through the window," one staff sex educator said, recalling the moment when she heard that Babeland was considering hiring a man to work on the sales floor. Employees wondered what might change if men, who have more social privilege and power, began working on the sales floor or in management positions. Whose voices would be heard and whose opinions would be considered valid? "[Men] have ways that they relate to women and they think they are right. It just changes the dynamics. It's just different," one staff sex educator noted. "It's not a level playing field. It's just not," another remarked.[35]

By virtue of being women-owned and, at the time, almost exclusively women-operated, Babeland had created a workplace culture that offered its female employees an escape from the sexism and gendered devaluation that many of them faced on a regular basis. As a result, they were extremely protective of the safe space that Babeland afforded them as women, as queers, and, importantly, as sexperts with the authority to speak openly about sex in a culture that often punishes women for doing so. As Babeland's Christine Rinki noted, "Sexuality is not defined around my experience, and there needs to be special attention paid to that and special places for me to feel safe and at home and with my community. I think it's really important that we, as queer women . . . and as women period, that we are the experts."[36]

At Good Vibrations, the question of whether or not to hire men or advertise to male customers was only resolved, at least to some extent, by taking a closer look at who its customers were. Good Vibrations conducted marketing surveys in the 1990s and learned that its customers were predominantly heterosexual, predominantly white, and predominantly middle class. Former Good Vibrations employee Terri Hague explained:

It was pretty much an echo of the staff, with more men. It was a pretty even fifty-fifty split of men and women. It was interesting, because that kind of helped solve the debate, because these are the people who are buying the stuff, so do you want to stop selling to men, because they are 50 percent of our customers? Do you want to stop selling to heterosexuals, because that is 75 percent of our customers? If you start narrowing it down to who *you* want the customers to be, you are looking at maybe 10 percent and that is just not realistic, so I think that helped a lot. But there was still tremendous debate.[37]

The first man hired to work on the sales floor at Good Vibrations was Charlie Glickman, who began working in the Berkeley store in 1996. Queer-identified, Glickman had a background that included volunteering at Alameda County's rape crisis center as the project coordinator for Men Overcoming Sexual Assault. He's slight of build, with small hands and an alto voice. As a result, it wasn't unusual for him to be mistaken as a trans guy. But he also knew how to act like someone's "gay BFF," he said. "You know, like Will and Grace." He never hit on customers and projected a nonthreatening vibe, which he thinks made it comfortable for many women to have him help them when they were shopping. And yet not all Good Vibrations customers were happy seeing a man on the sales floor. At least one woman wrote to the company to say, "Please take me off your mailing list. There's a man working there." However, Glickman found this response to be the exception and not the rule.[38]

Over time, Good Vibrations staff realized that the company's warm, welcoming, and sex-positive retail model appealed to many men and adjusted their business practices accordingly. "Men have had opportunities to get really crappy, cheap, hazardous products that are not good ones," explained Thomas Roche, the former director of marketing at Good Vibrations. "And so there are a lot of men who want to get higher-quality products and who want to come to us. As a result, we find that we have a lot of male customers. . . . It is not so wild to think about a man reading about us in *Maxim* and going on our website and ordering something for him to share with his girlfriend. That is not unusual."[39] According to Janell Davis, many men would say to her, "I love coming into your store so much more than going to the men's stores, because everything [there] is so huge and the assumption is that I know how to use it all and I want the biggest one there. Maybe I don't."[40] Other progressive sex shop owners, too, became aware that men also wanted an alternative to the stereotypical porno shop. "I think there are a lot of men, of all sexual orientations, that frankly don't feel comfortable in the traditional porn store, either," said Laura Haave, the owner of the Tool Shed in Milwaukee.[41] Ellen Barnard from A Woman's Touch in Madison, Wisconsin, agreed. The thing that surprised Barnard the most when she opened her store, she recalled, was the number of men who said, "Thank you, thank you, thank you for opening a store that makes me feel like it's okay to have sex with my wife."[42] Once Barnard realized that men were also looking for a place that validated their desires and didn't make them feel guilty, dirty, or ashamed for being sexual, she expanded the store's product mix to meet their needs. "We didn't know that men would be needing this [place] as much as women would," Barnard told me.[43]

Marketing to men was not only about meeting an existing need. It was also a practical gesture that acknowledged that many men had money, and many men also had female partners who stood to benefit from them shopping at sex-positive shops like Good Vibrations, Babeland, and A Woman's Touch. According to Carol Queen,

> I don't think it would be at all inappropriate to say that one of the reasons—one of the many reasons, not the only reason—that [Good Vibrations] is now a more pansexually oriented business, is because who can doubt that men's money is green? But there is more to it than that. It also is really important for us to expose as many men as we can to the way we think about sexuality, which was, granted, developed in a for-women context. We think that many men who don't even have sex with women will think it is relevant, but we certainly think that

men who do have sex with women will either find it relevant or ought to find it relevant, and that women who have sex with men will be glad if we have been able to give more men a vantage point around sex and women's sexuality—and everybody's sexuality—that is, if you will, more feminist, more women oriented, more women's pleasure oriented; just sort of more holistic. So it is part of the project to get guys on board with this.[44]

Good Vibrations' Estevez agreed, and argued that it didn't benefit the company's mission to be exclusive. "We could do a greater business if we allowed men, who have more money than women, to shop in our store. If we can sell our products to men and get men's money, then we can take that money and do this kinky, radical sex education. We had all kinds of fantasies about getting the GV-RV and doing a cross-country tour."[45] While it took Good Vibrations some time to reach this conclusion, for other companies, it was a no-brainer: welcoming men as customers benefited everyone—their businesses, the culture, and especially women who have sex with men. "My hope," said Estevez, "is that these men would leave the store and be transformed by their experience, and that they would go home to their partners and be better men for it."[46]

## Queering Heterosexuality

Felice Shays is an out and proud dyke—a New Yorker, a Jew, a leather woman, and a feminist, with a penchant for red lipstick and high heels. Confident and opinionated, she possessed more practical, hands-on knowledge about BDSM-related products than anyone else working on the sales floor at Babeland's Lower East Side store in the early 2000s. She was also a skilled sex educator, someone who could turn the task of talking about vibrators and butt plugs into a commanding piece of sex shop performance art.

Occasionally, when Shays gave customers tours of what she affectionately referred to as "dildo land," she would purposefully flaunt her queer-feminist sexuality. While showcasing this dildo or that one, she might casually mention to a customer that she sometimes wore a soft pack dildo underneath her mini-skirt, knowing full well that she was probably challenging someone's deeply felt assumptions about sex, gender, and bodies. In this and other ways, Shays saw herself as advancing Babeland's "queer agenda." "I'm not saying the person I am talking to should understand why, or think it's hot, or want to copy my cock-under-skirt reality, but the fact that I am presenting it as part of my tour is a definition of who I am as a pervert and a sex-positive kind of gal."[47]

Many at Babeland took pride in the company's queer orientation. "Feminism is my thing," co-owner Cavanah once told me, "but I think having queer people talk to straight people about sex . . . I think what we are doing is queering straight sex in a lot of ways. We are shaking up their assumptions about what sex is and bringing in all kinds of other information and possibilities and that is queering it. I think we queer them."[48]

What does it mean to queer something or someone, and what might this process look like in the context of a sex store? Sex educator, author, and former Good Vibrations education director Charlie Glickman suggested that one way that Good Vibrations and its sister stores queer sexuality is by "pushing past limits that really don't need to be there."[49] In this sense, the act of queering is about disassembling normative ideas about the relationship between gender, sexuality, and bodies, and creating alternative configurations and possibilities—what we might think of as queer rearticulations. For businesses like Good Vibrations and Babeland, these queer rearticulations might include any number of things: a lesbian employee describing how to go down on a silicone dildo during a blowjob workshop, a heterosexual female customer who expresses her preference for gay male pornography, or a trans man teaching a workshop on G-spot ejaculation.

Good Vibrations product and purchasing manager Coyote Days described the act of queering as a process of "breaking open boxes." When she began working at Good Vibrations in 2003 a manager told her, "Don't let what a toy is intended for stop you from thinking about all the different ways it can be used." Days began to queer sex toys by not attaching products to a specific sexual practice or gender. For example, male-female couples can use a vibrating cock ring during intercourse, but a cock ring also can be placed on a dildo or around a finger and used for manual stimulation of any number of body parts by people of any gender. Just because a manufacturer markets an item in a particular way doesn't mean that's how Good Vibrations staff have to talk about it or how customers must use it. "If I limit myself," Days explained, "I limit my sales, my reach, and who feels comfortable in our stores."[50]

For Days and others, queer is not just a sexual orientation; it's also a point of view, a perspective that informs how they think and talk about sexual products, information, and identities. "[Good Vibrations] hires a lot of young queer people [and] I feel like even the straight people we hire are a little queer," Days told me. As a result, she explains, Good Vibrations employees "have a different way of seeing relationships and gender," which invariably influences how they talk about sex and gender on the sales floor. Babeland's Dena Hankins agreed. "I think when you walk into [Babeland] or when you go on the website, you are looking at the sexual aspects of the world from a standpoint that is more open and accepting and excited about variation than a nonqueer standpoint." Babeland, according to Hankins, is "standing in a slightly different place to look at the world."[51]

That straight people are learning about sex from queer people has led some writers and sex educators to argue that the LGBT movement has influenced not just queer sexuality, but the sex lives of everyone. In fact, some cultural critics have suggested that a new sexual identity has emerged, that of the queer heterosexual. Perhaps not surprisingly, one of the places where the cross-pollination of sexual information and ideas is happening between straight people and their queer counterparts is on the sex shop floor. According to sex educator and writer Tristan Taormino, "When a dyke counsels a husband who asks, 'What's the best kind of toy for stimulating my wife's clitoris during penetration?' she gives him advice from experience. A lesbian sex tip is transmitted to a straight man, and lines begin to blur."[52]

This kind of boundary blurring is a daily occurrence at feminist and queer-owned sex-toy stores around the country, where employees often double as queer ambassadors who are exporting queer discourses and nonnormative sexual possibilities into the straight world. Jacq Jones, the former Babeland employee who now owns Sugar in Baltimore, described the "melting" of traditional identity categories and offered examples of how this sometimes played out on the sales floor. One time, she recounted, a female acquaintance came into the store and said, "I am *so* glad you are here. I started dating this guy and he is really wonderful and we are really fabulous together and we are being sexual, but you see, he is gay, so we need to figure out how to make this satisfying for him."[53]

Jones, for her part, learned to not make assumptions about what kind of genitals someone had underneath their clothes, or what kind of sex a person might be having or with whom. She also did not assume that a male and female couple was necessarily heterosexual, because they might not be. "What is it called when a gay man is dating a straight woman? Is that straight? Maybe but maybe not," she suggested. "Or this woman, who is a friend of mine who is bisexual and her lover is male, and flamingly femmy and cross-dresses all of the time. She says [to me], 'You cannot tell me if I am walking down the street with a man in high heels, fishnets and a dress, that that's not queer.'"[54]

In their roles as sex shop owners, authors, sex educators, and porn producers, lesbians and queer women have been on the front lines of helping to queer heterosexuality. According to Babeland's Laura Weide, "If you're talking about pleasing women sexually, who knows better than lesbians? It's one thing to have a women-owned sex store where you talk about self-pleasure, but when you talk about giving pleasure to women and being able to share information, there are just some added insights that dykes can offer and they do."[55]

Nowhere perhaps was the trend of lesbians queering straight sex more apparent than with the popularization of pegging, or the act of men being anally penetrated by their female partners. In an interview published in *On Our Backs* magazine in 2001, Jackie Strano and Shar Rednour, the creative forces behind the *Bend Over Boyfriend* films, discussed why they thought pegging had become so popular in such a short amount of time. "I think people's minds finally wrapped around the idea that being an open, receptive partner doesn't necessarily mean you're being passive, which in a lot of men's minds is not a good thing," Strano said. "Women are also coming into their own around being more aggressive. Men are discovering their assholes for pure, intense orgasmic pleasure. What's the latest millennium sex craze, the next hot thing? Boys with their asses in the air and feeling really powerful about it."[56]

"The younger generation," Rednour chimed in, "is demanding a lot more sex information and education. Instead of the woman just flopping around like a rag doll on the end of a stick, women are thrilled: 'I get to stick my finger somewhere and I get to do something.'"[57]

"*It's this new way that straight people are having lesbian sex*," Strano added. "He's orgasmic but not focused just on his dick being hard all the time and coming. She's staying orgasmic for a length of time because she's doing him, plus she feels powerful with a dick strapped on."[58]

For Strano, the act of pegging queers heterosexuality to such a degree that it becomes a version of lesbian sex. Pegging underscores the idea that sexual acts are not contingent upon sexual identities. Women can strap on a dildo and experience what it feels like to be in the driver's seat, and men can bend over and experience what it feels like to be a receptive partner. Conventional relationships between gender, power, and pleasure are unsettled, often inverted, and frequently mismatched, producing new, and indeed more queer, sexual possibilities.

Babeland owners and employees viewed the company's queer identity as central to the business's mission. "I think we are more queer [than other stores], because we are queer. I don't know how else to put it," Cavanah explained. (Indeed, a full-page ad that ran in *On Our Backs* magazine in the late 1990s and early 2000s foregrounded the owners' queer identity as a central organizing principle of the business, declaring that as lesbians, "We Want What You Want.") Dana Clark, the former manager of Babeland in New York, argued that Babeland's mission "wouldn't exist without queerness behind it":

> The mission wouldn't be what it is if it did not have queer people behind it. The reason why I say this is because it seems to me, in my experience with queer people and identifying as queer, is that we are more sexually open, that for some reason, we have permission to lay aside the rules that we have learned about sex and about being a woman, and create another set of rules that we are very comfortable with. . . . It is not that I don't think that is happening in other sex-toy stores across the nation, but I feel like we create this comfort to be whoever you are. Maybe the basis of that is that we have that in our staff: we are who we are. The queerness of it to me, or when I think of queer sexual politics, I guess, is that we are ridiculed or closeted in so many parts of our lives, that the importance of being queer within the store and having that representation within the store is also making a collective, queer feminist statement. We are here. We do acknowledge it. And we run the business from that place.[59]

In giving themselves "permission to lay aside the rules," feminist and queer-identified sex-toy retailers have constructed new norms — or counternorms, as the case may be — that inform how they think and talk about sex. Adler from Self Serve observed, "A lot of these women [who have started these businesses] are women who have already had to come out as sexual people and claim some alternative to what the norm is for pleasure, for relationships, for happiness."[60] Early to Bed's Deysach claimed that one advantage that queer women have over straight women is that "they don't have a preset idea of what sex is." When most straight people talk about sex, she explained, they are actually talking about intercourse. When a queer woman talks about sex, "she could be talking about a hundred different things. . . . I think [sex] is something that some straight people think we do better than them." Deysach pointed to the popularity of books like *Lesbian Sex Secrets for Men* as evidence that many straight people are interested in all the "big secrets that we know that [they] don't."[61]

Many Babeland employees felt that the company's queer standpoint doubled as a selling point that attracted both queers and nonqueers alike to

The queer identity of Babeland cofounders Claire Cavanah and Rachel Venning figured prominently in the company's early advertising and outreach.

the business. "I like the fact that we don't change our company drastically in order to bring more straight folks in or make more straight people comfortable," said Isaiah Benjamin. Instead, he added, "Babeland is drawing people who are maybe not already part of a sex-positive culture into what is already there, which is a very dyke-positive, very irreverent, very sex-positive environment." He continued,

I think that is partly manifested in the fact that a lot of our frontline customer service people are visibly queer, and people who are straight are coming into the store and interrupting a bunch of big old dykes a lot of the time. And yet, we have an approach that makes people comfortable, and we haven't made an attempt to seem more clean-cut or seem less queer in order to make people more comfortable. I think what we have found is that a lot of people are really into that—and not just queer people. We get a lot of great e-mails from straight men saying how great an experience that is and I like that about Babeland a lot.[62]

Babeland does not downplay or try to straighten its image to appeal to the sexual mainstream. According to former marketing manager Weide, "There is not a question at Babeland, 'Do we need to change our identity?' It is like, 'This is who we are,' [so] how do we communicate that to let people know more about us, and that we are here and that they are welcome here, rather than feeling like we have to change our look. . . . The conversation about how to represent the company to make more people feel welcome has just not been a conversation [that we have had]."[63]

Babeland's mantra could easily be, "We're here, we're queer, we own this sex store, get used to it." But as Benjamin and Weide noted, the business's queer identity was not something anyone in the company felt that customers needed to get used to. Rather, its queer orientation was a fundamental part of the business's identity and, by extension, its commercial appeal.

Much like the word "feminism," however, the term "queer" is also very much up for grabs. Shays, for example, described her struggles to come to grips with what the word "queer" even meant:

Part of it is my age. Queer was not a term that was really used when I was coming out. Queer really didn't exist and certainly not queer theory. So when queer hit the stands I was like, "I am a lesbian. I am a feminist." I was a feminist first and then I was a lesbian and then I became a dyke politically . . . so when queer came along, it felt like a dilution of lesbianism—and yet I loved when Susie Bright came out and said that she was a dyke who sleeps with men every once in a while. I was like, "Okay. This is blowing my mind. I don't understand this." It made me mad, because it felt like our tribe is being diluted once again. Dyke means you sleep with women and that's where it's at—your social, emotional, physical, and sexual realities are all about women. So it really confused me; and then I was meeting really young ones who were saying, "I am queer," and I was like, "Great. What does that mean?" "Well he's queer and she's queer." But what does that mean? "It means that we are all kinky and anything goes or it means that we are all whatever we are and that is totally cool." Well, that means everyone. "Well, yeah." Well, no. An open mind does not make you queer.[64]

Shays's account of navigating the often slippery slope of identity politics is instructive, because it points to the important role that identity categories play in organizing people's conceptual universes and lived experiences. Words such as "lesbian," "feminist," and "dyke" matter precisely because they are powerful articulations of political affiliation and community membership that mean something very specific; for example, "Dyke means you sleep with women." The lack of specificity attached to the word "queer," by comparison, left Shays with more questions than answers about how queerness functioned as a form of sexual politics.

And while an open mind might not make someone queer, as Shays contends, it is for many people an important first step in rethinking taken-for-granted assumptions about gender and sexuality, and imagining a different set of possibilities for themselves and their relationships. It might also be what motivates someone to venture into a sex-toy store like Good Vibrations or Babeland in the first place.

Author and literary critic Samuel Delany has written about the social significance of "contact encounters." Contact, he writes, "is the conversation that starts in the line at the grocery counter with the person behind you while the clerk is changing the paper roll in the cash register. It is the pleasantries exchanged with a neighbor who has brought her chair out to take some air on the stoop. It is the discussion that begins with the person next to you at the bar."[65] Contact is a form of social exchange—sometimes verbal, sometimes not—that occurs between otherwise unrelated people during the course of the day: an encounter with someone standing in line at Starbucks, the UPS delivery person knocking on your door, or the vibrator clerk at Babeland. Contact encounters are the result of people being "thrown together in public space through chance and propinquity."[66] For Delany, what is especially significant about these chance encounters is the degree to which they create opportunities for interclass, interracial, and intergenerational affiliations and exchanges, which either can be fleeting in nature or can turn into something more enduring.

Sex-toy stores like Good Vibrations and Babeland facilitate the cross-pollination of sexual information between different groups of people—lesbians and gays, queer-identified and straight people, transgender and cisgender individuals—who might otherwise never come into direct contact with each other. Individuals can—and very often do—turn to feminist and queer-friendly sex shops for sexual information and consumer experiences they might not find anyplace else, from people they might otherwise never encounter. This idea was captured by a male fan of Babeland, who noted, "It's funny how you just wind up in conversation while you are there—and not just with the people who work there, but other customers, too. You end up doing product review with the person who is standing next to you looking at vibrators." While debates about what constitutes feminism, or how best to appeal to men when "women-run" is often interpreted as "women-only" persist, Babeland and businesses like it have succeeded in cultivating a particular kind of sex public, a community of affiliation based on practices of consumption that are not necessarily bound by rigid categories of gender, race, class, sexual orientation, or age, helping to create new—and perhaps even more queer—networks for the social transmission of sexual information and knowledge.

*eight*

# PROFITABILITY AND
# SOCIAL CHANGE

———

It costs a lot of money to change the world.

ZIADEE WHIPTAIL
Good Vibrations


It was one of the most tense and uncomfortable store meetings in Babeland's history. It was June 2001 and Carrie Schrader, the company's general business manager, had just finished handing employees copies of a profit and loss statement showing that the Lower East Side store was losing money. Then she dropped a bomb: the store's assistant purchasing manager and longtime employee, Lucky, had been laid off.

I learned that day that I had started my fieldwork during a period of unprecedented financial crisis for Babeland. Schrader, who had flown to New York from the company's headquarters in Seattle the day before, explained that since the start of the year the New York store (there was only one in the city at the time) had been losing money and that cost-cutting measures needed to take place, effective immediately. "What are the possible ways that we can cut costs and remain profitable?" she asked.

In an effort to answer her own question, Schrader proceeded to outline several cost-cutting strategies: the salaries of the business's owners, including hers, would be cut; management raises and hiring would be frozen; the company's business loans would be restructured; and educational workshops and special events would be scaled back to one a month until the business's finances looked healthier. But what left everyone's mouths hanging open was the announcement that Lucky had been laid off—the first such layoff in the company's history.

Employees sat in stunned silence, quietly absorbing the news. As if to contextualize these changes, Schrader explained that retail businesses across the nation were experiencing their slowest sales in twelve years. This, combined with the recent expansion of the company's mail-order operation and its physical relocation from Seattle to Oakland, as well as the lease of a new point-of-sale system, had caused cash-flow problems. The first priority, Schrader explained, was to keep the store's doors open and the business's sex-positive feminist mission alive.

"What we are witnessing," she reported dryly, "is the very real struggle between capitalism and the mission. We cannot do the mission if we don't have the money, so the two need to be balanced."

Schrader paused and asked if anyone had anything to say. The two staff members sitting directly across from me shook their heads and said no, although their body language—crossed arms, pursed lips, and downcast eyes—indicated they were upset. Jamye Waxman, who had been hired only three weeks earlier, was the first to speak. Trying to defuse what was clearly a tense situation, she stated that layoffs were occurring everywhere and that the decision to eliminate Lucky's position should not be seen as anything personal. Felice Shays, one of the store's more outspoken employees, looked down and slowly shook her head.

"Why haven't we had access to the numbers before this point?" she asked, adding that she felt angry and betrayed by what she saw as the extremely "reactionary" decision to lay off Lucky. "Why weren't other solutions considered before letting someone go?"

Dan Athineos, the store's assistant manager, offered a different perspective. She told the group that since hearing the news about Lucky that morning, she had been forced to revisit what the company's mission meant to her. "This might sound wishy-washy," she said, "but you all know what the mission means to you. Working at Babeland has changed my life and I have political reasons for being here, but that does not change the fact that this is, after all, a business."

As the meeting drew to a close, the company's cofounder, Claire Cavanah, who had been sitting quietly throughout most of the discussion, turned to me and, looking dispirited, said, "Welcome to the world of retail."

Babeland's short-lived financial crisis, which began an immediate reversal after the business's cost-cutting measures were implemented, marked an important turning point for the company. For the first time since the business's humble beginnings in Seattle almost nine years earlier—when Cavanah and her business partner, Rachel Venning, used an old cigar box as a cash register and a spiral notebook to keep track of daily sales—there were open discussions about profit, loss, the bottom line, and the thorny relationship between consumer capitalism and the business's larger mission of changing the way the culture thinks and talks about sex. As Cavanah later explained, "[The business's mission] was all about changing the world and so the result is that if you don't put profitability in there, you don't remember to think about it."[1] The increasingly competitive nature of the sex-toy market, especially since the rise of online retailing, along with the company's continued growth, meant that profit needed to be added to its mission—at least in spirit—and built into the very fabric of the business. As far as the management team was concerned, money could no longer be treated as an afterthought or something that was antithetical to the business's larger mission of social change. Talking openly about profits needed to become as important as talking candidly about sex.

As a result of the business's heightened consciousness around money and profitability, staff members were taught to read and interpret monthly profit and loss reports; a greater emphasis was placed on meeting daily and monthly sales goals; and friendly notes began to appear in the store's daily log encouraging sex educators to push more expensive silicone products over rubber ones in an effort to increase sales. It appeared to be the dawn of a new, more profit-minded era, an occasion, Cavanah would later tell me, for employees to become as excited about making money as they were about selling sex toys and educating consumers.

For a researcher, it was a fascinating time to be conducting fieldwork. The conversations that began to take place around money not only revealed the ideological tensions between profitability and social change, but they also exposed the deeply felt ambivalences that many Babeland employees had about the business's relationship to consumer capitalism. Annie Michelson, a staff sex educator in Seattle, told me that she was "still in this phase of Babeland being this huge social justice organization, rather than a business."[2] For her and many other staff members, the issue of money had been almost entirely subsumed by the company's mission of making the world a better and more sexually open place. In fact, many Babeland employees described the business almost exclusively in terms of social altruism rather than sales and very often framed them as competing tendencies. According to Alicia Relles, "I really came [to the business] with a perspective of it not being so much about money or profit, but for education and really feeling like that is what we are doing. And that the mission doesn't explicitly say anything about profit makes it very easy to see the store almost exclusively in terms of its educational mission rather than a commercial mission."[3]

She wasn't the only person who felt this way. In the eyes of many Babeland employees, the company had ceased to exist as a commercial enterprise with very real profit-making concerns. (There was a period of time, for example, when the New York store had an open-till policy under which employees could "borrow" money for lunch or other incidentals and leave an IOU. This practice only stopped when the company's accountant indicated in a memo to staff that in other places this is called stealing "and we just can't tolerate it.")

It was money, and not sex, that was viewed as an impurity that risked tainting the business's larger mission of sex-positive social change. And, as I would eventually learn, Babeland was not alone in its struggles to figure out how to balance its commitment to social change with being a profitable business.

## The Trouble with Money

Eve's Garden's founder, Dell Williams, knew that she was not a good businesswoman, but it was not something she was especially eager to talk about. Instead, she wanted to tell me about her passion for women's liberation, how Eve's Garden came to be, and the many letters of acknowledgment and thanks she had received over the years from customers. We were sitting in her office at Eve's Garden in Midtown Manhattan, Williams on one side of the desk and me on the other. A poster of Betty Dodson's cover art from the 1973 NOW Conference on Female Sexuality hung on the wall behind her, and various papers and news clippings were scattered across her desk. In preparation for my visit, Williams had pulled old articles and mail-order catalogs from her filing cabinet. Every now and then, she would pass me something to read: an early draft of Eve's Garden's mission statement, an article she wrote for the *Journal of Sex Research*, a book of publicity that she had collected over the years; and while I sat and read them, she rummaged through her files, looking for more items to show me.

At the time of our interview in 2001, Williams was seventy-nine years old, rail thin, and not in particularly good health; but when she talked about her involvement with the women's movement and her belief in the power of women's orgasmic energy, her eyes lit up. This was her life's work and she wanted it to be documented. What she was not so keen to talk about were her struggles over the years to keep Eve's Garden financially solvent.

"I don't know if you need my whole business history," she said at one point, looking uncertain about whether she was revealing too much about her efforts to keep the business afloat.

"If you feel comfortable talking about it, yes, I'd like to hear it."

"I don't think I was very good at the business side of things," she admitted. "I always seemed to have problems with money and meeting payroll. Financially I should have gotten another partner or someone to handle that aspect of it, because it always seemed to be a struggle."[4]

Undercapitalized from the start, Williams made a series of missteps that hurt Eve's Garden financially and impeded its growth. A 1984 article in *Ms.* chronicled the various mistakes Williams made along the way, which included starting Eve's Garden without careful planning, expanding without a strong financial base, and relying on the well-intended but ultimately bad advice of others. Williams acknowledged that she was "more motivated by fervor than business sense," a factor that nearly caused the collapse of Eve's Garden in the early 1980s when a foray into venture capitalism and the relocation of mail-order operations to Boston left the business in a shambles.[5] Overworked, crippled with anxiety, and saddled with debt, including to the IRS, Williams brought the business back to New York City and tried to start over.

"At one point I felt I couldn't handle it anymore," Williams told me. "I kind of had a nervous breakdown, or some kind of breakdown, where I couldn't be involved [in the business] anymore. I was out of the picture for about two or three years."[6]

Although the financial hardships and punishing anxiety that Williams experienced were extreme, very few feminist retailers that I spoke with were comfortable describing themselves as businesswomen. In fact, ambivalence, if not outright antagonism, toward consumer capitalism shaped the narratives of many sex-positive feminist retailers, and perhaps no single individual exuded greater antipathy toward business than Good Vibrations founder Joani Blank.

Blank was not shy about expressing her disdain for the world of business and prided herself on the fact that she did not do "business as usual." When I asked her what she meant by this, she offered a one-sentence answer: "*I didn't give a damn about profits.*"[7] Profits, she explained, were secondary to everything that was important to her about running a successful business. By her own account, she was "extraordinarily fortunate" to be in a financially privileged position—she lived cheaply and had both savings and family money she could draw on—which meant that she did not have to keep as close an eye on the bottom line as other business owners might need to do. Having money to fall back on allowed her to be outwardly dismissive of money and yet, at the same time, not worry about whether or not she'd be able to pay the business's bills. As a result, Blank could infuse Good Vibrations with cash when needed. Indeed, several former employees who worked at Good Vibrations in the 1980s recalled that for a number of years Blank floated Good Vibrations when the company was operating at a loss and unable to pay all of its bills. "She had the luxury of not having to worry about the bottom line," former employee Anne Semans remarked.[8] Former Good Vibrations manager Cathy Winks agreed. "In the early years, everyone used to joke that Joani was 'Joani Bank' instead of Joani Blank, because she kept Good Vibrations going when by right its doors would have shut pretty quickly if it had been trying to support itself."[9]

Being the owner of a business in which profit and wealth accumulation were not primary motivations had some advantages, however. For one, it gave Blank the freedom to make business decisions that were not necessarily contingent on whether a specific item or project would be profitable. "I could just [run the business] in the way that felt right to me," Blank explained. This meant that Good Vibrations could carry products with virtually no profit margin simply because Blank felt it was important to make those items available to customers. Winks recalled that in the early days of Good Vibrations, Blank made regular trips to San Francisco's Japan Town to purchase cases of the Hitachi Magic Wand for resale. According to Winks, Blank would buy the vibrators at a slight discount only to turn around and sell them at Good Vibrations at the same price for which they were being sold in Japan Town, thereby making a profit of only about two dollars for every one sold.

The fact that Blank was not, as Semans described it, "a stressed-out businessperson" meant that Good Vibrations could pursue potentially unprofitable ventures simply because she thought they should exist. This was certainly the case with the launch of Good Vibrations' Sexuality Library in the late 1980s, a catalog dedicated to books and videos about sex. Semans, who spearheaded the Sexuality Library, described the project as essentially "hemorrhaging money" for its first year, in large part because of the challenges involved in turning a profit from a book catalog in which the markup on books was low and the printing costs high. At one staff meeting, Semans recalled, she got upset about the financially struggling catalog. Afterward, Blank took her aside and said, "Anne, don't take it so personally. What's the worst thing that's going to happen? We just decide not to have the catalog."[10]

"It always made me feel really good in this business capacity," Semans said. "Because it allowed me—and I think it allowed the rest of us—to have a more realistic relationship to our work and the success or failure of any given project."

Many employees who worked at Good Vibrations in the 1980s and early 1990s viewed Blank's unconventional attitude toward money as a gift. According to Winks, Blank "allowed us to have that spirit of abundance that I keep coming back to: 'We think this ought to exist, so let's make it exist.' There were books that she thought should be available, so she would just publish them. That sense of possibility is really an incredible gift to bequeath."[11]

Blank hired women to work at Good Vibrations—and initially it was all women—who were smart and passionate about the business's social mission. They had degrees in literature and religious studies from schools like Stanford University and Barnard College, but only rarely did they have any relevant business background or retail experience. According to Semans, "[Joani] hired you because she thought you were smart and then she said, 'This is my vision. Make it happen.' It was a great work experience for all of us. We all ended up learning so many different aspects of running a business, instead of going to business school."[12]

The downside of this, Semans acknowledged, was that "if anyone had had a business background, or had any more business savvy, we probably would've wasted a lot less time and been more strategic."

But business savvy and strategy were not prerequisites for working at Good Vibrations during this time. The emphasis, at least when Terri Hague worked there in the early to mid-1990s, was on what the business did as opposed to how much money it made. "Good Vibrations always made money despite itself," she explained. "Despite the efforts of the staff. It seemed like if it were any other business the staff would've driven it into the ground, just from inexperience. Just from lack of business knowledge and making mistakes."[13] Another Good Vibrations employee offered a similar assessment: "I don't think anybody verbally said in my presence that we don't care about profits back in 1994 or 1995. I think to some degree it was like, 'We have these other priorities.' But also to some degree there was a sense of not really knowing how to make a profit."[14]

Similar to what happened at Babeland, it took a series of financial shortfalls in the mid- to late 1990s for Good Vibrations to begin thinking anew about its relationship to profits. As Hague explained:

Year after year [Good Vibrations] would see these phenomenal sales records broken and year after year [we would] look at the bottom line and it was in the red. There were a couple of points when it got pretty dire and they said that we might not be able to pay certain bills. This is a really big deal. We have to get more serious about making money. [We need] to cut costs where we can and emphasize profit.... Good Vibrations had this real naiveté of thinking that it was always going to make money and it was always going to be profitable because sex sells. But unfortunately the business also has skyrocketing expenses.[15]

For both Good Vibrations and Babeland, an emerging culture of cost effectiveness and profit mindedness, which began in earnest in the early 2000s, dovetailed with a newfound commitment to retail professionalism. This shift included hiring general business managers — some with MBAs in hand — who were equipped with the necessary skills to lead these companies into a new era of controlled growth, financial stability, and profitability. As Ben Doyle, the general business manager at Good Vibrations in the early 2000s, explained, "We find [at Good Vibrations] that even if we don't want to worry about those things, we have no choice but to worry about those things because if we are not improving the business operationally — significantly and consistently — we are not going to survive in this market."[16] Babeland's Schrader expressed a similar sentiment: "In order to survive and keep doing the things we do, we have to sell. We have to create a market [and] we have to hold on to the market."[17]

The emerging culture of profit mindedness was, at least initially, dramatically at odds with the existing philosophy of these businesses. Blank had cultivated a commercial universe — and indeed a retail model — where ideas about access to information, social good, and ethical approaches to running a business trumped generating profits for the sheer sake of wealth accumulation. It was with a sense of satisfaction that Blank once recounted a story in which an acquaintance said, "Joani, you run your business like a social service." Without missing a beat, Blank replied, "Right. That is exactly it. Thank you. That is a compliment."[18] That Blank experienced this remark as a compliment rather than a condemnation of her business practices not only speaks to her understanding of herself as a businessperson, but it reflects the degree to which she muddied the taken-for-granted distinctions that typically characterize for-profit and not-for-profit enterprises — a blurring of values, practices, and ideologies that was for many years a hallmark of the Good Vibrations retail model.

## Sex Toys and Social Entrepreneurship

The kind of boundary blurring practiced by Blank, which eventually trickled down to other feminist retailers, is characteristic of social entrepreneurship. The concept of social entrepreneurship gained momentum in the 1980s due largely to the work of Bill Drayton at Ashoka, a not-for-profit organization dedicated to identifying and supporting individuals across the globe working to find creative solutions to social problems in the areas of health, education, microfinancing, and agriculture, with an eye toward "tackling chronic social problems."[19] Social entrepreneurs are committed to putting profits toward a larger social purpose. Their undertakings might assume any number of forms: innovative not-for-profits, social-purpose business ventures, and hybrid organizations that mix not-for-profit and for-profit elements, such as homeless shelters that start businesses to train and employ their residents. Blake Mycoskie, the founder of TOMS, for example, gives one pair of shoes to those in need for every pair that's purchased. Warby Parker, similarly, donates one pair of eyeglasses for every pair sold in an effort to make sure that people who need glasses get them. Headbands for Hope founder Jessica Ekstrom gives one headband to a child with cancer for every headband that is purchased.

In recent decades, as funding for the nonprofit sector has dwindled and competition for scarce resources has increased, the idea of social entrepreneurship and socially responsible businesses has gained popularity. In fact, it is now possible for companies to register as a benefit corporation, a type of corporate entity that includes having a positive social impact as part of its legal goals. Regardless of corporate structure, social entrepreneurs creatively combine elements from the not-for-profit and for-profit realms, mixing, for example, the idealism of a social worker with the fiscal aptitude of a seasoned CEO. The value of social entrepreneurship, according to experts, doesn't reside in efficiency (think assembly lines, for example) but in the ability to make the world a better, more equitable, sustainable, and, one could add, sex-positive place.[20]

Social entrepreneurs have been described as "mad scientists in the lab" and "do-gooders with savvy." Their ventures are not charities, but they are not traditional businesses, either. According to J. Gregory Dees, a pioneer in the field of social entrepreneurship, social entrepreneurs are innovators who are interested in finding the most effective means for furthering their social visions and are not constrained by the conventional boundaries thought to exist between the not-for-profit and for-profit worlds.[21] Dees argues that while making a profit, creating wealth, or serving the needs of customers may all be part of the business model used by social entrepreneurs, these things are a "means to a social end, not the end in itself."[22] For social entrepreneurs, success is ultimately measured by societal impact, not the size of one's bank account.

Decades before social entrepreneurship acquired the buzz that it has today, and long before universities like Stanford and Harvard were offering courses dedicated to developing this business strategy, feminist sex-toy stores like Eve's Garden and Good Vibrations were mixing utopian ideals with market forces to create mission-driven retail ventures committed to sex education and social transformation. These were not nonprofit entities, but in many ways they operated as though they were. And while these businesses did not give free vibrators to every customer who walked in the door, they offered, often at no charge, information and resources aimed at helping people improve their sex lives and enhance their sexual self-esteem. They provided education and outreach programs in the community, and routinely donated products to fund-raising raffles, community organizations, and other worthwhile causes. A decidedly not-for-profit mentality was promulgated by Williams and Blank during the first wave of feminist sex-toy retailing in the 1970s and early 1980s, which influenced how subsequent generations of feminist retailers thought about their businesses. For many, running a feminist sex shop was about doing social good, not getting rich. As Laura Haave, the owner of the Tool Shed in Milwaukee, would tell me years later in terms that echoed those of her predecessors: "I'm not doing this to make money. I don't pay myself. I don't make any money from the store. I also have a full-time job. The store is like my volunteer work or my child. Clearly, I'm not doing this to get rich."[23]

And yet not everyone affiliated with these businesses can afford this volunteer mind-set. Opening a business of any kind requires access to capital, and sex-related businesses are not strong contenders for bank loans. For most of the feminist retailers I interviewed, start-up money came from loans from family and friends, personal savings, or home equity; and the intertwining of race and socioeconomic status invariably means that white men and women are in stronger positions to have (or to be able to get) the capital they need to start a business in the first place. Indeed, Eve's Garden, Good Vibrations, and Babeland were founded by middle- to upper-middle-class white women, some of whom had elite educations and all of whom had forms of economic capital at their disposal. Thus, the opinion that profits are only marginally important is informed by, and produced through, a specific constellation of race and class privilege. The calculus can be very different for hourly retail workers living paycheck to paycheck and struggling to make ends meet in some of the most expensive cities in the United States. As one Good Vibrations employee explained, "If you are managing a multimillion-dollar company [as a worker-owner] and you can barely make your rent, that's hard."[24] The disconnect between how some store owners thought about money versus how their employees did would deepen over time, placing new kinds of pressures on what it meant to run a feminist business.

## Money Makes Things Dirty

The first sales transaction I made at Babeland involved a woman who purchased $420 worth of sex toys, books, and videos. She was white and middle-aged, with a pile of eye-catching red hair on top of her head. I remember watching her as she walked around the store with focused deliberation. She picked items up, held them in her hands, and occasionally peppered me with questions: "Do you sell many of these? Have you seen this film? Is this vibrator waterproof? What do you recommend?"

Before long, a stack of products began accumulating on the counter: a leather harness, a purple dildo, a glittery vibrator, another dildo, a blue feather tickler, books, videos, and more. The growing heap of merchandise began to unnerve me. I had just learned how to operate the computerized cash register and the thought of ringing up sales and dealing with other people's money—both customers' money and the store's—made me nervous. What if I rang up an item incorrectly and needed to void something? What if I gave the customer too little or too much change? What if my register did not balance at the end of my shift? I was thinking about all these things as I rang up the woman's sales, trying hard not to make any mistakes in the process.

It wasn't until after the customer had left the store that I realized I had forgotten to have her sign her credit card receipt. The list of things she had purchased was long and the total significant, but there was no signature at the bottom. Did this mean that the entire transaction was null and void? Was Babeland going to politely thank me for my scholarly interest but inform me that I was too much of a liability? Was my career as a vibrator clerk over just as it was beginning? Why, I wondered, did dealing with money—especially other people's money—make me so nervous?

Luckily, I didn't lose my job or access to my field site. The store manager simply called the customer the next morning and, to my relief, she authorized the sales transaction over the phone. The incident, however, signaled something important to me about my own unease around money; and it wasn't long before I realized that I was not the only one at Babeland who had a rather vexed relationship to money—spending it, watching others spend it, handling it, making it, or not making enough of it. Days later, when I told Cavanah about the woman who had purchased $420 worth of merchandise, she told me that she used to worry when people would spend money at Babeland. And although she had become more accustomed to it, she still wasn't entirely comfortable with it.

What was increasingly clear to me as my fieldwork progressed was that the retail culture at Babeland—and, as I would learn, many other sex-positive feminist retailers—was deeply influenced by a perpetual crisis of conscience around money, profitability, and the business's relationship to consumer capitalism. As one employee put it, there are "apologies at Babeland around profitability."

Many of my interviewees expressed anywhere from mild to extreme discomfort about being active participants in a capitalist system that they saw as closely aligned with exploitation and inequality. In conversation after conversation, I listened as employees described their struggles to reconcile the idea that money makes things dirty with their personal investment in and commitment to Babeland's success. One sex educator in New York pointedly told me that if the business ever became just about making money, she would leave. "I did not come to work at the store to be part of a retail experience," she said. "That isn't what it has ever been about for me. I have certainly become more comfortable with it—which makes me wonder if I have lost some critical edge—but I think that my experience being at the store and what brought me there and what has kept me there has everything to do with who the store is and the fact that it would even have a mission."[25]

Most employees were quick to dismiss the money side of the business in favor of its sex-positive mission. It was as though the business had two distinct parts—commerce and politics—that could be easily disarticulated from each other and understood on their own terms. It was a view shared by sales staff and owners alike. According to Cavanah, "I didn't go into this business as a businessperson. I went into it as a feminist and a women's liberationist, with my own understanding of how sex fits into that. The whole capitalist consumer thing has never been easy for me to deal with. I don't even shop. Not only did I not work in retail [before I opened Babeland] but I didn't even go into retail stores."[26]

Searah Deysach from Early to Bed echoed this discomfort. Deysach admitted that she, too, never wanted to be a businessperson; but to do what she ultimately wanted to do—provide people with information about sex in a supportive environment—she had to become one. "It's really hard to open a not-for-profit retail store," she told me. "If I could do that, I'd be a lot more comfortable."[27]

The act of keeping consumer capitalism at bay while simultaneously reaping the monetary and social benefits it makes possible involves a complicated set of negotiations and deferrals. Feminist retailers often find themselves operating both within and outside the dominant culture; they are at once hegemonic and counterhegemonic, mainstream and radical in their approach to both market capitalism and cultural transformation—a paradox that is not lost on them. Cavanah, for example, described herself as an "uneasy, accidental capitalist" but conceded that she is also very much part of the system that makes her so uncomfortable.[28] Her business partner, Rachel Venning, explained her discomfort in the following way: "Being a retailer in this culture is definitely like being a cultural player because [we live in] a consumer culture and it is so much of how people interact, and where they meet, and what they think about, and how they express themselves. I personally don't care for it. The whole shopping thing—buying and selling—is definitely not the highlight of anything; it is a kind of necessary evil or something."[29]

Venning, who has an MBA, admitted that she didn't like to think of herself as a businessperson, but acknowledged that there was no adequate language to describe what she did for a living. "If I go around and say, 'I am a sex educator and I own Babeland,' I feel like there is something kind of false there. But I also feel that if I say, 'I am a businessperson,' that is not the whole picture either. Both are true."[30] Finding ways to bridge what are often thought of as dueling identities, those of businesswoman and sex educator, or retailer and social activist, is an ongoing challenge that for many entrepreneurs never seems adequately resolved. While the idea that money makes things dirty is one way to understand why so many feminist retailers and sales staff admitted they were uncomfortable with the retail side of the business, this explanation ultimately fails to take into account the highly gendered nature of this discomfort—that is, the belief that as women and, moreover, as feminists committed to social change, they were not supposed to be concerned with matters of money and profitability. Interestingly, this position mirrors many of the concerns that some feminists articulated in the 1970s about whether or not there could be such a thing as feminist businesses. Heated debates emerged in the pages of the radical feminist publication *off our backs* (not to be confused with *On Our Backs*) between those who saw feminist businesses as innovations with the power to transform the very nature of capitalism and those who believed that feminism and business were fundamentally contradictory and that capitalism would inevitably "twist and bend any politic to the obedience of the laws of business."[31]

The belief that feminism and capitalism are incompatible still holds sway for many feminists. Babeland's Felice Shays, for example, explained that at least in theory, "feminism is not supposed to be money oriented." According to her, "Capitalism is often still thought of as the male domain and therefore bad. So how feminists can be capitalists is a very confusing dichotomy."[32] The gulf that is thought to exist between progressive politics and marketplace culture is one way to make sense of why so many feminist retailers and sales staff cling to the idea that feminist politics should remain untainted by the stain of capitalism.

"I think it is ridiculous to think that feminists are not supposed to make money or are not supposed to be profit minded," Babeland's Tyler Merriman said. "But I think a little bit of that history has stuck with us. There is this weird feminist, socialist blending around profit and how [unimportant] it has been in our culture." She continued,

> I feel like the only time that feminists really talked about money was in relationship to what women were making in relation to men. Not about what women are doing in business or what money feminists are making for themselves. I don't know what it was like when Claire and Rachel started this business but I don't think money was a motivating factor. I think it was more like, "Hey, we want to spread the good word." I think that making money wasn't very important. . . . It wasn't necessarily unimportant, but spreading the good word was more important.[33]

Venning herself went so far as to add, "Someone who is a hard-core feminist would never start a business in the first place, because the distribution of wealth is unfair."[34]

While sex-positive retailers have reclaimed sex as a feminist domain, consumer capitalism has not been similarly recuperated. Sex has been salvaged, redefined, and imbued with new cultural meanings by sex-positive feminist writers, pornographers, sex educators, and retailers. Consumer capitalism, on the other hand, has not experienced the same kind of feminist reclamation. For feminist sex-toy businesses, it is not sex that is constructed as dirty, but money and the marketplace that are viewed as potential contaminants that risk undermining, or at least sullying, their sex-positive missions. As Tristan Taormino noted in 2015 during one of her sex educator boot camps, "I think talking about money is even more taboo [than sex]."

The tension between feminism and capitalism is not the only ideological divide at play for these retailers. In fact, it is difficult to separate women's complicated relationship to money from the gendered ideology that structures the world of business and the work of doing social good. For Hague, the debates that took place at Good Vibrations around money and growth—how much, how quickly, and what kinds of growth—inevitably came back to the issue of women and money: women being afraid to make money; women not wanting to make a profit; women not wanting to profit at other women's expense or buying into the idea that women are simply not very good with money.[35] Taormino expressed a similar sentiment: "I think that there is still this weird feminist backlash within women-owned and -run businesses about money. I feel like there is still this devaluation, like [women] are not meant to make money, or we are not worth making money. I think that there are still a lot of issues around money."[36]

The concerns that many feminist retailers and employees have around money seem to be exacerbated by the emphasis on doing good. Working on behalf of social change is very often presented as a noble, selfless endeavor. Making money and accumulating wealth, on the other hand, are viewed as selfish, hollow, and misdirected uses of a person's time and talent. As Jacq Jones explained, "Women often tend to do work that is based around some sort of social good, and people who do work for social good are not supposed to make money off of that. You are not supposed to profit from doing social good. It is okay to profit from selling a car, but not from helping a woman get away from her abusive husband."[37]

Jones's observations situate women's complicated relationship to money within a broader ideological framework where doing good is understood primarily as women's work. This is not by any means a recent formulation. According to historian Lori Ginzberg, a powerful ideology of white, middle-class "benevolent femininity" emerged in the United States during the nineteenth century, suggesting that women "act to heal or transform the world."[38] Notions of morality and social good were grafted onto an "ideology of women's higher standard of virtue," which meant that in certain white, middle- and upper-class circles, an understanding of women's work arose that valued social transformation over monetary profits.[39] The dominant belief was that the work of benevolence should be unpaid. Ginzberg points out that the ideology of benevolent femininity was complicated. "The emphasis on benevolence as a peculiarly female 'impulse from the heart,' removed from crass economic considerations, tended to conceal the fact that benevolence and money went hand in hand," Ginzberg argues.[40]

Although the nature of benevolence work has certainly changed since this earlier era, a version of white, middle-class benevolent femininity based on the belief that women's work on behalf of social change should be unpaid or paid very little persists and continues to inform the ways that many feminist sex-toy retailers and sales staff understand their relationship to—and indeed the relationship between—money, consumer capitalism, and the very real work of social change that their businesses aim to promote.

Meanwhile, some feminist retailers have found ways to overcome or at least manage their discomfort with the capitalist imperatives of running a business by making sure that they give back to their communities. This might involve giving money, products, or time and expertise to causes they believe in, from Planned Parenthood to LGBT youth centers to HIV/AIDS organizations. Good Vibrations, for example, has partnered with a number of community organizations, donating products, advertising, and a percentage of sales to groups such as the Transgender Law Center and the Berkeley Free Clinic. Come for a Cause is the name of Babeland's philanthropy, which, according to the company's website, has raised over $200,000 over the years for more than three hundred different groups. For her part, Searah Deysach from Early to Bed makes a point to do outreach and educational programs for queer youth groups, colleges, and underserved populations, such as the women's group at a local AIDS organization. Regardless of whether or not these efforts translate into sales, Deysach is committed to making sure this kind of outreach remains part of the work that Early to Bed does. At the same time, as the sole proprietor of a small business she acknowledges that it is hard to step away from the sales floor to conduct workshops that will likely have no direct impact on the business's bottom line. "This is when I think if we could just have a nonprofit arm, where the business could help support these things and where we could get grants to pay people to do these workshops and get out in the community, that's my fantasy about what I'd love to see this place turn into."[41]

## "This Is America; Money Talks"

Some feminist retailers and employees did appreciate that generating a profit was an essential part of running a successful business, as well as a form of social power. "I have no problems whatsoever with the capitalist realities of our world," Jones told me. "I like money. I think money is good."[42]

Jones and a handful of others understood, as Good Vibrations' Roma Estevez put it, that "money can get you places."[43] The more money you have, the more you can pay your employees, the more stores you can open, the better website you can build, and the more people you can reach with your sex-positive message. Babeland's Brandie Taylor talked in frank and unapologetic terms about the relationship between money and the mission:

> The mission is for everyone and there is no way we can spread our mission louder and clearer and wider than if we have more money in our belt. So we have to sell a lot of these toys and make a profit so we can spread the vision to everyone and promote positive sexuality to the whole world. . . . Underneath it all we are a business. Yes, we are a feminist business and I think we are a queer business, but we are a business. Period. And what is the common thing [that businesses share]? Businesses make profits. That's what they do. They sell things. So we have to come here and sell vibrators. That is our job.[44]

For Taylor, money not only greases the wheels of social change, but it keeps the wheels spinning. For her, and in the context of Babeland, profit acquires a different meaning than it might otherwise have if wealth accumulation was the only desired outcome. In this sense, the project of social change advanced by Babeland and other feminist sex-toy businesses has the potential to recuperate, and to some degree transform, the capitalist underpinnings of these businesses, injecting them with newfound meaning and social value.

Cathy Winks described the moment when she realized just how important money was to advancing Good Vibrations' mission: "It wasn't really for me until about 1991 or 1992 when I suddenly realized that [Good Vibrations] had grossed a million dollars in revenues and it was like a light switch flipped and I was like, 'Oh for goodness sakes. We made a million dollars. We could easily make so much more.' Then my engines started revving up about how we could take this message out into the world and be successful."[45]

Roma Estevez described a similar experience. Her relationship to money began to shift during the nine years that she worked at Good Vibrations once she realized that if the company could make more money, it could "do bigger and better things in the world."[46] Winks echoed this idea: "This is America; money talks. If Good Vibrations hadn't grown as successful and profitable as it did," she continued, "we wouldn't have the impact on other retailers or adult novelty manufacturers. You have to prove that there is a market and that it is a big and profitable enough market to get changes made in the design of sex toys, the quality of sex toys, [and] the quality of videos."[47]

That money talks as loudly as it does implies that consumerism is a language that many people understand. By focusing on the act of shopping, sex-positive retailers strategically combine not-for-profit sensibilities with the logic of the marketplace, tapping into a way of organizing the world that most people are intimately familiar with. In other words, consumer capitalism—and by extension a commercialized version of feminist politics—brings with it a set of norms and a system of exchange that structures and mediates people's lives in absolutely fundamental ways. As Babeland's Venning explained, "People know what to do with stores. They really understand that you go in and you get to look around. You can ask questions, you can buy or not buy, and you get to leave. If it was just a drop-in sex education center," she continued, "I think that would be a lot more intimidating for people to go to. If you could just stop by and ask people questions, if there were toys there and you got information but there wasn't a consumer purpose, I don't think people would come as much because it would feel strange."[48]

The claim that people know what to do with stores—you can browse, ask questions, purchase items, or leave empty-handed—suggests that they might in fact be perfect settings for launching any number of educational initiatives or feminist undertakings, because they are places that people already frequent. Not only are stores a familiar cultural form, but in the early twentieth century, with the rise of department stores, shopping was transformed from a functional activity for women into a respectable, and indeed popular, form of leisure. While U.S. women's role as consumers has been presented as an almost natural one, encapsulated by the pithy phrases "born to shop" and "Mrs. Consumer," historian Kathy Peiss has observed that women's relationship to consumer culture is firmly rooted in historical developments, such as advertising, mass-circulating women's magazines, and new professional opportunities as "information brokers, interlocutors, and taste-makers who claimed to understand and communicate with women consumers effectively."[49] Throughout the twentieth century, shopping became an "extension of freedom," especially for middle-class female consumers—a point that resonates with women's participation in the sexual marketplace today.[50]

The normalization of shopping as a socially accepted leisure activity for women was evident in many discussions I had with both sex-toy store employees and customers. One twenty-something female customer I spoke with suggested that "shopping for sexual information" might be easier than going to a not-for-profit sexuality education center because stores are "mainstream" as opposed to being on the "fringe." Shopping, moreover, doesn't involve negotiating the various gatekeeping procedures that are a part of accessing social services, such as scheduling an appointment, dealing with a receptionist, or completing pages of intake paperwork that are not only time consuming but make preserving one's anonymity impossible. Nor do you have to present yourself as having a problem or being in need of a specific service when you go into a store. Thus, a very different kind of relationship exists between a sales assistant and a customer than between a social worker and a client. "It can be empowering to be a shopper," another Babeland customer once said. And the commonly accepted mantra that the "customer is always right," she continued, is an equalizer that helps establish a different dynamic than that which typically exists between, say, a health professional and a patient. "Perhaps people would feel more comfortable accessing social services if they were being sold as a product," a Babeland employee with a background in social services mused. Babeland's Laura Weide expressed a similar thought: "Because [Babeland] is a commercial locale, I think it gives us a kind of legitimacy that if we were some small women's sexuality and pleasure activist organization and education center we [would not have]."[51]

As explicitly commercial locations, feminist sex-toy stores invoke a range of signs, symbols, practices, and market-based interactions that constitute a familiar and, some argue, legitimate part of the cultural landscape. Despite many feminist retailers' discomfort with a commercial world where money talks and where consumer capitalism is accepted as the norm, packaging sexual information and ideas about sexual liberation as though they were commodities might in fact be a highly effective means of providing such things to people who might otherwise not have ready access to them outside of the context of market culture. "It is so American," a Babeland customer commented, "to be able to buy sexual liberation."

## Changing of the Guard

In August 2001, almost three months after Babeland implemented its program of cost cutting and profit mindedness, Carrie Schrader resigned from her position as the company's general business manager to pursue a career in filmmaking. Schrader's departure marked the end of an era. Schrader was home-grown. A product of Babeland, she had worked her way up the ranks from sales assistant to store manager to eventually to become the company's first general business manager. Schrader had played an integral role in implementing systems, creating new management positions, and helping to make Babeland's mission the backbone of the company's culture. Cavanah credited Schrader with "kicking" Babeland to another level. "We had our own personality to begin with, but she made it, like, the culture."[52] And yet the business had reached a point where, in order to be financially prosperous in an increasingly competitive industry, the company needed stronger financial leadership and more operational savvy than Schrader could offer.

The search for Babeland's new general business manager was an important turning point for the company. It was, in many ways, emblematic of the enduring tension between money and the mission—which had not disappeared simply because employees had started talking about it. Babeland was still in the early stages of trying to figure out how to be both a money-savvy and mission-driven sex-toy company, a challenge that involved learning how to balance the different yet overlapping parts of the business. It was an ongoing process and one that had direct implications for who would be hired as the company's new chief financial officer.

The most pressing issue facing the company was whether it could find someone who could be a strong financial leader—a person who could "deal with the numbers," as one employee put it—but who would also "get" the mission. In an e-mail to staff, Schrader described the kind of person she was hoping to hire as her successor. According to her, she was "calling on all the sexy spirits of this world to bring [Babeland] someone who can hold the mission in their hearts and has the business in their brain, and [who] can hold both consistently and with joy."

Babeland received more than 250 résumés from people expressing interest in a job that had been described in advertisements as a cross between a chief financial officer (CFO) and a "den mother."[53] Many résumés came from people with MBAs who at first glance looked qualified, but upon closer inspection had failed to realize that Babeland was a sex-toy store and not a children's store. (Its name at the time was still Toys in Babeland.) Other applicants seemed unable to grasp the meaning and purpose of Babeland's mission. Schrader told me that some people wrote in their cover letters things like, "I have a daughter and she is really important to me, so women's issues are important to me."

One of the last résumés that Babeland received was from Rebecca Denk. Denk had an MBA and a proven track record of coming into organizations and implementing systems, creating budgets, and strengthening their financial infrastructures. She also had a history of working for mission-driven companies and not-for-profits, including Seattle's Theater Schmeater, a company that Schrader had watched transform from a mediocre, struggling theater to one that was financially strong and well regarded in the community. Denk, however, was not the only one being considered for the job. Dana Clark, the store manager of Babeland in New York City, was also a finalist.

Denk and Clark brought very different strengths to the table. Denk had an MBA and a background in business. Clark, on the other hand, had firsthand knowledge of Babeland and the idiosyncrasies of the business's retail culture—all things that someone coming to the business from outside the company would need to learn. Whereas Denk's background and strengths spoke to the company's recent emphasis on profitability and financial stability, Clark's expertise reflected Babeland's ongoing commitment to its mission. In many ways, Denk was the CFO outlined in the job description and Clark was the den mother. The decision about who would be hired as Schrader's replacement, it seemed, would ultimately come down to where Babeland placed the most emphasis: finding a CFO who could appreciate the mission-driven character of the business, or hiring a den mother who could also run a multimillion-dollar company.

Hiring Denk was a moment of reckoning for Babeland. The financial difficulties of the previous year had exacted a psychological toll, especially for Cavanah and Venning, and the general consensus among those involved in the hiring process was that what the company needed, more than anything else, was someone who could come into the business and have an immediate impact on strengthening its financial prospects. According to Venning, the feeling was: "Let's get someone who has more professional experience and financial experience and who doesn't have to do so much on the job learning but who has already learned [what they need to know]. [For us] that was the moment of saying, 'Let's get more expertise in management.'"[54]

Bringing Denk on board was an opportunity to put into practice what many people inside the company had been struggling to come to terms with: that working within a capitalist system meant that you had to think about capitalist concerns in order to perpetuate the organization—whether you wanted to or not. "This is not a university or a community center or an affinity group," Cavanah later explained. "It is a store and we cannot keep doing what we are doing unless we turn a profit."[55] Babeland's Tyler Merriman concurred: "Part of this business *is* about making money. That is kind of what business is about. That is not what this business is *all* about but [it is part of it]."[56]

A year into her tenure as the company's general business manager, Denk and I talked about the kinds of changes that had occurred under her watch. She was hired at a time when Babeland was, as she put it, "leading with serious intention and social activism," but downplaying the fact that it was also a business that needed to make money in order to survive. As she saw it, her primary responsibility was to bring the company's business mission into a closer alignment with its educational mission. The most pressing question for her was, "Is what we are doing true to the mission *and* good for business?"[57]

Although Babeland's commitment to its sex-positive mission remained unchanged, Denk worked hard during her tenure to strengthen the company's financial infrastructure. She put new financial systems in place, revamped the company's benefit plan, and rewrote many of the business's documents, including its employee manual, to make them stronger and more legally binding. Denk wanted to maintain what she described as the "heart-driven" and "grassroots" ethos of Babeland, while also doing her best to ensure that the company was "more sophisticated" in its operations. Rather than relying on what she described as an "oral history" of "this is how we do things," which is how the company was run for many years, she made sure that policies, procedures, and even budgets were formally documented. According to Denk, "At this point everybody seems to want that. It doesn't seem like, 'Oh, we are getting too formal or businesslike'; [rather] it is like, 'We really need to get a handle on this stuff.'"[58] Employee Brandie Taylor agreed: "We are mission driven," she insisted, "but there is no way [Babeland] can be here without making money. If you want to support the mission you have to support the profit [because] we are not going to grow and we are not going to spread the mission if we are not making a profit."[59]

For Babeland and other feminist sex-toy businesses, changing the way the broader culture thinks and talks about sex requires not only entrepreneurial vision and missionary zeal but an ability to balance the books and pay the bills. As obvious as this statement may seem, it took a series of financial hardships in order for Good Vibrations and Babeland to bridge the ideological chasm that had long existed between money and the mission, feminism and capitalism, and profitability and social change, resulting in a new appreciation for how profit fueled and sustained their businesses.

Getting to this place, however, was not easy. Feminist sex-toy stores have historically relied on an alternative set of commercial visions, values, and practices, ones that emphasized what these businesses did in the world—providing sexual education, promoting sex positivity, and increasing sexual literacy—

as opposed to how much money they made. As a result, the demands of the marketplace frequently took a back seat to the goals of the mission, which simply reinforced the idea that commerce and politics, profitability and social change, were separate rather than interdependent spheres of activity and concern. And the fact that many employees viewed themselves as social workers and sex educators, rather than businesspeople and retail employees, only exacerbated these divisions, producing a business culture in which doing good consistently trumped profit making as a means of evaluating commercial success.

Feminist sex-toy stores have worked hard over the years to bridge this ideological divide and cultivate new forms of business expertise that can better support the goals of their missions while also turning a profit. As one staff member explained about Good Vibrations: "We have worked very hard to try to develop more expertise in the business, and I think we are at a place now where we understand how to be profitable and I think that we haven't [understood that] in the past. And I guess we worked really hard to do that because there was a shift in wanting to do that."[60]

Learning to see money as friend instead of foe required a major reorientation on the part of store owners and employees. Although the discomfort that many interviewees expressed regarding money and consumer capitalism has not entirely dissipated, store owners and sales staff are more inclined—or perhaps simply resigned—to concede that money and business savvy matter in an increasingly crowded and competitive marketplace where aspirations of sexual empowerment and social change alone are not enough to keep their businesses alive. They acknowledge that while feminist sex-toy stores might not do business as usual, especially compared to their more conventional retail counterparts, the business of sex education and social change that they promote does not exist outside of market forces, but depends upon sales, money, market shares, and profitability for its very survival.

# GROW OR DIE?

---

To some extent, we are the victims of our success.

FORMER GOOD VIBRATIONS CEO THERESA SPARKS
in "Competition Has Shaken Good Vibrations"

The news was spreading like wildfire, and my e-mail inbox was filled with messages from feminist retailers from around the country expressing shock and disbelief. Good Vibrations, the legendary San Francisco sex-toy emporium that had inspired so many of them, had been sold—the result of a financial crisis so severe that the company was on the brink of filing for bankruptcy or, worse, shutting its doors, because it had no money to pay vendors and restock shelves. As one feminist retailer told me, "I feel like a parent just died."

And it was not simply the fact that Good Vibrations had been sold that stunned so many fellow retailers and longtime customers, but the news of who had purchased it: General Video of America and Trans-World News (GVA-TWN), a Cleveland-based wholesaler and distributor of adult merchandise that had been around since the late 1950s. The company was better known for selling blow-up dolls and catering to the "trench coat crowd" than providing accurate information and quality sex toys to urban queers and suburban soccer moms. To many observers, it was exactly the kind of mainstream adult company that Good Vibrations had worked so hard to distinguish itself from since launching thirty years earlier as a quirky, educationally focused, and women-friendly vibrator shop. Had Good Vibrations sold out and "gone over to the dark side," as one person put it, or had it made a smart business decision in a rapidly changing marketplace? What had happened?

Good Vibrations, like other sex-toy retailers, had weathered financially tough times in the past, but in 2007, when the business was sold, things were different. Internet sales, which just years before had been robust, had dropped precipitously—the result, many within the company argued, of Google changing the algorithm it used to rank websites. Good Vibrations' position in search results for "sex toys" had plummeted from page 1 to page 8 and sales had dropped along with it. But that wasn't the only issue affecting the company's bottom line. The growing cultural acceptance and mainstreaming of sex toys, due in large part to the success of Good Vibrations and other sex-positive retailers, meant that these businesses were now competing with big companies like Amazon, which, due to economies of scale, could undercut smaller retailers and sell the same products for markedly less. It was also possible for anyone with a laptop to start an online sex-toy business without the costly overhead of running a brick-and-mortar store. The Internet, once considered a friend to sex-positive retailers, now seemed to have become an adversary. And some wondered what role, if any, mismanagement had played in exacerbating Good Vibrations' already shaky financial state.

The situation was so bad that a month before its sale to GVA-TWN, Good Vibrations, in an unusual move, posted a letter to its website outlining its business woes and asking for investors to help turn the company around. "Today, having almost completed our 30th year, we face the need to raise capital quickly in order to ensure that our business survives in its traditional form," board members Carol Queen and Charlie Glickman wrote.[1]

How ominous were things? A quick visit to Good Vibrations' website showed that almost every item was out of stock. The company had virtually nothing to sell, and it didn't take an MBA to know that the situation was dire.

The sale of Good Vibrations to GVA-TWN, which was presented in initial media reports as a merger, offered the sex-positive retailer a new lease on life, but it also benefited GVA-TWN. According to Rondee Kamins, GVA-TWN's owner, "everything that Good Vibrations is, GVA isn't and everything that GVA is, Good Vibrations isn't."[2] While GVA-TWN would be able to provide Good Vibrations with much-needed financial stability and access to inventory, in turn, Good Vibrations staff had the training and know-how to help GVA-TWN—which owns dozens of adult stores in the Midwest—retool its business model in an effort to court the growing women's and couples' market. As one Good Vibrations employee said about the union, "It's a marriage of two different worlds that I think need each other right now."

But questions remained: Would Good Vibrations continue to be the sex-positive, queer-friendly, and feminist-oriented business that its customers knew and loved? And what about its educational mission and outreach efforts? Was Good Vibrations destined to become the Walmart of sex toys, but with better politics?

"I'm glad they aren't going under," one feminist retailer told me, "but it must be so much harder to be a radical business under the umbrella of a mainstream powerhouse."[3]

What it means to "be a radical business" had also changed dramatically in the years since Good Vibrations' founding. When Joani Blank started Good Vibrations in 1977, and in the years that followed, the idea of competition, at least in any traditional sense, wasn't a concern. Blank's approach to running Good Vibrations, as I've discussed in earlier chapters, was intensely noncompetitive, and she freely shared information about the company's finances, vendor lists, and educational mission with entrepreneurs interested in opening stores of their own. But even if Blank had been a more traditional businessperson concerned about competitors cutting into the company's profit margins, the reality of the sexual marketplace in the 1970s and 1980s was such that Good Vibrations was essentially a unicorn. Its women-friendly and educational focus was so unique that Good Vibrations faced little to no direct competition from other retailers—and it remained that way for years.

By the time Searah Deysach decided to open Early to Bed in Chicago in the early 2000s, the tenor of the marketplace, even among feminist businesses, had changed dramatically. Armed with the knowledge that Good Vibrations had previously helped retailers Babeland and Grand Opening get their businesses off the ground, Deysach approached the company about the possibility of doing a similar internship to learn the ropes of running her own sex-positive store. "They just shot me down," she told me. "They said, 'We just cannot do that.'" Her takeaway? "This is not a friendly family of feminist stores."[4]

Perhaps Deysach's experience would have been different five years earlier, but by the start of the new millennium, retailers everywhere were expanding their operations and going online, which changed the way many businesses—including many feminist sex-toy stores—thought about competition. It was no longer the case that individual companies were bound by geography, with Good Vibrations commanding the lion's share of the market in the Bay Area, Babeland carving out profitable niches in Seattle and New York City, and Grand Opening serving the needs of the greater Boston area. Now these businesses were all competing for the same online customers located in geographically disparate places like rural Iowa and small-town Oklahoma. It was a whole new retail landscape, and information that had once been freely shared by Good Vibrations was now cast as trade secrets that needed to be protected so the company could keep an economic edge in an increasingly competitive marketplace—which, ironically, it had helped create. The era of sharing information and vendor lists—which had been a hallmark of Blank's entrepreneurial sisterhood, making it possible for other sex-positive retailers to follow so closely in Good Vibrations' footsteps—was over, replaced instead by the language of confidentiality clauses and noncompetition agreements (the latter of which I signed when I began my fieldwork at Babeland). As one staff member at Good Vibrations noted about the company's shift to a more proprietary relationship to information: "We decided that we need to protect the work that we have put into developing those things."[5]

These trends have only accelerated in recent years, making today's sexual marketplace virtually unrecognizable from the one that existed when Dell Williams and Blank founded their respective businesses in the 1970s. Now it's possible for a customer to browse the sales floor at a boutique retailer such as Good Vibrations and, without ever leaving the store, get on her smartphone to see which online competitor is selling the same item for less and order it right then and there.

So it's no surprise that Ellen Barnard from A Woman's Touch in Madison, Wisconsin, says she also keeps information about her business close to the vest. "I get inquiries all the time," she told me. "Somebody somewhere says they want to open a store like ours. I say, 'Go for it. Make sure you have enough money, good business sense, and a vision.' And that's pretty much all I'm willing to give, because otherwise I'd be giving all my information away."[6]

In retrospect, Deysach understands why companies weren't exactly jumping up and down at the prospect of helping a potential competitor build her business, but at the time, the rejections stung. Today, she makes a point to pay it forward when people approach her for information and advice. Whenever a new feminist sex shop opens, she sends the owner a note to say, "I am here. I've been doing this for years. I don't know everything, but if you ever need me, I want you to feel comfortable approaching me."[7] For her, it's about cultivating the kinds of relationships and sense of community that she wants to see among her fellow feminist sex shop owners.

It turns out that other feminist store owners wanted to see that, too. In 2009 Molly Adler and Matie Fricker of Self Serve in Albuquerque founded the Progressive Pleasure Club (PPC), a network of like-minded, independent brick-and-mortar sex shops dedicated to providing accurate sexuality resources and safe, quality products. The club arose from a desire to foster a community of peers who understood the unique challenges of running a small, socially conscious sex shop. But Adler and Fricker also wanted to flip the script regarding how feminist businesses approached information sharing and competition.

The duo wrote what Fricker described as a "collaboration manifesto" and circulated it among other progressive sex shop owners. The response, according to Fricker, was immediate and enthusiastic. Everyone, she said, "was looking for this kind of space."[8]

The PPC, which includes ten sex-positive retailers from around the country, from Portland, Maine, to Portland, Oregon, currently exists primarily as a private networking list for members to figure out how to run their businesses in ways they can feel good about, while also providing a livelihood for themselves and their employees.

"Functioning within a capitalist system can be challenging," Fricker explained, "so we spend a lot of time talking about how we can do this in an ethical way."

Undergirding all of this is what Fricker describes as a "belief in abundance," an approach, interestingly enough, that circles back to the open, community-oriented ideas about how to run a successful business popularized by Blank during the first wave of feminist sex-toy retailing decades earlier: there is no need to fear competition; sharing resources means there is more for everybody, not less for us; more businesses providing accurate information and talking openly about sex will create a better, more sex-positive world for everyone. Abundance, in other words, breeds abundance.

Two businesses that are notably absent from the list of PPC members are Good Vibrations and Babeland. Because they are larger, more established companies that have been around for years, "their challenges are just so different than ours," Fricker explained.[9] Most PPC stores have fewer than ten employees and some have only two or three. Good Vibrations and Babeland, on the other hand, are multimillion-dollar operations with multiple retail locations that can buy in bulk and therefore offer customers deeper discounts and early release products, making it harder for PPC members such as Self Serve, Sugar, Smitten Kitten, Early to Bed, Feelmore, and others to compete on the same level. While Good Vibrations and Babeland are certainly not behemoths like Amazon, smaller feminist sex shops regard them as retailing giants nonetheless. "We have a good relationship with Babeland," Fricker readily acknowledged, "but they are just a different animal that's not in our zoo."[10]

Labor issues and workers' rights have also emerged as concerns for feminist sex store employees and owners. In a move that garnered national media attention, workers at Babeland's New York City stores voted to unionize in May 2016, becoming part of the Retail, Wholesale and Department Store Union (RWDSU). The action was heralded in the press as a win for sex shop employees everywhere, and Babeland supporters took to social media, using the hashtags #FistsUpForBabeland and #DildosUnited in a show of solidarity. Lena Solow, a Babeland employee who was active in the unionizing efforts, explained in a telephone interview that there was not one particular incident that sparked the organizing efforts; rather, it was a confluence of worker concerns about transparency, communication, better pay, job security, and safety on the sales floor, including more training to help staff deal with inappropriate customers. All of these things, she argued, disproportionately affected workers who were already marginalized by society, including transgender employees. After months of voicing their concerns in meetings and e-mails, workers decided to pursue collective action in an effort to effect structural changes that they hoped would make Babeland the best workplace it could be.[11]

The move stunned owners Claire Cavanah and Rachel Venning. While they were aware of employee concerns regarding pay, training, and safety, and had begun taking steps to address them—including rewriting the employee manual and raising the starting hourly wage from $12 to $14—they had no idea that unionizing efforts were underway until they received the courtesy call from the RWDSU telling them it was filing papers with the National Labor Relations Board. As lesbian business owners, it had always been important to them that Babeland be a good place to work, especially for queer employees, and claims that this was not necessarily the case cut deeply. What Cavanah and Venning had viewed as a perk of working at Babeland, that the job was fun and meaningful because of the potentially transformative interactions employees had with customers, was now a source of friction. Sales staff felt burdened by the emotional labor these interactions often entailed and were fed up with customers, especially men, who did not always interact with them in ways that felt respectful. Babeland's owners had always emphasized the importance of providing a safe space for customers; now employees were using that same concept to make their case for a safe workplace. What had once felt like a united front of sex-positive warriors joined together in a common fight against sex negativity and sexism now seemed like it was crumbling under the pressure of an internal divide that pitted sales staff against management.[12]

Babeland was not the first sex shop in the United States to unionize. In 2004, workers at Grand Opening in Boston voted to join Unite Here. Similar to employees at Babeland, workers were seeking greater workplace rights and protections, including standard pay rates, uniform policies regarding disciplinary actions, and raises to reward employee loyalty and longevity. A generous employee discount on sex toys, they argued, had limited value if they could not pay their rent. Devastated by the employees' vote to unionize without first addressing their concerns with her, owner Kim Airs lost some of her spark for running the business. Due largely to the unionization drive, she gave up Grand Opening's lease shortly thereafter and moved the business entirely online. For Airs, letting go of the store after more than a decade of success was, she told me, "more painful than the death of my mother."[13]

But for Self Serve owner Matie Fricker, who was a union leader at Grand Opening during that time, the fight to unionize changed her life. "For a brief and shining moment," she said, "we were the only unionized sex shop in the world." Fricker maintains that Self Serve would not be the business it is today without that experience. "Every time someone tells me that Self Serve is a good place to work, I am humbled. I want to create a space where employees feel heard and respected . . . where the front of the house and the back of the house can work together." For Fricker, investing in her employees, which includes providing paid sick leave and vacation time to anyone working more than twenty hours a week, is as important to the business's feminist foundation as sex education and sex positivity.[14]

As feminist sex-toy stores have become more mainstream, what it means to be a feminist business in the context of capitalism is being redefined. It's no longer as radical as it once was to advocate for sexual pleasure; as a result, what it means to work at place like Babeland has also changed. Employees are demanding to be treated as workers who are laboring under capitalist conditions as opposed to do-gooders who are pursuing a part-time passion project for pin money. These efforts are drawing sharp attention to class contradictions and workers' rights and, at the same time, staking a claim to what types of issues count as feminist. "It's not enough to just respect people's pronouns," Babeland's Solow argued. "A trans person not being able to take sick time is a feminist issue."

Babeland workers are pointing to a question that has plagued the feminist movement since the 1970s, namely, what counts as a feminist issue and how important is it for feminists to deal with class? Working-class feminists were extremely vocal in the early 1970s about the importance of bringing a class analysis to feminist causes, challenging the idea, as feminist thinker bell hooks has pointed out, that the concerns of privileged white women were the only ones that mattered.[15] Issues of class were not separate from patriarchy; nor were they divorced from women's everyday experiences of sexism and racism. Indeed, the conflicts at Babeland have brought matters of class to the forefront of sex-positive retail activism; and yet, at the same time, these struggles are also emblematic of a number of key tensions that have dogged feminist sex-toy businesses for decades: How do you balance money and the mission? Retail labor and sex education? How welcoming are these businesses to men? And finally, what does it mean to create a safe space, and who is included?

It is perhaps not surprising that at a time when workers' rights have assumed greater importance in debates across the country, including the campaign for a living wage, these issues have also become more prominent in the context of feminist and queer-run sex shops. While it might be easy to chalk these shifts up to growing pains, it is also the case that the cultural landscape around selling sex toys has changed dramatically since Babeland opened its small Seattle store in 1993. According to Venning, it's no longer a "David and Goliath thing" where feminist sex-toy stores are duking it out with the mainstream sexual marketplace for a place at the table. "[What we do] is now far more ordinary," she acknowledged. "It's not as special [as it once was], so it makes sense that employees would feel more like employees."[16]

For Babeland's Solow, the vote to unionize is another example of feminism in action; it is also part of a larger story about present-day labor organizing in which queer-identified and transgender employees are making their voices heard and having an impact. Sex toys and sex positivity are "awesome," Solow acknowledged, but they are not enough if workers do not feel respected. Her bigger goal? "I want every sex shop to be unionized."[17]

## When Co-ops Go Corporate

When I first caught a glimpse of Joel Kaminsky at Good Vibrations' downtown Oakland headquarters in November 2013, he was in the middle of a phone call with the adult industry trade organization Free Speech Coalition, whose board of directors he serves on. Slim and stylish, with graying hair pulled back in a ponytail and a silver earring in his left ear, he waved a quick hello before returning to his call. A cell phone in one hand and a Bluetooth hooked around his ear, he struck me as someone who knew how to multitask and get things done.

Kaminsky, an adult industry veteran, began working for the family porno business as a teenager growing up in Cleveland, Ohio, so he has seen firsthand the industry's evolution from back alleys to boutique shopping districts. Kaminsky was the chief operating officer of GVA-TWN when it acquired Good Vibrations in 2007; by 2009, he owned Good Vibrations outright and had relocated to the Bay Area to focus his energies exclusively on running the company.

Over lunch at a restaurant across the street, Kaminsky and Good Vibrations' executive vice president Jackie Rednour-Bruckman (Jackie Strano) talked about what it had been like to bring the company back from the edge of financial ruin and not only stabilize operations, but grow the business and open new stores.

Kaminsky acknowledged that he gets offers "all the time" to buy companies, especially from people looking to unload their brick-and-mortar stores; and yet there was something about Good Vibrations, its history and mission, that captivated his imagination. Good Vibrations was "meaningful in the industry," he said—"they helped people"—and he wanted to play a role in developing the company and keeping it relevant.[18]

Kaminsky described Good Vibrations at the point he took over as being similar to a house in foreclosure: Not only was it behind on its mortgage, but it was also overdue on all the maintenance needed to keep the company, and the individual stores, in tip-top shape. "We are building a new house, a new foundation," he told me. Kaminsky streamlined operations, trimmed a top-heavy payroll, eliminated staff redundancies—there were sometimes two or three people doing essentially the same job—and got rid of employees who were not on board with him or the company's new business-oriented direction. He also instituted what he called a "culture of discipline." In his view, the former co-op structure had given people too much freedom to set their own schedules to the point where some employees worked very little. "You have to clean up in order for things to grow."[19]

And grow they have. Good Vibrations now boasts nine sleekly branded retail locations—seven in the Bay Area and two in the Boston area. It also has a thriving wholesale business. Despite these achievements, the sale of Good Vibrations struck a nerve with some customers. In a pointed 2014 Yelp review, Amy Luna, who described herself as a Bay Area sex educator and longtime Good Vibrations customer, lamented that the company's women-centered philosophy and marketing had changed "for the worse." "I felt it as soon as I walked in [the store] and so did my guests." Luna pointed to the "gender normative pandering" of selling what she labeled as "porny" lingerie and having it take up the bulk of floor space, which she claimed was "offensive in principle to all the women who helped build your brand over the decades."[20] She continued,

When you start pandering to the general public's ideas of sexuality (like that how women "look" is more important than how they "feel") you stop becoming the alternative sex shop that was why you built a loyal following in the first place. Good Vibes initially CREATED the alternative women-centered trends, and didn't FOLLOW mass media conditioning. You were PROACTIVE for sexual education, not REACTIVE for profit. You taught me to be the subject of my own sexuality and then turned the tables on me, marketing women as sexual objects, just like every other sex shop. And, even more disturbing . . . you believe that press kit talking points will prevent your clientele from noticing. That's what happens when co-ops go corporate. . . . It feels exactly as if Larry Flint [sic] just bought *Ms.* magazine and the cover story is touting cosmetic genital surgery as the newest "liberation" for women because women are "asking for it." . . . Well, it was good while it lasted. No, actually it was EPIC and world changing. Thanks for that. I will try to keep the torch lit in my work. Hopefully others will, too.[21]

The review gutted longtime employees who had weathered uncertainty and "enormous grief," according to one person, to keep Good Vibrations and its mission alive during what was arguably one of the most tumultuous periods in the company's history. Not only did they feel the reviewer had grossly misrepresented the business, but they also thought she showed little understanding or appreciation of the larger market forces that had almost caused the company to close its doors forever.

Concerns regarding the business's future, however, were not coming just from customers. Some workers left when Good Vibrations was sold, fearing that Kaminsky was going to "cram adult's old business model onto GV's broken business model as a solution"[22]—although he steadfastly maintained this was never his intention. Even some who stayed said they felt a difference. One employee who had experienced the company's transition from a worker-owned co-op, to a corporation with shareholders, to a business run by a more conventional capitalist, claimed that there had been an inversion of emphasis: people working in the stores used to be sex educators who also happened to sell things. Now, they were sales assistants that also provided sex education.

Yet other longtime employees, including product and purchasing manager Coyote Days, saw things differently. For Days, the sale was a "lifeline"; it meant that Good Vibrations, a company she loved, now had a chance at survival, and she was going to do everything in her power to make sure it thrived. It also meant that Good Vibrations could pay its vendors, which to her was significant. These were people she had gotten to know over the years. She had met their families and, in some cases, been to their homes. With the sale, Good Vibrations had an influx of cash it could use to pay its outstanding bills and get inventory onto its empty shelves. According to Days, "We could actually say, 'We want to place an order. Here's a credit card.'"

The sale of Good Vibrations also presented the company with new opportunities. It was now possible, for example, for Days to call up a distributor and say, "Hi, we are owned by Joel Kaminsky." The industry veteran was well regarded among his peers, and channels of distribution that had not formerly been available to Good Vibrations suddenly were. There were other positive changes, too, Days said. Kaminsky promoted some long-standing employees to new positions and gave more power and responsibility to others, demonstrating that he had not only a knack for recognizing untapped talent but, according to Days and others, "deep respect" for the people who loved Good Vibrations so much they had stayed during such a turbulent and uncertain time. "We are doing the things we've always done," Days told me, "but now we are doing them bigger."

While some people viewed the sale of Good Vibrations as akin to entering into a deal with the devil, others saw it as a new lease on life, as a way for the company to honor its sex-positive legacy and move forward into the future under more financially secure conditions. But it was Good Vibrations' founder, Joani Blank, who had left the company more than a decade earlier, who offered perhaps the most pragmatic view of the situation. "They did what they had to do," she said, with a shrug of her shoulders.[23]

## From Margins to Mainstream

If success has changed feminist sex-toy stores, these businesses have in turn profoundly reshaped both the adult industry and the culture at large. For decades, feminist sex-toy retailers made it their mission to put a vibrator on the bedside table of every woman, of every age, everywhere, because they believed that sexual pleasure was a birthright. Today, due largely to the success of their sex-positive educational and outreach efforts, we live in a world in which women-friendly sex shops are increasingly the norm, even in places like Las Vegas—a city hardly known for its progressive sexual politics. And yet feminist business owner Karoline Khamis refused to be deterred—despite restrictive zoning ordinances and other obstacles—when she opened Toyboxx

Toyboxx founder Karoline Khamis in her Las Vegas store, 2016. Courtesy of Karoline Khamis.

in 2014 in the hope of bringing a version of the Good Vibrations model to one of the world's biggest adult playgrounds.

Nowadays, there's nothing unusual about publications like *Bitch* magazine running full-page ads for feminist sex-toy businesses or publishing stories about the history of the dildo.[24] The availability of how-to books about sex that discuss everything from male prostate play to strap-on sex, from open relationships to sex during pregnancy, has exploded. More and better-made sex toys for people with penises exist than ever before. Sex-related podcasts such as Sex Out Loud and Sex Nerd Sandra examine the intersection of sex and culture, while a growing cadre of sex-toy bloggers review what they see as the best and worst that the industry has to offer.

Budding sex educators looking to hone their skills and market themselves as sex professionals can enroll in Tristan Taormino's Sex Educator Boot Camp and Reid Mihalko's Sex Geek Summer Camp. Representations of sex toys can be found on television with increasing frequency, including depictions of dildos and strap-ons in shows like *Transparent* and *Broad City*; and one Australian university is now offering a course on sex-toy design.[25] The 2012 publication of *Fifty Shades of Grey*, the runaway best seller about an emotionally distant billionaire and his young female paramour, generated a boom in sex-toy sales across the globe. British retailer Love Honey introduced the official *Fifty Shades* "pleasure collection" and the Adult Entertainment Expo (AEE) held business seminars on how retailers could better capitalize on the "*Fifty Shades* Frenzy" by hosting special "ladies nights" and BDSM workshops geared toward first-time customers.[26]

These cultural shifts did not happen overnight. The increasing availability of sex toys and the growth of the women's market are the result of decades of efforts on the part of feminist retailers, manufacturers, and educators to make sexual products more respectable—and therefore more acceptable—to segments of Middle America that previously would never have dreamed of venturing into an adult store. Sex-toy packaging with sultry images of porn stars has been replaced with softer and more sanitized imagery, an expensive but worthwhile undertaking for companies hoping to appeal to women on the basis of "friendly, colorful and informative packaging devoid of bodies";[27] discourses of sexual health and education, rather than titillation, are regularly used as marketing platforms; and new breeds of sex-toy manufacturers, such as Tantus and NJoy, are bringing sleek design, quality manufacturing, and lifestyle branding to an industry that historically has not been known for these things. "What we are seeing is a confluence of cultural shifts," explained

NJoy's Greg DeLong. "What started thirty years ago with Joani Blank and Good Vibrations—that it's okay for women to use sex toys—has continued to evolve. The Internet has also helped spread information and normalize sex for a new generation of consumers."[28]

Perhaps the most dramatic shift has been the widespread acknowledgment on the part of mainstream retailers, manufacturers, and porn producers that the adult industry is no longer a world of men. When Betty Dodson stood on-stage at the 1973 NOW Women's Sexuality Conference and boasted about her relationship to her vibrator, she could hardly have anticipated a time when adult industry leaders would ask feminist sex-toy store owners like Babeland's Rachel Venning for business insight and merchandising tips. But that's exactly what has happened at industry gatherings since the mid-2000s, where, far from being ignored, women hold the microphone in seminar rooms filled to capacity with wholesalers, distributors, retailers, and content producers eager to mine—and some might argue, co-opt—their expertise. In an industry that is increasingly interested in cashing in on the buying power of women, their status as experts, CEOs, educators, trend makers, and, importantly, consumers has continued to grow.

These gains were hard won. "When I began," Metis Black, the founder of sex-toy manufacturer Tantus said, recalling the industry in the late 1990s, it "was really a boys' club. Men were the important buyers, salesmen, manu-facturers, and store owners. Women might be on their arms, but the decision makers were almost always men."[29]

Black remembers being at one adult novelty trade show in the early 2000s and watching as a product buyer for Good Vibrations was ignored as she went from booth to booth. "She couldn't get the time of day from the big boys, and here was a woman who spends well over $1,000,000 a year, $3,000,000 was probably her budget . . . and no one would pay any attention to her."[30]

It was not just that women found themselves marginalized in an indus-try dominated by men and steeped in sexism, but that their perspectives and contributions were often completely disregarded. When feminist porn pio-neer Candida Royalle first started making porn for women and couples in the early 1980s, she was unable to find distributors willing to place her films in retail stores because they could not wrap their heads around the products she was making. When she approached retailers about carrying her movies, they raised their eyebrows and scratched their heads in confusion. "The market was not listening [to women], but I was," Royalle recounted.[31]

Feminist retailers, manufacturers, and porn producers had become accustomed to existing on a different planet — in their own galaxy, really — their orbit only occasionally overlapping with that of the larger adult industry, because they were such outliers. Babeland cofounder Venning, for example, didn't attend the AEE, the largest adult industry showcase in the United States, until 2007 — fourteen years after Babeland opened its doors for business. "I didn't think [the AEE] was relevant to what we were about," she explained. "I thought it seemed like porn, porn stars, and the objectification of women. For years, I really didn't see Babeland as part of the adult industry. I've always seen us as significantly different, more akin to a bookstore or a community center or something in health and wellness . . . so even though the [AEE] show had been going on for years, I just didn't really notice or care."[32]

As mainstream adult retailers with dollar signs in their eyes adopt parts of the Good Vibrations retail model, it has raised questions for Venning and others about the politics of co-optation — the practice of taking or adopting an idea as one's own, often without giving credit where due. Their concerns mirror some of the same ones that feminists had in the 1970s, namely that feminist businesses "serve as scouts for new markets and as outlets for products created by larger industries."[33] According to Venning, "I think it's great for women that their needs are being considered, [but] sometimes I feel what we're doing is being co-opted — folks talk the talk, but don't walk the walk. . . . They may claim to be doing sex education, but it's really just a sales pitch. From a business perspective it makes things more competitive, which isn't as fun. I still feel that we are the best of the best, though, so that's a comfort."[34]

Feminist entrepreneurs are divided about what the mainstreaming of sex toys and the co-optation of their business models mean for the future. Some have doubled down on the mantra "grow or die" as a marketplace reality. Others, like the members of the PPC, are leading with cooperation and community building as strategies to ensure the health and longevity of their businesses. And for Good Vibrations, survival has meant cultivating new and strategic business alliances in an effort to better monetize operations and remain relevant in a rapidly evolving industry.

Some retailers are confident that the cornerstones of the Good Vibrations retail model, its in-store experience and overall sex-positive philosophy, cannot be easily duplicated by copycat businesses that are looking for the "secret sauce," as one person put it. In other words, appealing to women takes more than painting one's store lavender and hiring a woman to run the cash register. "What makes us a place where women want to shop comes from multiple things, but I think it starts with our ethics," Sugar's Jacq Jones said. "We normalize sex in a powerful way. We make available quality information, a clean and welcoming environment, and staff that really care about what they do. I don't see that occurring on a massive scale without a huge cultural shift in attitudes about sex."[35]

If co-optation is the industry practice du jour, it may be the price feminists have paid for a world in which, as retailer Jones notes, "folks that were terrified to walk into a store that sold toys will now happily walk in and post about it on Facebook."[36] Thanks to early feminist businesses like Eve's Garden and Good Vibrations, you can find elements of the alternative, women-friendly, and educationally oriented retail model they developed even at establishments like Las Vegas's Adult Superstore. That's where twenty-six-year-old Amber, a Las Vegas transplant, headed after her dog ate her favorite vibrator. Amber grew up in a small Midwestern farming town of six thousand people, a place where sex "was shunned" and sex toys were never discussed. If she wanted to find a sex-toy store back home, it would mean driving forty miles to St. Louis. Now, at the Adult Superstore, a large sex-toy emporium—think clothing retailer H&M but for sex toys—she knows that she'll not only have many options to choose from, but once there she'll be treated with respect by a knowledgeable staff.[37]

It's a far cry from the humiliation Dell Williams experienced in the early 1970s when she walked into Macy's department store to purchase the Hitachi Magic Wand. The culture that Williams and her contemporaries fought so hard to transform was one that rarely viewed women as sexual agents and consumers who were entitled to take their pleasure—and their orgasms—seriously and expect that others would, too.

Judging by Amber's attitude toward her vibrator errand, they seem to have succeeded. For Amber, there's nothing dirty or sleazy about it—no stigma, no embarrassment. Shopping for a sex toy is like any other business transaction, akin to buying any other consumer product to meet a perceived need. "Things are changing," she told me. "It's now okay for women to be more open about our sexuality, to have an opinion, to talk about it."[38]

Feminists changed the sex-toy industry and, over time, the industry changed their businesses, forcing them to become more profit-minded and fiscally conscious whether they wanted to or not. For many people, myself included, there's a palpable nostalgia for an earlier time when feminist entrepreneurs like Williams and Blank led with conviction and intention and shunned conventional ways of doing business. The images of Williams standing in her kitchen opening letters from customers thanking her for starting Eve's Garden, or Blank sitting in Good Vibrations' tiny shop in San Francisco's Mission District, stamping brown paper bags with the tongue-in-cheek phrase Plain Brown Wrapper, are undeniably quaint and harken back to a simpler time when having a feminist vision and the compunction to bring it to life were all that mattered.

It is no longer the case that money takes a backseat to the mission, and the absorption of sex positivity—or at least a version of it—into the cultural mainstream means that in some instances the feminist messages that these stores hold so near and dear are being diluted. While it is uncertain what the future holds for feminist sex-toy stores, the model of sex-positive capitalism that they promote, one that leads with sex education and frank conversations about sex, is not going away and in fact has become the industry standard. Indeed, the history of feminist sex-toy stores reveals both the promises and limitations of working within a capitalist system where commercial pressures and political idealism form an uneasy and sometimes acrimonious relationship. These businesses have succeeded in bringing the sexual revolution into the bedrooms of countless women and men who might never have attended a political rally or sexuality conference, but who feel comfortable—and indeed entitled—to shop for sexual information and products. They demonstrate that it is possible to reconfigure the relationships between feminist politics and marketplace culture, activism and capitalism, and social change and profitability, creating in the process new commercial and political realities designed to educate, empower, and transform people's sexual lives—although perhaps not always in ways their founders imagined.

*appendix*

# STUDYING SEXUAL CULTURE
# AND COMMERCE

Researching the history of feminist sex-toy stores sent me down a rabbit hole. It took years and multiple methods of data collection—ethnographic fieldwork, in-depth interviews, and archival research—to weave together the various historical threads, cultural currents, and political influences that have shaped these businesses and the larger women's market for sex toys and pornography.

As a gender and sexuality scholar with a background in communication and media studies, I am interested in understanding the processes by which things acquire meaning, how these meanings circulate, and how they are consumed. In this regard, my research is indebted to what sociologist Paul du Gay describes as the "language of culture," including the ways that people "think, feel and act in organizations."[1]

Scholars have noted the methodological challenges of studying phenomena related to sexuality, especially its commercial organization and industrial dynamics.[2] Georgina Voss, for example, has called for sexuality researchers to go "further behind the scenes" and "seek out material from further inside the industry."[3] For me, heeding this call required a kind of methodological promiscuity: I talked to as many retailers, employees, and industry insiders as I could; visited as many relevant field sites as possible; and amassed a research archive teeming with corporate documents, internal memos, advertisements, and other ephemera, all of which I drew upon to produce a multidimensional account of the history of feminist vibrator businesses and the women who pioneered them.

## Ethnographic Fieldwork

I spent six months and countless hours in 2001 conducting fieldwork at feminist retailer Babeland's Lower East Side store in New York City, where I was given unfettered access to the business, both on the sales floor and behind the scenes. I sold vibrators and dispensed practical information about sex; attended staff, marketing, and management meetings; learned to read profit and loss reports; and participated in interviews for the hiring of new staff. I immersed myself in Babeland's retail universe in an effort to better understand how store owners and staff worked to advance the company's mission of sex education and personal empowerment and, at the same time, maintain a commercially viable business.

Had I been conducting a more traditional ethnography, my research might have ended there, but in actuality it was just beginning. By "empirically following the thread of cultural process," namely the emergence and circulation of the Good Vibrations retail model, I engaged in a version of "mobile ethnography" that took me to sex-toy shops in cities across the country, from Good Vibrations in San Francisco, Grand Opening in Boston, and Self Serve in Albuquerque, to Early to Bed in Chicago, A Woman's Touch in Madison, the Tool Shed in Milwaukee, and Feelmore in Oakland.[4] As a counterpoint, I sought out variations of the traditional adult store in suburban enclaves and urban meccas whenever I could. I spent a day at a dildo factory and toured a lubricant manufacturing plant. I sat in on more than a dozen in-store sex education workshops at various retail establishments on topics as varied as Sex Toys 101, Strap-on Sex, and How to Give a Good Blowjob. Over the years, I attended more than fifteen adult industry trade shows, including the annual AVN Adult Entertainment Expo in Las Vegas (2008–2016), the International Lingerie Show in Las Vegas (2008–2013), and the XBiz Show in Los Angeles (2014), where I met and spoke with sex-toy manufacturers, distributors, and retailers, and attended dozens of business seminars on topics that included sex education in retail settings, the growing power and influence of women in the adult industry, and the *Fifty Shades* consumer frenzy. In 2010 and 2011, I also moderated the women's seminar at the Adult Entertainment Expo, a role that placed me squarely within the discourses I was analyzing.

My fieldwork resembled what sociologist Michael Burawoy has described as the "extended case method," an approach that is especially well suited for examining the influence of macro processes (e.g., industry forces and constraints) on specific cultural scenes and contexts (e.g., feminist vibrator shops).[5] The extended case method also offers ethnographers a way to mitigate what Burawoy sees as two fundamental weaknesses of traditional ethnography, that of significance and the level of analysis. While individual case studies may reveal interesting findings, they are often highly particular rather than generalizable, producing analyses that are inherently microsocial and frequently ahistorical. The extended case method addresses these limitations by moving between multiple sites of cultural activity, while also focusing on the interactions between macro and micro processes. As a result, researchers are better situated to capture the interplay between different levels of social activity across multiple locations, detailing the "patterns of power" that are woven throughout everyday life, including, in this case, the sexual marketplace.[6]

## Interviews

I conducted in-depth interviews with more than eighty feminist entrepreneurs, CEOs, sales staff, manufacturers, marketers, and pornographers, and talked informally with dozens of individuals working in various sectors of the adult industry. In some cases, this involved multiple interviews with key informants over the course of many years. I tape-recorded and transcribed all of them, with the exception of just a few. Interviewing people who occupied different positions—and positions of power—within a company, including former employees, allowed me tell a multigenerational and multivocal story spanning several waves of feminist sex-toy retailing, from the early 1970s to the present.

Interviewees were excited to talk about their businesses, their jobs, and their visions for sex-positive social change. Many of them, such as Eve's Garden founder Dell Williams, who was seventy-nine when I met her in 2001, knew that feminist history was often glossed over or misrepresented and were therefore eager to have their contributions documented. Store owners were also aware that they were being asked to take part in a research project that included other businesses that were essentially their competitors—and they did not want to be left out. I sometimes felt as though retailers viewed my research as a potential promotional vehicle, an academic public relations machine for feminist sex-toy businesses and their products. They knew that I would be presenting my findings at conferences and that I would eventually publish my results. Thus, I was not immune from the larger commercial and promotional concerns that shaped the businesses I was studying.

My research had other effects, too, including reminding many retailers that their efforts mattered; that in addition to selling products, they were engaged in a version of sex-positive retail activism that had the potential to impact people's lives in profoundly meaningful ways. For store owners who were at times beleaguered and often bogged down with the day-to-day responsibilities and minutiae of running a business—endless meetings, personnel issues, marketing concerns, and inventory management, including counting every last condom in the store—it was sometimes easy to forget what had inspired them to open a sex-toy store in the first place. One owner, for example, told me that my research had "restarted her brain" and "brought her back to her original passion" for the business. Another said it had helped her "get her vision for a progressive company together." She admitted that she had felt burned out by all the problems, issues, and criticisms facing the business over the years and that her job had become a chore. "Your enthusiasm really infected me, and I regard my newfound dedication to the business as in part due to you. . . . I realize that inspiring me was not part of your plan, but that just goes to show that the influence of researchers on the researched cultures can be salutary."

## Archival Research

Archival research was a rich and invaluable source of data. I accessed records stored in basement file cabinets, corporate scrapbooks filled with media clippings, unprocessed boxes of documents at community-based archives, and papers housed in university collections. I examined customer letters, mission statements, ad copy, print catalogs, company newsletters, marketing materials, internal memos, and minutes from staff meetings, among other items and ephemera. Internal company memos were especially revealing. These documents provided evidence of cost-cutting measures, interpersonal tensions, organizational growing pains, and, from time to time, employee dissatisfaction. They exposed details about the less glamorous and sometimes contested parts of running a feminist business, supplementing the information that interviewees typically shared—or felt comfortable sharing—during one-on-one interviews.

## Identity, Hybridity, and Feminist Objectivity

I shared many points of connection with my research subjects, especially those who came of age and discovered feminism at the height of the feminist sex wars in the early to mid-1980s. The political language and cultural references they used to talk about their businesses offered a familiar interpretive framework for understanding their subject positions and worldviews. Like many feminist sex-toy store owners and employees, I am also white, middle class, and college educated, with a fluid sexuality and a sex-positive sensibility.

These points of identification not only helped me gain access to and negotiate the commercial world I was studying, they also influenced what I saw and how I made sense of it.

I wore multiple hats in the field: ethnographer, vibrator clerk, and sexual consumer. Because of this, my identity was complicated and shifting. When I began my fieldwork at Babeland, for example, I identified as a researcher who was also working on the sales floor. Somewhere along the way—I think it was when I was given my own set of keys to the store—the relationship blurred. One day I realized that I had become a Babelander; it was an identity I inhabited as much, if not sometimes more, it seemed, than that of a researcher. My ethnographic lens had shifted from participant observation toward what anthropologist Barbara Tedlock has described as the "observation of participation," a research position in which ethnographers both "experience and observe their own and others' coparticipation in the ethnographic encounter."[7] Much like turning a kaleidoscope, my vantage point and object chamber had changed.

My success in the field ultimately hinged on my ability to do my job well. I worked hard to learn the ropes—which included obtaining a vast amount of product knowledge and sexual information. The learning curve was steep, especially early on when I was figuring out how to change the register tape, redeem a gift certificate, and settle a batch of credit cards. I was determined to show my coworkers that I was dependable and trustworthy, and that I could cover their backs when the store got busy. This was important not only because working on the sales floor was my entry into the world of Babeland, but also because I believed in the business's mission and enjoyed being part of it. I found it inspiring to come to work every day and be surrounded by a group of smart, strong, predominantly queer-identified women who were committed to sex education and social justice. The business was not without its shortcomings and imperfections—for example, some employees expressed frustration about what they saw as the gap between the business's political ideals and the day-to-day operations of the company; others felt the business was run too much like a family, involving a "Kumbaya" style of lesbian-feminist processing that sought consensus in decision making but routinely fell back on its hierarchical structure; and yet, it was also ripe with a sense of utopian possibility, which I found incredibly seductive. Thus, the biggest challenge I faced, and one that I tried to reconcile to the best of my ability, was striking a balance between sex-positive advocacy and scholarly objectivity, while also maintaining the critical distance that good research, feminist or otherwise, ultimately demands.

NOTES

## introduction

1. As quoted in "B2B Means Business," in *The AVN Adult Entertainment Expo Show Guide*, January 2008, 50. Copy on file with author.

2. For a discussion of *Sex and the City's* infamous vibrator episode, see Lynn Comella, "(Safe) *Sex and the City*: On Vibrators, Masturbation, and the Myth of 'Real' Sex," *Feminist Media Studies* 3, no. 1 (2003): 107–110; for a discussion of the economy of *Fifty Shades of Grey*, see Lynn Comella, "Fifty Shades of Erotic Stimulation," *Feminist Media Studies* 13, no. 3 (2013): 563–566; for discussions regarding the emergence of a women's market for sexual products, see Feona Attwood, "Fashion and Passion: Marketing Sex to Women," *Sexualities* 8, no. 4 (2005): 392–406; Clarissa Smith, *One for the Girls: The Pleasures and Practices of Reading Women's Porn* (Bristol, U.K.: Intellect, 2007); Merl Storr, *Latex and Lingerie: Shopping for Pleasure at Ann Summers Parties* (Oxford: Berg, 2003).

3. Debby Herbenick, Michael Reece, Stephanie A. Sanders, Brian Dodge, Annahita Ghassemi, and J. Dennis Fortenberry, "Prevalence and Characteristics of Vibrator Use by Women in the United States: Results from a Nationally Representative Study," *Journal of Sexual Medicine* 6 (2009): 1857–1866.

4. Hilary Howard, "Vibrators Carry the Conversation," *New York Times*, April 20, 2011, http://www.nytimes.com/2011/04/21/fashion/21VIBRATORS.html?_r=0.

5. Emma Gray, "Vibrator Sales Up—Are Sex Toys a Woman's Best Friend?" *Huffington Post*, May 8, 2012, http://www.huffingtonpost.com/2012/05/08/vibrator-sales-sex -toys-women_n_1501352.html. Sherri Shaulis, senior editor of pleasure products at *Adult Video News*, noted in a personal correspondence that it is necessary to contextualize this $15 billion figure. This number reflects sales globally, not nationally, and includes everything from $10 bullet vibrators to $7,000 sex dolls. It also includes sexual lubricants, sex furniture, and so on. And while it is very likely that this often-quoted figure is exaggerated, Shaulis acknowledges that "no real [sales] data exist." For articles citing this figure, see David Rosen, "What the $15 Billion Sex Toy Industry Tells Us about Sexuality Today," *Alternet*, March 7, 2013, http://www.alternet.org/sex-amp -relationships/what-15-billion-sex-toy-industry-tells-us-about-sexuality-today; Janet Burns, "How the 'Niche' Sex Toy Market Grew into an Unstoppable $15B Industry," *Forbes*, July 16, 2016, http://www.forbes.com/sites/janetwburns/2016/07/15/adult-expo -founders-talk-15b-sex-toy-industry-after-20-years-in-the-fray/#5d2b394f38a1.

6. Betty Friedan, *The Feminine Mystique* (New York: Norton, 2001 [1963]).

7. Sara Evans, *Personal Politics: The Roots of Women's Liberation in the Civil Rights Movement and the New Left* (New York: Vintage, 1979), 12.

8. John D'Emilio and Estelle Freedman, *Intimate Matters: A History of Sexuality in America* (Chicago: University of Chicago Press, 1997), 286.

9. Barbara Ehrenreich, *The Hearts of Men: American Dreams and the Flight from Commitment* (New York: Anchor, 1983), 42.

10. Evans, *Personal Politics*, 11.

11. According to historian Lillian Faderman, lesbian pulp novels "helped spread the word about lesbian lifestyles to women who may have been too sheltered otherwise to know that such things existed." See Faderman's *Odd Girls and Twilight Lovers: A History of Lesbian Life in Twentieth-Century America* (New York: Penguin, 1991), 147.

12. Friedan, *Feminine Mystique*, 258.

13. Friedan, *Feminine Mystique*, 261.

14. Elaine Tyler May, *America and the Pill: A History of Promise, Peril, and Liberation* (New York: Basic Books, 2010), 6.

15. David Allyn, *Make Love, Not War: The Sexual Revolution, an Unfettered History* (Boston: Little, Brown, 2000), 243.

16. Allyn, *Make Love, Not War*, 243.

17. D'Emilio and Freedman, *Intimate Matters*, 327.

18. Barbara Ehrenreich, Elizabeth Hess, and Gloria Jacobs, *Re-making Love: The Feminization of Sex* (Garden City, NY: Anchor Press/Doubleday, 1986), 105.

19. Ehrenreich, Hess, and Jacobs, *Re-making Love*, 105.

20. Ehrenreich, Hess, and Jacobs, *Re-making Love*, 109.

21. Commission on Obscenity and Pornography, *The Report of the Commission on Obscenity and Pornography* (New York: Bantam, 1970), 1.

22. Commission on Obscenity and Pornography, *Report*, 53.

23. "Is Smut Good for You?," *Time*, October 12, 1970.

24. Gerard Damiano, dir., *Deep Throat* (Gerard Damiano Film Productions, 1972).

25. Carolyn Bronstein, *Battling Pornography: The American Feminist Anti-pornography Movement, 1976–1986* (Cambridge: Cambridge University Press, 2011), 82.

26. Following Georgia's lead, Texas amended its antiobscenity laws in 1979 and was soon joined by Colorado (1981), Mississippi (1983), Louisiana (1985), Kansas (1986), Alabama (1998), and Virginia (2000). Most of the statutes were challenged, and while some were found to be unconstitutional by state courts, others were upheld. In 2008, the U.S. Fifth Circuit Court of Appeals overturned the Texas ban, making Alabama the only state where the sale of vibrators and other "obscene devices" remains illegal. For a discussion of these bans, see Tristan Taormino, "Dallas Dildo Defiance," in *Tristan Taormino's True Lust: Adventures in Sex, Porn and Perversion* (San Francisco: Cleis, 2002), 13–15; Danielle J. Lindemann, "Pathology Full Circle: A History of Anti-vibrator Legislation in the United States," *Columbia Journal of Gender and Law* 15, no. 1 (2006):

326–346; Alana Chazan, "Good Vibrations: Liberating Sexuality from the Commercial Regulation of Sexual Devices," *Texas Journal of Women and the Law* 18, no. 2 (2009): 263–305; Karthik Subramanian, "It's a Dildo in 49 States, but It's a Dildon't in Alabama: Alabama's Anti-obscenity Enforcement Act and the Assault on Civil Liberty and Personal Freedom," *Alabama Civil Rights and Civil Liberties Law Review* 1, no. 111 (2011): 111–139.

27. Lynn Raridon, interview with author, March 26, 2002.

28. Claire Cavanah, interview with author, August 30, 2001.

29. Joani Blank, "Closing Keynote Plenary" (Catalyst Con West, Burbank, California, September 13, 2015).

30. For discussions regarding private versus public representations of sexuality, see Jane Juffer, *At Home with Pornography: Women, Sex, and Everyday Life* (New York: New York University Press, 1998); Dangerous Bedfellows, *Policing Public Sex: Queer Politics and the Future of AIDS Activism* (Boston, MA: South End, 1996).

31. Aileen Journey, interview with author, October 25, 1998.

32. For discussion of these debates, see Bronstein, *Battling Pornography*; Lisa Duggan and Nan Hunter, *Sex Wars: Sexual Dissent and Political Culture* (New York: Routledge, 1995); Carole Vance, *Pleasure and Danger: Exploring Female Sexuality* (New York: Routledge and Kegan Paul, 1984).

33. Originally named Toys in Babeland, the company rebranded in 2005 and dropped the "Toys in." According to Babeland cofounder Rachel Venning, "We wanted to get away from being just about toys and identify as a place of sexual empowerment." Rachel Venning, e-mail message to author, June 4, 2015.

34. Lisa Henderson, "Sexuality, Cultural Production, and Foucault" (paper presented at Sexuality after Foucault, Manchester University, Manchester, U.K., November 2003).

35. For analyses of the making of TV talk shows, see Josh Gamson, *Freaks Talk Back: Tabloid Talk Shows and Sexual Nonconformity* (Chicago: University of Chicago Press, 1998); Laura Grindstaff, *The Money Shot: Crass, Class, and the Making of TV Talk Shows* (Chicago: University of Chicago Press, 2002). For discussions regarding the making of consumer markets, see Katherine Sender, *Business, Not Politics: The Making of the Gay Market* (New York: Columbia University Press, 2004); Arlene Davila, *Latinos, Inc.: The Marketing and Making of a People* (Berkeley: University of California Press, 2001). For an examination of the making of *Ms.* magazine, see Amy Erdman Farrell, *Yours in Sisterhood: Ms. Magazine and the Promise of Popular Feminism* (Chapel Hill: University of North Carolina Press, 1998).

36. For examples, see Mireille Miller-Young, *A Taste for Brown Sugar: Black Women in Pornography* (Durham, NC: Duke University Press, 2014); Margot Weiss, *Techniques of Pleasure: BDSM and the Circuits of Sexuality* (Durham, NC: Duke University Press, 2011); Barb G. Brents, Crystal A. Jackson, and Kate Hausbeck, *The State of Sex: Tourism, Sex, and Sin in the New American Heartland* (New York: Routledge, 2010); Katherine

Frank, *G-Strings and Sympathy: Strip Club Regulars and Male Desire* (Durham, NC: Duke University Press, 2002).

37. Although online retailing and home sex-toy parties are important revenue streams for many feminist sex-toy companies, these retail channels have their own logic and produce consumer experiences that are different from the ones I examine in this book. Home sex-toy parties, which are based on a model of direct selling popularized by companies such as Tupperware, occur in the privacy of individuals' homes and typically rely on preexisting networks of friends and acquaintances; and for many people, shopping for sex toys online is as much about anonymity as it is convenience.

38. For discussions regarding the history of department stores and the rise of American consumer culture, see Susan Porter Benson, *Counter Cultures: Saleswomen, Managers, and Customers in American Department Stores 1890–1940* (Urbana: University of Illinois Press, 1986); William Leach, *Land of Desire: Merchants, Power, and the Rise of a New American Culture* (New York: Pantheon, 1993); Elaine Abelson, *When Ladies Go A-Thieving: Middle-Class Shoplifters in the Victorian Department Store* (Oxford: Oxford University Press, 1989); Kathy Peiss, *Hope in a Jar: The Making of America's Beauty Culture* (New York: Metropolitan, 1998).

39. Michel Foucault, *The History of Sexuality*, vol. 1: *An Introduction* (New York: Vintage, 1978), 18.

40. Jacq Jones, interview with author, April 12, 2002.

41. For a discussion of sex negativity and its effects, see Gayle Rubin's groundbreaking essay, "Thinking Sex: Notes for a Radical Theory of the Politics of Sexuality," in *The Lesbian and Gay Studies Reader*, ed. Henry Abelove, Michelle A. Barale, and David M. Halperin (New York: Routledge, 1993), 3–44.

42. Carol Queen and Lynn Comella, "The Necessary Revolution: Sex-Positive Feminism in the Post-Barnard Era," *Communication Review* 11, no. 3 (2008): 278.

43. See Andi Zeisler, *We Were Feminists Once: From Riot Grrrl to Covergirl®, the Buying and Selling of a Political Movement* (New York: PublicAffairs, 2016); Alexandra Chasin, *Selling Out: The Gay and Lesbian Movement Goes to Market* (Basingstoke, U.K.: Palgrave, 2000).

44. See Gail Dines, *Pornland: How Porn Has Hijacked Our Sexuality* (Boston: Beacon, 2010); Julia Long, *Anti-porn: The Resurgence of Anti-pornography Feminism* (London: Zed, 2012); Robert Jensen, *Getting Off: Pornography and the End of Masculinity* (Cambridge, MA: South End, 2007).

45. Michael Warner, *The Trouble with Normal: Sex, Politics, and the Ethics of Queer Life* (Cambridge, MA: Harvard University Press, 1999), 4.

## *one* The Business of Masturbation

1. Betty Dodson, *My Romantic Love Wars: A Sexual Memoir* (New York: Betty Dodson, 2010), 177.

2. Betty Dodson, "Remarks," in *Women's Sexuality Conference Proceedings*, ed. NOW (New York: NOW, 1974), 10. Photocopy on file with author.

3. Lorrien, "Remarks," in *Women's Sexuality Conference Proceedings*, 38.

4. Lorrien, "Remarks," 38.

5. Laurie Johnson, "Women's Sexuality Conference Ends in School Here," *New York Times*, June 11, 1973; Lindsay Miller, "Women Confer on Sex," *New York Post*, June 11, 1973.

6. Barbara, "Remarks," in *Women's Sexuality Conference Proceedings*, 33.

7. Laura Scharf, "On Planning the Sexuality Conference," in *Women's Sexuality Conference Proceedings*, 36.

8. Dell Williams, "To Explore, Define and Celebrate Our Own Sexuality (Or the Resurrection of Eve)," in *Women's Sexuality Conference Proceedings*, 6.

9. Ruth Rosen, *The World Split Open: How the Modern Women's Movement Changed America* (New York: Penguin, 2006), 143.

10. Judy Wenning, "Opening Remarks," in *Women's Sexuality Conference Proceedings*, 9.

11. Sigmund Freud, *New Introductory Lectures on Psychoanalysis* (New York: Norton, 1965), 104.

12. Anne Koedt, "The Myth of the Vaginal Orgasm," in *Notes from the Second Year: Women's Liberation*, ed. Shulamith Firestone and Anne Koedt (New York: Radical Feminists, 1970), 38.

13. Koedt, "The Myth of the Vaginal Orgasm," 38.

14. Alix Shulman, "Organs and Orgasms," in *Woman in Sexist Society: Studies in Power and Powerlessness*, ed. Vivian Gornick and Barbara K. Moran (New York: Mentor, 1971), 292.

15. Shulman, "Organs and Orgasms," 291.

16. Alfred C. Kinsey, *Sexual Behavior in the Human Female* (Philadelphia: Saunders, 1953).

17. Janice M. Irvine, *Disorders of Desire: Sex and Gender in Modern American Sexology* (Philadelphia: Temple University Press, 1990), 63.

18. Kinsey, *Sexual Behavior*, 582.

19. Kinsey, *Sexual Behavior*, 584.

20. Irvine, *Disorders of Desire*, 59.

21. William H. Masters and Virginia Johnson, *Human Sexual Response* (Boston: Little, Brown, 1966), 45.

22. Rebecca Chalker, *The Clitoral Truth: The Secret World at Your Fingertips* (New York: Seven Stories, 2000), 14.

23. Joani Blank, "Closing Keynote Plenary" (Catalyst Con West, Burbank, California, September 13, 2015).

24. Federation of Feminist Women's Health Centers, *A New View of a Woman's Body: A Fully Illustrated Guide* (West Hollywood, CA: Feminist Health, 1991), 33.

25. Federation of Feminist Women's Health Centers, *A New View of a Woman's Body*, 46.

26. Ti-Grace Atkinson, "The Institution of Sexual Intercourse," in *Notes from the Second Year: Women's Liberation*, ed. Shulamith Firestone and Anne Koedt (New York: Radical Feminists, 1970), 42–47.

27. Shulman, "Organs and Orgasms," 301.

28. Dell Williams, Eve's Garden catalog, 1975. Photocopy on file with author.

29. Dodson, *My Romantic Love Wars*.

30. Betty Dodson, *Liberating Masturbation* (New York: Betty Dodson, 1974), 2.

31. Betty Dodson, *Sex for One: The Joy of Selfloving* (New York: Three Rivers, 1996), 19.

32. Dodson, *Sex for One*, 22.

33. Betty Dodson, "Having Sex with Machines: The Return of the Electric Vibrator," Betty Dodson's Blog, June 8, 2010, http://dodsonandross.com/blogs/betty-dodson/2010/06/having-sex-machines-return-electric-vibrator.

34. Medical practitioners believed that hysteria was caused by a disturbance of the uterus, which was thought to wander the body causing problems of various kinds. This theory dated back thousands of years to the time of Hippocrates and continued to have currency until 1952, when the American Psychiatric Association dropped the diagnosis altogether. For discussions about the history of vibrators, see Rachel Maines, *The Technology of Orgasm: "Hysteria," the Vibrator, and Women's Sexual Satisfaction* (Baltimore, MD: Johns Hopkins University Press, 1999); Hallie Lieberman, "Taboo Technologies: Sex Toys in America since 1850" (PhD diss., University of Wisconsin, Madison, 2014).

35. In 1981, Down There Press published a facsimile edition of *The Relief of Pain and the Treatment of Disease by Vibration: Shelton Electric Vibrator* (New York: Shelton Electric Company, 1917), 4.

36. Betty Dodson, "Porn Wars," in *The Feminist Porn Book: The Politics of Producing Pleasure*, ed. Tristan Taormino, Celine Parreñas Shimizu, Constance Penley, and Mireille Miller-Young (New York: Feminist Press, 2013), 24.

37. Betty Dodson, telephone interview with author, December 3, 1999.

38. Evans Holt, *A New Look at Masturbation* (Las Vegas: Griffon, 1970), 8.

39. Thomas W. Laqueur, *Solitary Sex: A Cultural History of Masturbation* (New York: Zone, 2003), 397.

40. Boston Women's Health Book Collective, *Our Bodies, Ourselves: A Course by and for Women* (Boston: New England Free Press, 1971), 13.

41. Toni Ayers, Maggi Rubenstein, and Carolyn Haynes Smith, *Masturbation Techniques for Women/Getting In Touch* (San Francisco: Multimedia Resource Center, 1972).

42. Ayers, Rubenstein, and Smith, *Masturbation Techniques for Women*, 6.

43. For an overview of humanistic sexology, see Leonore Tiefer, "Sex Therapy as Humanistic Enterprise," *Sexual and Relationship Therapy* 21, no. 3 (2006): 359–375.

44. Irvine, *Disorders of Desire*, 106–107.

45. Ayers, Rubenstein, and Smith, *Masturbation Techniques for Women*, 2.

46. Dodson, *Liberating Masturbation*, 13.

47. For a discussion regarding the history of genital portraiture and masturbation demonstrations in feminist self-help and body education workshops, see Eithne Johnson, "Loving Yourself: The Specular Scene in Sexual Self-Help Advice for Women," in *Collecting Visible Evidence*, ed. Jane M. Gaines and Michael Renov (Minneapolis: University of Minnesota Press, 1999), 216–240.

48. Dodson, interview.

49. Mimi Lobell, "Last Word," n.d. Photocopy on file with author.

50. Dodson, *My Romantic Love Wars*, 167.

51. Suzie Saliga Vavrek, letter to the editor, *Ms.*, December 1974, 8.

52. Kay Kling, letter to the editor, *Ms.*, December, 1974, 8.

53. Susie Bright, telephone interview with author, June 18, 2010.

54. Dodson, *Liberating Masturbation*, 7.

55. Kathy Davis, *The Making of* Our Bodies, Ourselves: *How Feminism Travels across Borders* (Durham, NC: Duke University Press, 2007), 2.

56. Dell Williams, interview with author, November 20, 2001.

57. Dell Williams and Lynn Vannucci, *Revolution in the Garden: Memoirs of the Garden Keeper* (Santa Rosa, CA: Silverback, 2005), 142.

58. Williams, interview.

59. As quoted in Katie Monagle, "All about Eve's Garden," *Ms.*, November–December 1995, 54.

60. Williams, interview.

61. Williams, interview.

62. Williams, interview.

63. Williams, interview.

64. Wilhelm Reich, *The Function of the Orgasm: Sex-Economic Problems of Biological Energy*, trans. V. R. Carfagno (New York: Farrar, Straus and Giroux, 1973).

65. Reich, *The Function of the Orgasm*, 201.

66. David Allyn, *Make Love, Not War: The Sexual Revolution, An Unfettered History* (Boston: Little, Brown, 2000), 45.

67. Dell Williams, Eve's Garden catalog, 1986. Copy on file with author.

68. Williams, interview.

69. Williams, interview.

70. Alice Echols, *Daring to Be Bad: Radical Feminism in America 1967–1975* (Minneapolis: University of Minnesota Press, 1989), 269.

71. Williams and Vannucci, *Revolution in the Garden*, 190.

72. Williams, interview.

73. Williams, interview.

74. Herme Shore, "Dell Williams Caters to Woman's Right to Sexuality," *Women's Week*, February 27, 1978, 10.

75. Williams, interview.

76. As quoted in Eve's Garden catalog, 1986. Copy on file with author.

77. Customer correspondence to Dell Williams, 5 April 1975, box 5, folder 1, Dell Williams papers, #7676, Division of Rare and Manuscript Collections, Cornell University Library.

78. Customer correspondence to Dell Williams, 8 April 1980, box 5, folder 1; customer correspondence, 18 June 1980; customer correspondence, n.d., box 5, folder 2, Dell Williams papers.

79. Customer correspondence to Dell Williams, n.d., box 5, folder 13 (1985–1989), Dell Williams papers.

80. Customer correspondence to Dell Williams, 21 September 1986, box 5, folder 14, Dell Williams papers.

81. Customer correspondence to Dell Williams, 25 May 1976, box 5, folder 4, Dell Williams papers.

82. Customer correspondence to Dell Williams, 28 January 1991, box 5, folder 15, Dell Williams papers.

83. Customer correspondence to Dell Williams, n.d., box 5, folder 15, Dell Williams papers.

84. Customer correspondence to Dell Williams, February 1982, box 5, folder 2; correspondence to Dell Williams, n.d., box 5, folder 6; correspondence to Dell Williams, February 1982, box 5, folder 2, Dell Williams papers.

85. Customer correspondence to Dell Williams, 1 August 1976; Dell Williams correspondence to customer, n.d., box 5, folder 3, Dell Williams papers.

86. Customer correspondence to Dell Williams, 5 August 1983, box 5, folder 2, Dell Williams papers.

87. Customer correspondence to Dell Williams, 23 January 1984, box 5, folder 3; correspondence to Dell Williams, 3 April 1975, box 5, folder 2; correspondence to Dell Williams, 6 November 1975, box 5, folder 2, Dell Williams papers.

88. Dell Williams correspondence to customer, 11 November 1975, box 5, folder 2, Dell Williams papers.


## *two*  Out of the Therapist's Office, into the Vibrator Shop

1. For a detailed sexual history of San Francisco neighborhoods, including the Mission District, see Josh Sides, *Erotic City: Sexual Revolutions and the Making of Modern San Francisco* (Oxford: Oxford University Press, 2009).

2. Adi Gevins, "She's Bringing You Good Vibrations," *Berkeley Barb*, June 17, 1977.

3. Gevins, "She's Bringing You Good Vibrations."

4. Joani Blank, telephone interview with author, October 20, 1999.

5. Joani Blank, conversation with author, December 9, 2015.

6. Joani Blank, interview with author, November 13, 2013.

7. Joani Blank, "Closing Keynote" (Catalyst Con West, Los Angeles, September 13, 2015).

8. Blank, interview, November 13, 2013.

9. Barbach and her staff used the term "preorgasmic" rather than "nonorgasmic" or "frigid" to describe women who weren't having orgasms, because they fully expected that the women who entered the program would be orgasmic by the time it ended. For a description of the treatment program, see Lonnie Barbach, *For Yourself: The Fulfillment of Female Sexuality* (New York: Signet, 1975).

10. Joani Blank, telephone interview with author, February 6, 2002.

11. As quoted in Meika Loe, "Feminism for Sale: Case Study of a Pro-Sex Feminist Business," *Gender and Society* 13, no. 6 (1999): 711.

12. Blank, interview, February 6, 2002.

13. Blank, interview, February 6, 2002.

14. Joani Blank, *My Playbook for Women about Sex* (Burlingame, CA: Down There Press, 1975), 7.

15. Joani Blank, *Good Vibrations: The Complete Woman's Guide to Vibrators* (Burlingame, CA: Down There Press, 1976).

16. Blank, *Good Vibrations*, 4.

17. Blank, *Good Vibrations*, 9.

18. Blank, *Good Vibrations*, 18.

19. Cathy Winks, telephone interview with author, June 27, 2002.

20. Susie Bright, telephone interview with author, June 18, 2010.

21. Bright, interview.

22. Bright, interview.

23. Bright, interview.

24. Bright, interview.

25. Susie Bright, *Big Sex Little Death: A Memoir* (Berkeley: Seal, 2011).

26. Bright, interview.

27. For a detailed history of antipornography feminist organizing, see Carolyn Bronstein, *Battling Pornography: The American Feminist Anti-pornography Movement, 1976–1986* (Cambridge: Cambridge University Press, 2011).

28. Bronstein, *Battling Pornography*, 285.

29. Bronstein, *Battling Pornography*, 287.

30. Heather Findlay, "Freud's 'Fetishism' and the Lesbian Dildo Debates," *Feminist Studies* 18, no. 3 (1992): 563.

31. Sophie Schmuckler, "How I Learned to Stop Worrying and Love My Dildo," in *Coming to Power: Writings and Graphics on Lesbian S/M*, ed. Samois (Boston: Alyson, 1981), 102.

32. As quoted in Jill Nagle, "My Big Fat Dick," *On Our Backs*, June–July 1998, 29.

33. Debi Sundahl and Nan Kinney, "From the Desk of the Publishers," *On Our Backs*, September–October 1989, 4.

34. As described by Susie Bright, *Susie Sexpert's Lesbian Sex World* (Pittsburgh: Cleis, 1990), 16.

35. Susie Bright, "Toys for Us," *On Our Backs*, summer 1984, 13.

36. Shar Rednour and Jackie Strano, "Steamy, Hot, and Political: Creating Radical Dyke Porn," in *New Views on Pornography: Sexuality, Politics, and the Law*, ed. Lynn Comella and Shira Tarrant (Santa Barbara, CA: Praeger, 2015), 176.

37. Bright, interview.

38. Bright, interview.

39. Roma Estevez, interview with author, November 22, 1999.

40. Briarpatch Community, eds., *The Briarpatch Book: Experiences in Right Livelihood and Simple Living* (San Francisco: New Glide, 1978), viii.

41. Gary Warne, "Demystifying Business," in *The Briarpatch Book: Experiences in Right Livelihood and Simple Living*, ed. Briarpatch Community (San Francisco: New Glide, 1978), 64.

42. Joani Blank, interview with author, July 14, 2008.

43. Winks, interview.

44. Blank, conversation with author, December 9, 2015.

45. Anne Semans, telephone interview with author, June 25, 2002.

46. Winks, interview.

47. Carol Queen, interview with author, June 8, 2002.


## *three* Living the Mission

1. Carrie Schrader, interview with author, June 21, 2001.

2. Schrader, interview.

3. Schrader, interview.

4. Claire Cavanah, interview with author, August 30, 2001.

5. Cavanah, interview.

6. Cavanah, interview.

7. Rachel Venning, telephone interview with author, March 14, 2002.

8. Cavanah, interview.

9. Schrader, interview.

10. James Twitchell, *Branded Nation: The Marketing of Megachurch, College Inc., and Museumworld* (New York: Simon and Schuster, 2004), 48.

11. Twitchell, *Branded Nation*, 4.

12. Marc Gobé, *Emotional Branding: The New Paradigm for Connecting Brands to People* (New York: Allworth, 2001), xiv.

13. Gobé, *Emotional Branding*, xxiii.

14. Tony Hsieh, *Delivering Happiness: A Path to Profits, Passion, and Purpose* (New York: Grand Central, 2010), 151.

15. Babeland Employee Handbook, 2001, 5. Copy on file with author.

16. Cavanah, interview.

17. Heather, interview with author, August 1, 2001.

18. See Bernd Schmitt, *Experiential Marketing: How to Get Customers to Sense, Feel, Think, Act, and Relate to Your Company and Brands* (New York: Free Press, 1999).

19. Juawana, interview with author, July 1, 2015.

20. Juawana, interview.

21. Juawana, interview.

22. Carrie Schrader, interview with author, November 21, 2001.

23. Rebecca Denk, telephone interview with author, October 12, 2003.

24. Jacq Jones, interview with author, April 12, 2002.

25. Amy Andre, telephone interview with author, July 10, 2008.

26. Andre, interview.

27. By many accounts, Blank had the business appraised for only a fraction of what it was worth. The recapitalization plan included a note for $462,252, payable over fifteen years, with interest at 7 percent compounded monthly. According to legal documents, the original group of worker-owners included Leigh Davidson, Laura Miller, Anne Semans, Cathy Winks, Amy Ottinger, Asha Gunabalan, Carol Queen, Caroline Streeter, Deborah Mayer, Roma Estevez, Staci Haines, and Terri Hague.

28. Terri Hague, telephone interview with author, March 28, 2002.

29. Cathy Winks, telephone interview with author, June 27, 2002.

30. Anne Semans, telephone interview with author, June 25, 2002.

31. Winks, interview.

32. Winks, interview.

33. Charlie Glickman, telephone interview with author, November 2, 2007.

34. Semans, interview.

35. Sarah Kennedy, interview with author, June 13, 2002.

36. Isaiah Benjamin, interview with author, June 7, 2002.

37. Matie Fricker, interview with author, June 25, 2008.

38. "Jacq Jones on Her Baltimore Sex-Positive Shop Sugar and Selling Sex Toys in the Age of the Internet," *Sex Out Loud* Radio with Tristan Taormino on VoiceAmerica, November 14, 2014.

39. Jacq Jones, telephone interview with author, October 11, 2007.

40. Jones, telephone interview.

41. Jones, telephone interview.

## *four* Repackaging Sex

1. Peter Stallybrass and Allon White, *The Politics and Poetics of Transgression* (Ithaca, NY: Cornell University Press, 1986), 3.

2. Rita Mae Brown, "The Last Straw," in *Class and Feminism*, ed. Charlotte Bunch and Nancy Myron (Baltimore, MD: Diana Press, 1974), 15.

3. Lisa Henderson, *Love and Money: Queers, Class, and Cultural Production* (New York: New York University Press, 2013), 5.

4. Claire Cavanah, interview with author, August 30, 2001.

5. Cathy Winks, telephone interview with author, June 27, 2002.

6. Candida Royale, "What's a Nice Girl Like You . . . ," in *The Feminist Porn Book: The Politics of Producing Pleasure*, ed. Tristan Taormino, Celine Parreñas Shimizu, Constance Penley, and Mireille Miller-Young (New York: Feminist Press, 2013), 62.

7. I borrow the idea of sexual vernaculars from communication scholar Cindy Patton, who argues that sexual performances, identities, and networks are constructed in and as sexual languages or vernaculars. Rather than being universal, sexual vernaculars are intimately connected to specific communities and subcultures of people who have their own ways of speaking about sex and organizing sexual knowledge and meanings. See Cindy Patton, "Safe Sex and the Pornographic Vernacular," in *How Do I Look? Queer Film and Video*, ed. Bad Object-Choices (Seattle: Bay Press, 1991), 31–50.

8. Alicia Relles, interview with author, October 25, 2001.

9. Charlie Glickman, interview with author, June 15, 2002.

10. Carol Queen, interview with author, June 8, 2002.

11. Kim Airs, interview with author, August 4, 1999.

12. Queen, interview, emphasis added.

13. Roma Estevez, interview with author, November 7, 1999.

14. Winks, interview.

15. Anne Semans, telephone interview with author, June 25, 2002.

16. Pierre Bourdieu, *Distinction: A Social Critique of the Judgement of Taste*, trans. Richard Nice (Cambridge, MA: Harvard University Press, 1984), 56.

17. Laura Weide, telephone interview with author, February 2, 2002.

18. See Beverley Skeggs, *Formations of Class and Gender: Becoming Respectable* (London: Sage, 1997).

19. Jacq Jones, telephone interview with author, October 11, 2007.

20. Ellen Barnard, interview with author, June 25, 2007.

21. Merl Storr, *Latex and Lingerie: Shopping for Pleasure at Ann Summers Parties* (Oxford: Berg, 2003), 126.

22. Storr, *Latex and Lingerie*, 126.

23. Amy Andre, telephone interview with author, July 10, 2008.

24. Aileen Journey, interview with author, October 25, 1998.

25. Searah Deysach, interview with author, June 24, 2007.

26. Jones, interview.

27. Tracy Clark-Flory, "Mixed Vibes from Good Vibrations," *Salon*, April 3, 2006, http://www.salon.com/2006/04/03/goodvibes/.

28. Estevez, interview.

29. Cavanah, interview.

30. Winks, interview.

31. Journey, interview.

32. Cavanah, interview.

33. Laura Kipnis, *Bound and Gagged: Pornography and the Politics of Fantasy in America* (Durham, NC: Duke University Press, 1999).

34. Kipnis, *Bound and Gagged*, 130.

35. Candida Royalle, telephone interview with author, November 7, 2001.

36. Royalle, interview.

37. Winks, interview.

38. Juawana, interview with author, July 1, 2015.

39. Brian Caulfield, "New Business Raises 'Adult-Oriented' Issue," *Berkeley Voice*, February 16, 1995.

40. Queen, interview.

41. For a discussion of zoning and its effects, see Lynn Comella, "Reinventing Times Square: Cultural Value and Images of 'Citizen Disney,'" in *Critical Cultural Policy Studies: A Reader*, ed. Justin Lewis and Toby Miller (Malden, MA: Blackwell, 2003), 316–326.

42. Matie Fricker, interview with author, June 26, 2008.

43. As quoted in Christie Chisholm, "Self Serve Created a Community That Celebrates Sexuality," *Albuquerque Business First*, February 14, 2010.

44. Fricker, interview.

## *five* The Politics of Products

1. Tyler Merriman, interview with author, February 19, 2002.

2. Merriman, interview.

3. Rachel Venning, telephone interview with author, March 14, 2002.

4. Searah Deysach, e-mail to author, December 11, 2012.

5. Searah Deysach, interview with author, June 24, 2007.

6. Searah Deysach, interview with author, April 24, 2015.

7. Joani Blank, conversation with author, December 9, 2015.

8. Anne Semans, telephone interview with author, June 25, 2002.

9. Susie Bright, telephone interview with author, June 18, 2010.

10. Bright, interview.

11. Bright, interview.

12. Roma Estevez, "Good Vibrations" (unpublished paper, University of Massachusetts, Amherst, 2000), 20.

13. Cathy Winks, *The Good Vibrations Guide to Adult Videos* (San Francisco: Down There Press, 1998), vii.

14. Carol Queen, "Good Vibrations, Women, and Porn: A History," in *New Views on Pornography: Sexuality, Politics, and the Law*, ed. Lynn Comella and Shira Tarrant (Santa Barbara, CA: Praeger, 2015), 184.

15. Queen, "Good Vibrations," 186.

16. Roma Estevez, interview with author, November 7, 1999.

17. Queen, "Good Vibrations," 187.

18. Queen, "Good Vibrations," 189.

19. Marilyn Bishara, interview with author, June 5, 2002.

20. Bishara, interview.

21. Cathy Winks, telephone interview with author, June 27, 2002.

22. Marlene Hoeber, telephone interview with author, August 27, 2015.

23. Tristan Taormino, telephone interview with author, December 17, 2015.

24. Bishara, interview.

25. Bright, interview.

26. Metis Black, telephone interview with author, April 1, 2008.

27. Winks, interview.

28. Greg DeLong, interview with author, December 1, 2010.

29. DeLong, interview.

30. Laura Haave, telephone interview with author, November 20, 2013.

31. Haave, interview.

32. Jennifer Pritchett, interview with author, September 16, 2012.

33. Nils H. Nilsson, Bjørn Malmgren-Hansen, Nils Bernth, Eva Pedersen, and Kirsten Pommer, "Survey and Health Assessment of Chemical Substances in Sex Toys," Danish Ministry of the Environment, 2006.

34. Pritchett, interview.

35. Alliyah Mirza, telephone interview with author, August 22, 2010.

36. Ellen Barnard, interview with author, June 25, 2007.

37. Metis Black, telephone interview with author, August 22, 2010.

38. Carol Queen, e-mail to author, August 23, 2010.

39. Mirza, interview.

40. Queen, e-mail.

41. Pritchett, interview.

## six Sexperts and Sex Talk

1. Molly Adler, interview with author, June 25, 2008.

2. Michelle Fine, "Sexuality, Schooling, and Adolescent Females: The Missing Discourse of Desire," *Harvard Education Review* 58, no. 1 (1988): 29–53.

3. Fine, "Sexuality, Schooling, and Adolescent Females," 33.

4. Fine, "Sexuality, Schooling, and Adolescent Females," 35.

5. Amy T. Schalet et al., "Invited Commentary: Broadening the Evidence for Adolescent Sexual and Reproductive Health and Education in the United States," *Journal of Youth and Adolescence* 43 (2014): 1596.

6. See Douglas B. Kirby, "The Impact of Abstinence and Comprehensive Sex and

STD/HIV Education Programs on Adolescent Sexual Behavior," *Sexuality Research and Social Policy* 5, no. 3 (2008): 18–27.

7. Research suggests that the sexual double standard, which encourages and celebrates heterosexual behavior in teenage boys while stigmatizing sexual experience in teenage girls, can harm girls by reducing their ability to negotiate in sexual encounters and by conditioning them to believe their sexual desires are less important than those of their male partners. Gender ideologies also hurt boys and men by suggesting that their sex drives and sexual prowess define them.

8. See Victor C. Strasburger and Sarah S. Brown, "Sex Education in the 21st Century," *Journal of the American Medical Association* 312, no. 2 (2014): 125–126.

9. Debby Herbenick and Michael Reece, "Sex Education in Adult Retail Stores," *American Journal of Sexuality Education* 2, no. 1 (2006): 57–75.

10. Herbenick and Reece, "Sex Education in Adult Retail Stores," 70.

11. Metis Black, "Bridging Sex Education and Adult Retail," *American Journal of Sexuality Education* 7, no. 4 (2012): 482.

12. For a useful discussion of the differences between a sexpert, expert, and sexologist, see Carol Queen, "Sexperts, Experts and Sexologists . . . Oh My," *Adult Video News*, October 1, 2009, http://business.avn.com/articles/novelty/Sexperts-Experts-and-Sex ologists-Oh-My-368942.html.

13. Jamye Waxman, "The New Sex Educators," *Adult Video News*, May 5, 2008, http://business.avn.com/articles/novelty/The-New-Sex-Educators-52605.html.

14. Susie Bright, telephone interview with author, June 18, 2010.

15. Joani Blank, interview with author, June 12, 2002.

16. Susie Bright, e-mail to author, June 15, 2015.

17. Lizz Randall, interview with author, February 22, 2002.

18. Tristan Taormino, telephone interview with author, November 2, 1999.

19. Alicia Relles, interview with author, October 25, 2001.

20. Ellen Barnard, interview with author, June 25, 2007.

21. Claire Cavanah, interview with author, August 30, 2001.

22. Janell Davis, telephone interview with author, November 9, 2001.

23. Carol Queen, "Continuing Education" (draft for Good Vibrations newsletter), n.d. Photocopy on file with author.

24. Queen, "Continuing Education."

25. Queen, "Continuing Education."

26. Roma Estevez, interview with author, November 7, 1999.

27. Carol Queen, "Memo to Staff," December 1, 1993. Photocopy on file with author.

28. For a detailed discussion about what sex positivity is and is not, see Carol Queen's discussion in *The Sex and Pleasure Book: Good Vibrations Guide to Great Sex for Everyone* (Concord, CA: Barnaby, 2015), 29–31.

29. Claire Cavanah, "Sex Toys 101" (lecture, Bluestockings, New York City, September 7, 2001).

30. Blank, interview.

31. Rachel Venning, telephone interview with author, March 14, 2002.

32. Cavanah, interview.

33. Randall, interview.

34. Venning, interview.

35. Carol Queen and Lynn Comella, "The Necessary Revolution: Sex-Positive Feminism in the Post-Barnard Era," *Communication Review* 11, no. 3 (2008): 287.

36. Carol Queen, interview with author, June 8, 2002.

37. Christine Rinki, interview with author, October 16, 2001.

38. Isaiah Benjamin, interview with author, June 7, 2002.

39. Michel Foucault, *The History of Sexuality*, vol. 1: *An Introduction* (New York: Vintage, 1978), 18.

40. Searah Deysach, interview with author, June 24, 2007.

41. Blank, interview.

42. Charlie Glickman, interview with author, June 15, 2002.

43. Randall, interview.

44. Davis, interview.

45. Amy Andre, telephone interview with author, July 10, 2008.

46. Andre, interview.

47. Andre, interview.

48. John Stagliano and Ernest Greene, dirs., *The Ultimate Guide to Anal Sex for Women* (Evil Angel Video, 1999), DVD.

49. Tristan Taormino, *Down and Dirty Sex Secrets* (New York: Ragan, 2001), 1.

50. Taormino, *Down and Dirty Sex Secrets*, 3.

51. Robert Eberwein, *Sex Ed: Film, Video, and the Framework of Desire* (New Brunswick, NJ: Rutgers University Press, 1999).

52. Taormino, interview.

53. Shar Rednour and Jackie Strano, dirs., *Bend Over Boyfriend* (Fatale Video, 1998), DVD.

54. Jackie Strano, interview with author, June 7, 2002.

55. Shar Rednour and Jackie Strano, "Steamy, Hot, and Political: Creating Radical Dyke Porn," in *New Views on Pornography: Sexuality, Politics, and the Law*, ed. Lynn Comella and Shira Tarrant (Santa Barbara, CA: Praeger, 2015), 169.

56. Shar Rednour, interview with author, June 7, 2002.

57. Rednour and Strano, "Steamy, Hot, and Political," 169.

58. Rednour and Strano, "Steamy, Hot, and Political," 170.

## *seven* Selling Identity

1. Letter from customer to Babeland, December 1999. Unprocessed corporate document. Retrieved from Babeland Seattle, February 2002.

2. Himani Bannerji, *Thinking Through: Essays on Feminism, Marxism and Anti-racism* (Toronto: Women's Press, 1995), 17.

3. Dell Williams and Lynn Vannucci, *Revolution in the Garden: Memoirs of the Garden Keeper* (Santa Rosa, CA: Silverback, 2005), 203.

4. Dell Williams, interview with author, November 28, 2001.

5. Alice Echols, *Daring to Be Bad: Radical Feminism in America 1967–1975* (Minneapolis: University of Minnesota Press, 1989), 245.

6. Norma Alarcón, "The Theoretical Subject(s) of *This Bridge Called My Back* and Anglo-American Feminism," in *Making Face, Making Soul: Haciendo Caras*, ed. G. Anzaldúa (San Francisco: Aunt Lute, 1990), 360.

7. Janell Davis, telephone interview with author, November 9, 2001.

8. Amy Andre, telephone interview with author, July 10, 2008.

9. Nenna Joiner, interview with author, July 14, 2008.

10. Nenna Joiner, interview with author, September 16, 2011.

11. Nenna Joiner, *Never Let the Odds Stop You* (Oakland, CA: Nenna Feelmore, 2015), 4.

12. Joiner, interview, September 16, 2011.

13. Nenna Joiner, telephone interview with author, October 11, 2015.

14. Joiner, interview, October 11, 2015.

15. Joiner, interview, September 16, 2011.

16. Babeland Roundtable, group interview with author, November 23, 2002.

17. Babeland Roundtable, interview.

18. Babeland Roundtable, interview.

19. Paula Gilovich, interview with author, February 19, 2002.

20. Davis, interview.

21. Lizz Randall, interview with author, February 22, 2002.

22. Randall, interview.

23. Felice Shays, interview with author, November 27, 2001.

24. Archer Parr, interview with author, June 7, 2002.

25. Babeland Roundtable, interview.

26. Searah Deysach, interview with author, April 24, 2015.

27. Molly Adler, interview with author, June 25, 2008.

28. Adler, interview.

29. Adler, interview.

30. Rachel Venning, telephone interview with author, March 14, 2002.

31. Kim Airs, interview with author, August 4, 1999.

32. Robert Lawrence, telephone interview with author, August 25, 2015.

33. Carol Queen, interview with author, June 8, 2002.

34. Queen, interview.

35. Babeland Roundtable, interview.

36. Babeland Roundtable, interview.

37. Terri Hague, telephone interview with author, March 28, 2002.

38. Charlie Glickman, interview with author, June 15, 2002.

39. Thomas Roche, interview with author, June 17, 2002.

40. Davis, interview.

41. Laura Haave, telephone interview with author, November 20, 2013.

42. Ellen Barnard, interview with author, June 25, 2007.

43. Barnard, interview.

44. Queen, interview.

45. Roma Estevez, interview with author, November 22, 1999.

46. Estevez, interview.

47. Babeland Roundtable, interview.

48. Claire Cavanah, interview with author, August 30, 2001.

49. Glickman, interview.

50. Coyote Days, interview with author, March 18, 2008.

51. Dena Hankins, interview with author, June 10, 2002.

52. Tristan Taormino, "The Queer Heterosexual," *Village Voice*, May 6, 2003, http://www.villagevoice.com/news/the-queer-heterosexual-6410490.

53. Jacq Jones, interview with author, April 12, 2002.

54. Jones, interview.

55. Laura Weide, interview with author, June 11, 2002.

56. Strano quoted in Tristan Taormino, "Dyke Porn Moguls Shar Rednour and Jackie Strano," *On Our Backs*, June–July 2000, 31.

57. Rednour quoted in Taormino, "Dyke Porn Moguls," 31.

58. Strano quoted in Taormino, "Dyke Porn Moguls," 31, emphasis mine.

59. Dana Clark, interview with author, August 24, 2001.

60. Adler, interview.

61. Deysach, interview with author, June 24, 2007.

62. Isaiah Benjamin, interview with author, June 7, 2002.

63. Weide, interview.

64. Shays, interview.

65. Samuel R. Delany, *Times Square Red, Times Square Blue* (New York: New York University Press, 1999), 123.

66. Delany, *Times Square Red*, 128.

## *eight* Profitability and Social Change

1. Claire Cavanah, interview with author, August 30, 2001.

2. Annie Michelson, telephone interview with author, February 25, 2002.

3. Alicia Relles, interview with author, October 25, 2001.

4. Dell Williams, interview with author, November 20, 2001.

5. As quoted in "A New Breed of Entrepreneur," *Ms.*, January 1984.

6. Williams, interview.

7. Joani Blank, telephone interview with author, February 6, 2002.

8. Anne Semans, telephone interview with author, June 25, 2002.

9. Cathy Winks, telephone interview with author, June 27, 2002.

10. Semans, interview.

11. Winks, interview.

12. Semans, interview.

13. Terri Hague, telephone interview with author, March 28, 2002.

14. Ziadee Whiptail, telephone interview with author, March 29, 2002.

15. Hague, interview.

16. Ben Doyle, interview with author, June 17, 2002.

17. Carrie Schrader, interview with author, June 21, 2001.

18. Joani Blank, interview with author, June 12, 2002.

19. Skoll World Forum, "The Rise of Social Entrepreneurship Suggests a Possible Future for Global Capitalism," *Forbes*, May 2, 2013, http://www.forbes.com/sites/skoll worldforum/2013/05/02/the-rise-of-social-entrepreneurship-suggests-a-possible -future-for-global-capitalism/#e5d7b4ee13bd.

20. Mee-Hyoe Koo, "Interview with Bill Drayton, Pioneer of Social Entrepreneur-ship," *Forbes*, September 30, 2013, http://www.forbes.com/sites/meehyoekoo/2013/09 /30/interview-with-bill-drayton-pioneer-of-social-entrepreneurship/#67101eb4692b.

21. J. Gregory Dees, "The Meaning of Social Entrepreneurship," Duke Innovation and Entrepreneurship, October 31, 1998, https://entrepreneurship.duke.edu/news-item /the-meaning-of-social-entrepreneurship/.

22. Dees, "The Meaning of Social Entrepreneurship," 5.

23. Laura Haave, telephone interview with author, November 20, 2013.

24. Hague, interview.

25. Christine Rinki, interview with author, October 16, 2001.

26. Cavanah, interview.

27. Searah Deysach, interview with author, June 24, 2007.

28. Cavanah, interview.

29. Rachel Venning, telephone interview with author, March 14, 2002.

30. Venning, interview.

31. Brooke William and Hannah Darby, "God, Mom, and Apple Pie: 'Feminist' Busi-nesses as an Extension of the American Dream," *off our backs*, February 28, 1976; on the debate, Jennifer Woodhul, "What's This about Feminist Businesses?," in *Feminist Frameworks: Alternative Theoretical Accounts of the Relationships between Women and Men*, ed. A. M. Jaggar and P. Rothenberg (New York: McGraw-Hill, 1978): 196–204.

32. Felice Shays, interview with author, November 27, 2001.

33. Tyler Merriman, interview with author, February 19, 2002.

34. Venning, interview.

35. Hague, interview.

36. Tristan Taormino, telephone interview with author, November 2, 1999.

37. Jacq Jones, interview with author, April 12, 2002.

38. Lori D. Ginzberg, *Women and the Work of Benevolence: Morality, Politics, and Class in the Nineteenth-Century United States* (New Haven, CT: Yale University Press, 1990), 34.

39. Ginzberg, *Women and the Work of Benevolence*, 13.

40. Ginzberg, *Women and the Work of Benevolence*, 42.

41. Deysach, interview.

42. Jones, interview.

43. Roma Estevez, interview with author, November 7, 1999.

44. Brandie Taylor, interview with author, February 21, 2002.

45. Winks, interview.

46. Estevez, interview.

47. Winks, interview.

48. Venning, interview.

49. Kathy Peiss, "American Women and the Making of Modern Consumer Culture," *Journal for MultiMedia History* 1, no. 1 (fall 1998), http://www.albany.edu/jmmh/vo11no1/peiss-text.html.

50. David Chaney, "The Department Store as a Cultural Form," *Theory, Culture and Society* 1, no. 3 (1983): 22.

51. Laura Weide, interview with author, June 11, 2002.

52. Cavanah, interview.

53. The advertisement read as follows: "[Babeland], the woman owned sex-toy store, is seeking a General Business Manager. This is a job you can put both your heart and your mind into. Responsibilities include planning, managing, and controlling the profitable operation of two far flung retail stores and an e-commerce site in a manner consistent with the values and mission of the company. The basic function of this position is to achieve revenue and income goals, while maintaining a positive work environment for the staff. It is a CFO crossed with den mother. The ability to lead and inspire a team of 6 or more managers and a staff of 30+ employees is essential."

54. Venning, interview.

55. Cavanah, interview.

56. Merriman, interview.

57. Rebecca Denk, telephone interview with author, October 12, 2003.

58. Denk, interview.

59. Taylor, interview.

60. Whiptail, interview.

## conclusion

1. Ilana DeBare, "Competition Has Shaken Good Vibrations," *San Francisco Chronicle*, September 7, 2007, http://www.sfgate.com/business/article/Competition-has-shaken-Good-Vibrations-2504754.php.

2. As quoted in Heather Cassell, "Good Vibrations Announces Merger," *Bay Area Reporter*, October 4, 2007, http://www.ebar.com/news/article.php?sec=news&article=2281.

3. Searah Deysach, e-mail to author, October 2, 2007.

4. Searah Deysach, interview with author, June 24, 2007.

5. Ziadee Whiptail, telephone interview with author, March 29, 2002.

6. Ellen Barnard, interview with author, June 25, 2007.

7. Deysach, interview, June 24, 2007.

8. Matie Fricker, telephone interview with author, December 18, 2015.

9. Fricker, interview, December 18, 2015.

10. Fricker, interview, December 18, 2015. Other PPC stores include Good for Her, Nomia, Oh My, She Bop, and the Tool Shed.

11. Lena Solow, telephone interview with author, July 8, 2016.

12. Rachel Venning, telephone interview with author, July 19, 2016.

13. Kim Airs, personal correspondence with author, July 18, 2016.

14. Matie Fricker, telephone interview with author, July 7, 2016.

15. bell hooks, *Feminism Is for Everybody: Passionate Politics* (Cambridge, MA: South End, 2000).

16. Venning, interview.

17. Solow, interview.

18. Joel Kaminsky, interview with author, November 14, 2013.

19. Kaminsky, interview.

20. Amy Luna, "Good Vibes Has Gone from Progressive to Regressive," Yelp review, March 31, 2014, https://www.yelp.com/user_details?userid=qKySbE7IgoJ-Muo_xFb32w.

21. Luna, "Good Vibes."

22. Violet Blue, "Phil Bronstein on Good Vibrations: Not for Women Anymore?" Tiny Nibbles (blog), August 17, 2009, http://www.tinynibbles.com/blogarchives/2009/08/phil-bronstein-on-good-vibrations-not-for-women-anymore.html.

23. Joani Blank, conversation with author, December 10, 2015.

24. Hallie Lieberman, "If You Mold It, They Will Come," *Bitch*, summer 2015, 20–22.

25. Tom Major, "Melbourne's RMIT University Runs a Design Course on How to Make Sex Toys," *Sydney Morning Herald*, January 22, 2016, http://www.smh.com.au/national/melbournes-rmit-university-runs-design-course-on-how-to-make-sex-toys-20151224-glulcj.html.

26. Bianca London, "Is This Fifty Shades Too Far? New Book-Themed Collection of Sex Toys Aimed at the Frustrated Housewives of Middle England," *Mail Online*, Octo-

ber 2, 2012, http://www.dailymail.co.uk/femail/article-2211596/50-Shades-Of-Grey
-sex-toys-The-collection-E-L-James-hopes-spice-Middle-England.html.

27. For an interesting discussion regarding the difference between so-called pornographic marketing and more female-friendly approaches, see Shelly Ronen, "Properly
Selling the Improper," *Thresholds* 44 (2016): 122.

28. Greg DeLong, interview with author, April 8, 2008.

29. Metis Black, e-mail to author, December 17, 2015.

30. Black, e-mail.

31. Candida Royalle interview, 2008, YouTube video, https://www.youtube.com
/watch?v=lpVBgk_EJrw.

32. Rachel Venning, e-mail to author, January 24, 2008.

33. Brooke William and Hannah Darby, "God, Mom, and Apple Pie: 'Feminist' Businesses as an Extension of the American Dream," *off our backs*, February 28, 1976.

34. Venning, e-mail.

35. Jacq Jones, e-mail to author, January 24, 2008.

36. Jacq Jones, e-mail to author, December 17, 2015.

37. Amber, telephone interview with author, December 29, 2015.

38. Amber, interview.

## *appendix*

1. Paul du Gay, *Production of Culture/Cultures of Production* (London: Sage, 1997), 1.

2. Georgina Voss, "'Treating It as a Normal Business': Researching the Pornography
Industry," *Sexualities* 15, no. 3–4 (2012): 391–410; also see Lynn Comella and Katherine
Sender, "Doing It: Methodological Challenges of Communication Research on Sexu-
ality," *International Journal of Communication* 7 (2013): 2560–2574; Lynn Comella,
"Studying Porn Cultures," *Porn Studies* 1, no. 1–2 (2014): 64–70.

3. Voss, "'Treating It as a Normal Business,'" 404.

4. George Marcus, "Ethnography in/of the World System: The Emergence of Multi-
sited Ethnography," *Annual Review of Anthropology* 24 (1995): 97.

5. Michael Burawoy, "The Extended Case Method," in *Ethnography Unbound: Power
and Resistance in the Modern Metropolis* (Berkeley: University of California Press), 271–
300.

6. Burawoy, "The Extended Case Method," 278.

7. Barbara Tedlock, "From Participant Observation to the Observation of Participation: The Emergence of Narrative Ethnography," *Journal of Anthropological Research*
47 (1991): 69.

# SELECTED
# BIBLIOGRAPHY

Alarcón, Norma. "The Theoretical Subject(s) of *This Bridge Called My Back* and Anglo-American Feminism." In *Making Face, Making Soul: Haciendo Caras*, edited by Gloria Anzaldúa, 356–369. San Francisco: Aunt Lute, 1990.

Allyn, David. *Make Love, Not War: The Sexual Revolution, An Unfettered History.* Boston: Little, Brown, 2000.

Atkinson, Ti-Grace. "The Institution of Sexual Intercourse." In *Notes from the Second Year: Women's Liberation*, edited by Shulamith Firestone and Anne Koedt, 42–47. New York: Radical Feminists, 1970.

Attwood, Feona. "Fashion and Passion: Marketing Sex to Women." *Sexualities* 8, no. 4 (2005): 392–406.

Ayers, Toni, Maggi Rubenstein, and Carolyn Haynes Smith. *Masturbation Techniques for Women/Getting in Touch.* San Francisco: Multimedia Resource Center, 1972.

Bannerji, Himani. *Thinking Through: Essays on Feminism, Marxism and Anti-racism.* Toronto: Women's Press, 1995.

Barbach, Lonnie. *For Yourself: The Fulfillment of Female Sexuality.* New York: Signet, 1975.

Benson, Susan Porter. *Counter Cultures: Saleswomen, Managers, and Customers in American Department Stores 1890–1940.* Urbana: University of Illinois Press, 1993.

Black, Metis. "Bridging Sex Education and Adult Retail." *American Journal of Sexuality Education* 7, no. 4 (2012): 480–482.

Blank, Joani. "Good Business Vibrations." In *The Woman-Centered Economy: Ideals, Reality, and the Space in Between*, edited by Loraine Edwalds and Midge Stocker, 205–208. Chicago: Third Side Press, 1995.

Blank, Joani. "Good, Good, Good, Good Vibrations." In *That Takes Ovaries! Bold Females and Their Brazen Acts*, edited by Rivka Solomon, 82–85. New York: Three Rivers, 2002.

Blank, Joani. *Good Vibrations: The Complete Woman's Guide to Vibrators.* Burlingame, CA: Down There Press, 1976.

Blank, Joani. *The Playbook for Women about Sex.* Burlingame, CA: Down There Press, 1975.

Boston Women's Health Book Collective. *Our Bodies, Ourselves: A Course by and for Women*. Boston: New England Free Press, 1971.

Bourdieu, Pierre. *Distinction: A Social Critique of the Judgement of Taste*. Translated by Richard Nice. Cambridge, MA: Harvard University Press, 1984.

Brents, Barb G., Crystal A. Jackson, and Kate Hausbeck. *The State of Sex: Tourism, Sex, and Sin in the New American Heartland*. New York: Routledge, 2010.

Bright, Susie. *Big Sex Little Death: A Memoir*. Berkeley: Seal, 2011.

Bright, Susie. *Susie Sexpert's Lesbian Sex World*. Pittsburgh: Cleis, 1990.

Bronstein, Carolyn. *Battling Pornography: The American Feminist Anti-pornography Movement, 1976–1986*. Cambridge: Cambridge University Press, 2011.

Brown, Rita Mae. "The Last Straw." In *Class and Feminism*, edited by Charlotte Bunch and Nancy Myron, 14–23. Baltimore, MD: Diana, 1974.

Burawoy, Michael, et al. *Ethnography Unbound: Power and Resistance in the Modern Metropolis*. Berkeley: University of California Press, 1991.

Chalker, Rebecca. *The Clitoral Truth: The Secret World at Your Fingertips*. New York: Seven Stories, 2000.

Chaney, David. "The Department Store as a Cultural Form." *Theory, Culture and Society* 1, no. 3 (1983): 22–31.

Chasin, Alexandra. *Selling Out: The Gay and Lesbian Movement Goes to Market*. Basingstoke, U.K.: Palgrave, 2000.

Chazan, Alana. "Good Vibrations: Liberating Sexuality from the Commercial Regulation of Sexual Devices." *Texas Journal of Women and Law* 18 (2009): 263–305.

Comella, Lynn. "Fifty Shades of Erotic Stimulation." *Feminist Media Studies* 13, no. 3 (2013): 563–566.

Comella, Lynn. "Re-inventing Times Square: Cultural Value and Images of 'Citizen Disney.'" In *Critical Cultural Policy Studies: A Reader*, edited by Justin Lewis and Toby Miller, 316–326. Malden, MA: Blackwell, 2003.

Comella, Lynn. "(Safe) *Sex and the City*: On Vibrators, Masturbation, and the Myth of 'Real' Sex." *Feminist Media Studies* 3, no. 1 (2003): 107–110.

Comella, Lynn. "Studying Porn Cultures." *Porn Studies* 1, no. 1–2 (2014): 64–70.

Comella, Lynn, and Katherine Sender. "Doing It: Methodological Challenges of Communication Research on Sexuality." *International Journal of Communication* 7 (2013): 2560–2574.

Comella, Lynn, and Shira Tarrant, eds. *New Views on Pornography: Sexuality, Politics, and the Law*. Santa Barbara, CA: Praeger, 2015.

Commission on Obscenity and Pornography. *The Report of the Commission on Obscenity and Pornography*. New York: Bantam, 1970.

Davila, Arlene. *Latinos, Inc.: The Marketing and Making of a People*. Berkeley: University of California Press, 2001.

Davis, Kathy. *The Making of* Our Bodies, Ourselves: *How Feminism Travels across Borders*. Durham, NC: Duke University Press, 2007.

Delany, Samuel R. *Times Square Red, Times Square Blue*. New York: New York University Press, 1999.

D'Emilio, John, and Estelle Freedman. *Intimate Matters: A History of Sexuality in America*. Chicago: University of Chicago Press, 1997.

Dines, Gail. *Pornland: How Porn Has Hijacked Our Sexuality*. Boston: Beacon, 2010.

Dodson, Betty. *Liberating Masturbation: A Meditation on Self Love*. New York: Betty Dodson, 1974.

Dodson, Betty. *My Romantic Love Wars: A Sexual Memoir*. New York: Betty Dodson, 2010. PDF e-book.

Dodson, Betty. "Porn Wars." In *The Feminist Porn Book: The Politics of Producing Pleasure*, edited by Tristan Taormino, Celine Parreñas Shimizu, Constance Penley, and Mireille Miller-Young, 23–31. New York: The Feminist Press, 2013.

Dodson, Betty. *Sex for One: The Joy of Selfloving*. New York: Three Rivers, 1996.

du Gay, Paul. *Production of Culture/Cultures of Production*. London: Sage, 1997.

Duggan, Lisa, and Nan Hunter. *Sex Wars: Sexual Dissent and Political Culture*. New York: Routledge, 1995.

Eberwein, Robert. *Sex Ed: Film, Video, and the Framework of Desire*. New Brunswick, NJ: Rutgers University Press, 1999.

Echols, Alice. *Daring to Be Bad: Radical Feminism in America 1967–1975*. Minneapolis: University of Minnesota Press, 1989.

Edwalds, Loraine, and Midge Stocker, eds. *The Woman-Centered Economy: Ideals, Reality and the Space in Between*. Chicago: Third Side, 1995.

Ehrenreich, Barbara. *The Hearts of Men: American Dreams and the Flight from Commitment*. New York: Anchor, 1983.

Ehrenreich, Barbara, Elizabeth Hess, and Gloria Jacobs. *Re-making Love: The Feminization of Sex*. Garden City, NY: Anchor Press/Doubleday, 1986.

Evans, Sara. *Personal Politics: The Roots of Women's Liberation in the Civil Rights Movement and the New Left*. New York: Vintage, 1979.

Faderman, Lillian. *Odd Girls and Twilight Lovers: A History of Lesbian Life in Twentieth-Century America*. New York: Penguin, 1991.

Farrell, Amy Erdman. *Yours in Sisterhood: Ms. Magazine and the Promise of Popular Feminism*. Chapel Hill: University of North Carolina Press, 1998.

Federation of Feminist Women's Health Centers. *A New View of a Woman's Body: A Fully Illustrated Guide*. West Hollywood, CA: Feminist Health, 1991.

Feelmore, Nenna. *Never Let the Odds Stop You*. Oakland, CA: Nenna Feelmore, 2015.

Findlay, Heather. "Freud's 'Fetishism' and the Lesbian Dildo Debates." *Feminist Studies* 18, no. 3 (1992): 563–579.

Fine, Michelle. "Sexuality, Schooling, and Adolescent Females: The Missing Discourse of Desire." *Harvard Education Review* 58, no. 1 (1988): 29–53.

Foucault, Michel. *The History of Sexuality*, vol. 1. New York: Vintage, 1978.

Frank, Katherine. *G-Strings and Sympathy: Strip Club Regulars and Male Desire*. Durham, NC: Duke University Press, 2002.

Freud, Sigmund. *New Introductory Lectures on Psychoanalysis*. Translated by J. Strachey. New York: Norton, 1965.

Friedan, Betty. *The Feminine Mystique*. New York: Norton, 2001 (1963).

Ginzberg, Lori D. *Women and the Work of Benevolence: Morality, Politics, and Class in the Nineteenth-Century United States*. New Haven, CT: Yale University Press, 1990.

Gobé, Marc. *Emotional Branding: The New Paradigm for Connecting Brands to People*. New York: Allworth, 2001.

Hardy, Kate, Sarah Kingston, and Teela Sanders, eds. *New Sociologies of Sex Work*. Farnham, U.K.: Ashgate, 2010.

Henderson, Lisa. *Love and Money: Queers, Class, and Cultural Production*. New York: New York University Press, 2013.

Herbenick, Debby, and Michael Reece. "Sex Education in Adult Retail Stores." *American Journal of Sexuality Education* 2, no. 1 (2006): 57–75.

Herbenick, Debby, Michael Reece, Stephanie A. Sanders, Brian Dodge, Annahita Ghassemi, and J. Dennis Fortenberry. "Prevalence and Characteristics of Vibrator Use by Women in the United States: Results from a Nationally Representative Study." *Journal of Sexual Medicine* 6 (2009): 1857–1866.

Herbenick, Debby, Michael Reece, Stephanie A. Sanders, Brian Dodge, Annahita Ghassemi, and J. Dennis Fortenberry. "Women's Vibrator Use in Sexual Partnerships: Results From a Nationally Representative Survey in the United States." *Journal of Sex and Marital Therapy* 36, no. 1 (2010): 49–65.

Holt, Evans. *A New Look at Masturbation*. Las Vegas: Griffon, 1970.

hooks, bell. *Feminism Is for Everybody: Passionate Politics*. Cambridge, MA: South End, 2000.

Hsieh, Tony. *Delivering Happiness: A Path to Profits, Passion, and Purpose*. New York: Grand Central, 2010.

Irvine, Janice M. *Disorders of Desire: Sex and Gender in Modern American Sexology*. Philadelphia: Temple University Press, 1990.

Jensen, Robert. *Getting Off: Pornography and the End of Masculinity*. Cambridge, MA: South End, 2007.

Johnson, Eithne. "Loving Yourself: The Specular Scene in Sexual Self-Help Advice for Women." In *Collecting Visible Evidence*, edited by Jane M. Gaines and Michael Renov, 216–240. Minneapolis: University of Minnesota Press, 1999.

Juffer, Jane. *At Home with Pornography: Women, Sex, and Everyday Life*. New York: New York University Press, 1998.

Kinsey, Alfred C. *Sexual Behavior in the Human Female*. Philadelphia: Saunders, 1953.

Kipnis, Laura. *Bound and Gagged: Pornography and the Politics of Fantasy in America*. Durham, NC: Duke University Press, 1999.

Kirby, Douglas B. "The Impact of Abstinence and Comprehensive Sex and STD/HIV

Education Programs on Adolescent Sexual Behavior." *Sexuality Research and Social Policy* 5, no. 3 (2008): 18–27.

Koedt, Anne. "The Myth of the Vaginal Orgasm." In *Notes from the Second Year: Women's Liberation*, edited by Shulamith Firestone and Anne Koedt, 37–41. New York: Radical Feminists, 1970.

Laqueur, Thomas W. *Solitary Sex: A Cultural History of Masturbation*. New York: Zone, 2003.

Leach, William. *Land of Desire: Merchants, Power, and the Rise of a New American Culture*. New York: Pantheon, 1993.

Loe, Meika. "Feminism for Sale: Case Study of a Pro-Sex Feminist Business." *Gender and Society* 13, no. 6 (1999): 705–732.

Long, Julia. *Anti-porn: The Resurgence of Anti-pornography Feminism*. London: Zed, 2012.

Maines, Rachel. *The Technology of Orgasm: "Hysteria," the Vibrator, and Women's Sexual Satisfaction*. Baltimore, MD: Johns Hopkins University Press, 1999.

Marcus, George E. "Ethnography in/of the World System: The Emergence of Multi-sited Ethnography." *Annual Review of Anthropology* 24 (1995): 95–117.

Masters, William H., and Virginia Johnson. *Human Sexual Response*. Boston: Little, Brown, 1966.

May, Elaine Tyler. *America and the Pill: A History of Promise, Peril, and Liberation*. New York: Basic Books, 2010.

Miller-Young, Mireille. *A Taste for Brown Sugar: Black Women in Pornography*. Durham, NC: Duke University Press, 2014.

Mukherjee, Roopali, and Sarah Banet-Weiser, eds. *Commodity Activism: Cultural Resistance in Neoliberal Times*. New York: New York University Press, 2012.

Nilsson, Nils H., Bjørn Malmgren-Hansen, Nils Bernth, Eva Pedersen, and Kirsten Pommer. "Survey and Health Assessment of Chemical Substances in Sex Toys." Danish Ministry of the Environment, 2005.

Patton, Cindy. "Safe Sex and the Pornographic Vernacular." In *How Do I Look? Queer Film and Video*, edited by Bad Object-Choices, 31–50. Seattle: Bay Press, 1991.

Peiss, Kathy. "American Women and the Making of Modern Consumer Culture." *Journal for MultiMedia History* 1, no. 1 (fall 1998), http://www.albany.edu/jmmh/vol1no1/peiss-text.html.

Peiss, Kathy. *Hope in a Jar: The Making of America's Beauty Culture*. New York: Metropolitan, 1998.

Queen, Carol. "Good Vibrations, Women, and Porn: A History." In *New Views on Pornography: Sexuality, Politics, and the Law*, edited by Lynn Comella and Shira Tarrant, 179–190. Santa Barbara, CA: Praeger, 2015.

Queen, Carol, and Lynn Comella. "The Necessary Revolution: Sex-Positive Feminism in the Post-Barnard Era." *Communication Review* 11, no. 3 (2008): 274–291.

Queen, Carol, and Shar Rednour. *The Sex and Pleasure Book: Good Vibrations Guide to Great Sex for Everyone*. Concord, CA: Barnaby, 2015.

Rednour, Shar, and Jackie Strano. "Steamy, Hot, and Political: Creating Radical Dyke Porn." In *New Views on Pornography: Sexuality, Politics, and the Law*, edited by Lynn Comella and Shira Tarrant, 165–177. Santa Barbara, CA: Praeger, 2015.

Reece, Michael, Debby Herbenick, and Catherine Sherwood-Puzzello. "Sexual Health Promotion and Adult Retail Stores." *Journal of Sex Research* 41, no. 2 (2004): 173–180.

Reich, Wilhelm. *The Function of the Orgasm: Sex-Economic Problems of Biological Energy*. Translated by V. R. Carfagno. New York: Farrar, Straus and Giroux, 1973.

Ronen, Shelly. "Properly Selling the Improper." *Thresholds* 44 (2016): 117–130.

Rosen, Ruth. *The World Split Open: How the Modern Women's Movement Changed America*. New York: Penguin, 2006.

Royalle, Candida. "What's a Nice Girl Like You . . ." In *The Feminist Porn Book: The Politics of Producing Pleasure*, edited by Tristan Taormino, Celine Parreñas Shimizu, Constance Penley, and Mireille Miller-Young, 58–69. New York: Feminist Press, 2013.

Rubin, Gayle. "Thinking Sex: Notes for a Radical Theory of the Politics of Sexuality." In *The Lesbian and Gay Studies Reader*, edited by Henry Abelove, Michele A. Barale, and David Halperin, 3–44. New York: Routledge, 1993.

Samois. *Coming to Power: Writings and Graphics on Lesbian s/M*. Boston: Alyson, 1981.

Sarachild, Kathie. "A Program for Feminist 'Consciousness Raising.'" In *Notes from the Second Year: Women's Liberation*, edited by Shulamith Firestone and Anne Koedt, 78–80. New York: Radical Feminists, 1970.

Schalet, Amy T., John S. Santelli, Stephen T. Russell, Carolyn T. Halpern, Sarah A. Miller, Sarah S. Pickering, Shoshana K. Goldberg, and Jennifer M. Hoenig. "Invited Commentary: Broadening the Evidence for Adolescent Sexual and Reproductive Health and Education in the United States." *Journal of Youth and Adolescence* 43 (2014): 1595–1610.

Schmitt, Bernd. *Experiential Marketing: How to Get Customers to Sense, Feel, Think, Act, and Relate to Your Company and Brands*. New York: Free Press, 1999.

Schmuckler, Sophie. "How I Learned to Stop Worrying and Love My Dildo." In *Coming to Power: Writings and Graphics on Lesbian s/M*, edited by Samois. Boston: Alyson, 1981.

Sender, Katherine. *Business, Not Politics: The Making of the Gay Market*. New York: Columbia University Press, 2004.

Shulman, Alix. "Organs and Orgasms." In *Woman in Sexist Society: Studies in Power and Powerlessness*, edited by Vivian Gornick and Barbara K. Moran, 292–303. New York: Mentor, 1971.

Sides, Josh. *Erotic City: Sexual Revolutions and the Making of Modern San Francisco*. Oxford: Oxford University Press, 2009.

Skeggs, Beverley. *Formations of Class and Gender: Becoming Respectable*. London: Sage, 1997.

Smith, Clarissa. *One for the Girls: The Pleasures and Practices of Reading Women's Porn*. Bristol, U.K.: Intellect, 2007.

Stallybrass, Peter, and Allon White. *The Politics and Poetics of Transgression*. Ithaca, NY: Cornell University Press, 1986.

Storr, Merl. *Latex and Lingerie: Shopping for Pleasure at Ann Summers Parties*. Oxford: Berg, 2003.

Strasburger, Victor C., and Sarah S. Brown. "Sex Education in the 21st Century." *Journal of the American Medical Association* 312, no. 2 (2014): 125–126.

Taormino, Tristan. *Down and Dirty Sex Secrets*. New York: Regan Books, 2001.

Taormino, Tristan. *True Lust: Adventures in Sex, Porn and Perversion*. San Francisco: Cleis, 2002.

Taormino, Tristan. *The Ultimate Guide to Anal Sex for Women*. San Francisco: Cleis, 1998.

Taormino, Tristan, Celine Parreñas Shimizu, Constance Penley, and Mireille Miller-Young, eds. *The Feminist Porn Book: The Politics of Producing Pleasure*. New York: Feminist Press, 2013.

Tedlock, Barbara. "From Participant Observation to the Observation of Participation: The Emergence of Narrative Ethnography." *Journal of Anthropological Research* 47 (1991): 69–94.

Tiefer, Leonore. "Sex Therapy as Humanistic Enterprise." *Sexual and Relationship Therapy* 21, no. 3 (2006): 359–375.

Twitchell, James B. *Branded Nation: The Marketing of Megachurch, College Inc., and Museumworld*. New York: Simon and Schuster, 2004.

Vance, Carole. *Pleasure and Danger: Exploring Female Sexuality*. New York: Routledge and Kegan Paul, 1984.

Voss, Georgina. "'Treating It as a Normal Business': Researching the Pornography Industry." *Sexualities* 15, no. 3–4 (2012): 391–410.

Warne, Gary. "Demystifying Business." In *The Briarpatch Book*, edited by the Briarpatch Community. San Francisco: New Glide, 1978.

Warner, Michael. *The Trouble with Normal: Sex, Politics, and the Ethics of Queer Life*. Cambridge, MA: Harvard University Press, 1999.

Weiss, Margot. *Techniques of Pleasure: BDSM and the Circuits of Sexuality*. Durham, NC: Duke University Press, 2011.

Weitzer, Ronald, ed. *Sex for Sale: Prostitution, Pornography, and the Sex Industry*, 2nd ed. New York: Routledge, 2010.

William, Brooke, and Hannah Darby. "God, Mom, and Apple Pie: 'Feminist' Businesses as an Extension of the American Dream." *off our backs*, February 28, 1976.

Williams, Dell. "Roots of the Garden." *Journal of Sex Research* 27, no. 3 (1990): 461–466.

Williams, Dell, and Lynn Vannucci. *Revolution in the Garden: Memoirs of the Garden Keeper*. Santa Rosa, CA: Silverback, 2005.

Winks, Cathy. *The Good Vibrations Guide to Adult Videos*. San Francisco: Down There Press, 1998.

Woodul, Jennifer. "What's This about Feminist Businesses?" In *Feminist Frameworks:*

*Alternative Theoretical Accounts of the Relationships between Women and Men*, edited by Alison M. Jaggar and Paula A. Rothenberg, 196–204. New York: McGraw-Hill, 1978.

Zeisler, Andi. *We Were Feminists Once: From Riot Grrrl to Covergirl®, the Buying and Selling of a Political Movement*. New York: PublicAffairs, 2016.

## Interviews

Molly Adler (cofounder, Self Serve), June 25, 2008, Albuquerque, NM.

Kim Airs (founder, Grand Opening), August 4, 1999, Boston; May 26, 2014, Las Vegas.

Amber (customer), December 29, 2015, telephone.

Amy Andre (former sex educator/sales assistant [SESA]/education department, Good Vibrations), July 10, 2008, telephone.

Dan Athineos (assistant store manager, Babeland NYC), October 19, 2001, New York City.

Babeland Roundtable Discussion (cofounder Claire Cavanah and staff sex educators Christine Rinki, Felice Shays, Saul Silva, and Jamye Waxman), November 23, 2002, New York City.

Ellen Barnard (cofounder and owner, A Woman's Touch), June 25, 2007, Madison, WI.

Stephanie Basile (organizer, Retail, Wholesale and Department Store Union), July 6, 2016, telephone.

Isaiah Benjamin (mail order employee, Babeland), June 7, 2002, Oakland, CA.

Marilyn Bishara (founder, Vixen Creations), June 5, 2002, San Francisco.

Metis Black (founder and president, Tantus), April 1, 2008, telephone; August 22, 2010, telephone.

Joani Blank (founder, Good Vibrations), October 20, 1999, telephone; February 6, 2002, telephone; June 12, 2002, Oakland; May 9, 2003, telephone; July 14, 2008, Oakland; November 13, 2013, Oakland.

Susie Bright (former manager, Good Vibrations), June 18, 2010, telephone.

Claire Cavanah (cofounder and owner, Babeland), August 30, 2001, New York City.

Dana Clark (store manager, Babeland NYC), July 30, 2001; August 24, 2001, New York City.

Janell Davis (former SESA, Good Vibrations), November 9, 2001, telephone.

Coyote Days (product and purchasing manager, Good Vibrations), March 18, 2008, San Francisco; July 5, 2016, telephone.

Greg DeLong (founder, NJoy), April 8, 2008, Las Vegas; December 1, 2010, telephone.

Rebecca Denk (general business manager, Babeland), January 10, 2002, telephone; October 12, 2003, telephone.

Searah Deysach (founder, Early to Bed), June 24, 2007, Chicago; April 24, 2015, Chicago.

Betty Dodson (author/artist), December 3, 1999, telephone.

Erin Doherty (mail order manager, Babeland), June 6, 2002, Oakland, CA.

Ben Doyle (general business manager, Good Vibrations), June 17, 2002, San Francisco.

Andy Duran (educational outreach and affiliate manager, Good Vibrations), July 18, 2016, telephone.

Roma Estevez (former SESA/porn reviewer and buyer, Good Vibrations), November 9, 1999; November 22, 1999, Northampton, MA.

Matie Fricker (cofounder and owner, Self Serve), June 25, 2008, Albuquerque, NM; December 18, 2015, telephone; July 7, 2016, telephone.

Kristina Garcia (sex educator, Babeland Seattle), February 25, 2002, telephone.

Paula Gilovich (sex educator, Babeland Seattle), February 19, 2002, Seattle.

Gina (customer), March 18, 2008, San Francisco.

Charlie Glickman (SESA, Good Vibrations), June 15, 2002, San Francisco; November 2, 2007, telephone.

Phoebe Grott (senior buyer, Babeland), January 17, 2013, Las Vegas.

Laura Ann Haave (owner, Tool Shed), November 20, 2013, telephone.

Terri Hague (former SESA, Good Vibrations), March 28, 2002, telephone.

Candy Halikas (former sales clerk, Forbidden Fruit), November 30, 2001, New York City.

Dena Hankins (marketing associate, Babeland), June 10, 2002, Okaland, CA.

Heather (customer, Babeland), August 1, 2001, New York City.

Marlene Hoeber (former designer, Vixen Creations), August 27, 2015, telephone.

Nenna Joiner (founder and owner, Feelmore), July 14, 2008, San Francisco; September 16, 2011, Oakland, CA; October, 11, 2015, telephone.

Jacq Jones (assistant store manager, Babeland), April 12, 2002, New York City; (founder and owner, Sugar), October 11, 2007, telephone.

Aileen Journey (founder, Intimacies), October 20, 1998; October 25, 1999, Northampton, MA.

Juawana (customer, Babeland), July 1, 2015, Las Vegas.

Joel Kaminsky (owner, Good Vibrations), November 14, 2013, Oakland, CA.

Sarah Kennedy (producer, Sexpositive Productions/SESA, Good Vibrations), June 13, 2002, San Francisco.

Karoline Khamis (founder and owner, Toyboxx), August 15, 2015, Las Vegas.

Robert Lawrence (customer, Good Vibrations), August 25, 2015, telephone.

Dan Martin (owner, Vibratex), April 9, 2013, Las Vegas.

Eve Meelan (president, board of directors/porn reviewer-buyer, Good Vibrations), June 17, 2002.

Gene Menger (marketing manager, Forbidden Fruit), May 21, 2002, Austin, TX.

Tyler Merriman (purchasing manager, Babeland Seattle), February 19, 2002, Seattle.

Annie Michelson (sex educator, Babeland Seattle), February 25, 2002, telephone.

Alliyah Mirza (founder, Earth Erotics), August 22, 2010, telephone.

Gail Monat (manager, Intimacies), August 29, 2001, Northampton, MA.

Amanda Morgan (sexual health educator), August 22, 2010, Las Vegas.

Chephany Navarro (sales clerk, Pink Pussycat), October 12, 2001, New York City.

Susan Ott (sales clerk, Intimacies), May 5, 2001, Northampton, MA.

Archer Parr (mail order, Babeland Oakland), June 7, 2002, Oakland, CA.

Jennifer Pritchett (founder and owner, Smitten Kitten), September 16, 2012, Long Beach, CA.

Carol Queen (staff sexologist, Good Vibrations), June 8, 2002, San Francisco.

Lizz Randall (store manager, Babeland Seattle), February 22, 2002, Seattle.

Lynn Raridon (owner, Forbidden Fruit), March 26, 2002, Austin, TX.

Shar Rednour (cofounder, SIR Video/former part-time SESA, Good Vibrations), June 7, 2002, Berkeley, CA.

Alicia Relles (sex educator, Babeland NYC), October 25, 2001, New York City.

Christine Rinki (sex educator, Babeland NYC), October 16, 2001, New York City.

Thomas Roche (marketing manager, Good Vibrations), June 17, 2002, San Francisco.

Candida Royalle (founder, Femme Productions), November 7, 2001, telephone.

April Sanchez (sales clerk, Forbidden Fruit), June 1, 2002, Austin, TX.

Carrie Schrader (general business manager, Babeland), June 21, 2001; November 21, 2001, New York City.

Anne Semans (former employee, Good Vibrations), June 25, 2002, telephone.

Sherri Shaulis (senior editor of pleasure products at Adult Video News), June 20, 2016, telephone.

Felice Shays (sex educator, Babeland NYC), November 27, 2001, New York City.

Lamalani Siverts (sex educator/assistant purchasing manager, Babeland Seattle), February 22, 2002.

Lena Solow (sex educator, Babeland NYC), July 8, 2016, telephone.

Angelique Stacy (store manager, Good Vibrations), March 21, 2008, San Francisco.

Jackie Strano (cofounder, SIR Video; executive vice president, Good Vibrations), June 7, 2002, Berkeley, CA; November 14, 2013, Oakland, CA.

Tristan Taormino (author and sex educator), November 2, 1999, telephone; December 17, 2015, telephone.

Brandie Taylor (assistant store manager, Babeland Seattle), February 21, 2002, Seattle.

Rachel Venning (cofounder and owner, Babeland), March 14, 2002, telephone; July 19, 2016, telephone.

Jamye Waxman (sex educator, Babeland NYC), November 29, 2001, New York City.

Laura Weide (marketing manager, Babeland), February 1, 2002, telephone; June 11, 2002, San Francisco.

Ziadee Whiptail (manager, education department, Good Vibrations), March 29, 2002, telephone.

Dell Williams (founder, Eve's Garden), November 20, 2001; November 28, 2001, New York City.

Cathy Winks (former manager, Good Vibrations), June 27, 2002, telephone.

# INDEX

*Italic page numbers refer to figures.*

A–Action Adult Books, 88–89, *90–91*, 97

Abzug, Bella, 30

Adler, Molly, *137*, 183; co-founding Progressive Pleasure Club, 214–15; co-founding/running Self Serve, 110–11, 136–38, 160, 173. *See also* Self Serve

Adult Entertainment Expo (AEE), 1–2, 223, 225, 230

Adults Only, 91–92

Adult Superstore, 75–76, 108, 226

Agnew, Spiro, 6

AIDS, 53–54, 109; activism, 149, 166, 168, 203. *See also* San Francisco AIDS Project

Airs, Kim, 1, 62, 97, *137*, 174, 217. *See also* Grand Opening

Alabama: antiobscenity laws, 6, 236n26

Alarcón, Norma, 163

Albuquerque, NM, 7, 84, 110–*11*, 133, 136–38, *137*, 173, 214, 230

Allyn, David, 5

Amazon, 212, 215

Amber (customer), 226

Andre, Amy, 78–79, 101, 154–55, 165

Andrews, Kathy, 175

Angel, Buck, 2

Ann Summers, 101

Anzaldúa, Gloria, 163

archival research, 8, 229, 232

Ashoka, 196

Athineos, Dan, 152–53, 189

Atkinson, Ti-Grace, 22

*AVN Novelty Business*: "The New Sex Educators," 140

Babeland, 2, *68*, 83, 102, 213–14; advertisements, *62*, *70*, *72*, *184*, 254n53; *Babelander's Report*, 71; brand, 71–75, 93, 96, 103–5, 108, 113–15, 169–72, 174, 176–77, 179–87, 230, 237n33; business model, 69–70, 78, 85–86, 147–49, 188–91, 194–95, 198–99, 203–9; catalogs, 63, *70*; Come for a Cause, 203; customers, 75–77, 103–5, 108, 152–53, 161–62, 178, 187, 198; employees, 10–12, 63–65, 68, 74–78, 84–85, 99, 104–5, 140–42, 149–50, 152–54, 156–57, 161–62, 176–77, 179–83, 188–91, 198–201, 204, 206–9, 215–18, 229–30, 233, 254n53; founders, 66, *70*, 93, 142, 147–49, 169–70, 174, *184*, 197–200, 205, 216, 224–25; mission, 7, 11–12, 65, *67*, 71–78, *72*, 113, 115, 153–54, 168, 174, 182–83, 189–91, 199, 204, 207–9, 230, 233, 254n53; products, 65, *67*, *94*, *106*, 113–15, 125; unionization, 215–218; workshops, 147–48

Baltimore, MD, 7, 78, 85, 100, 102, 181

Bannerji, Himani, 162

Barbach, Lonnie, 47, 243n9; *For Yourself*, 37, 40

Barnard, Ellen, 100, 133, 178, 214. *See also* A Woman's Touch

BDSM, 9, 12, 74, 152–53; anti-BDSM activism, 53–54; organizations, 53; products, 36, 110, 145, 179; workshops, 223

Bedroom Kandi, 3

*Behind the Green Door*, 122

*Bend Over Boyfriend* series, 11, 13, 137, 157–60, 182

benevolent femininity, 202–3

Benjamin, Isaiah, 84, 151, 184–85

*Berkeley Barb*, 45

Berkeley Free Clinic, 203

birth control pill. *See* contraception

bisexuality, 16, 46, 78, 89, 122–23, 157, 181

Bishara, Marilyn, 13, 124–26. *See also* Vixen Creations

*Bitch* magazine, 11, 72, 223

Black, Metis, 127, 130, 134, 140, 224. *See also* Tantus

Blank, Joani, 44, 164, 175, 221; business model, 57–62, 69, 192–97, 213–15, 226–27; founding/running Good Vibrations, 7–8, 43–46, 50–53, 56, 83–84, 91, 95–96, 116–21, 140–41, 148, 150–52, 224; funding *Bend Over Boyfriend* series, 158; funding Feelmore, 167; *Good Vibrations: The Complete Woman's Guide to Vibrators*, 49–50; *Herotica* book series, 56; *The Playbook for Women about Sex*, 48–49; selling Good Vibrations to employees, 79–82, 245n27; on women's sexual agency, 21, 43–48, 54. *See also* Good Vibrations; *Herotica* book series

Bodysex workshops, 23, 29

Bourdieu, Pierre, 88, 99

boutique culture, 92–93, 102, 103, 214, 218

Brancusi, Constantin, 125

branding, 104, 122, 128, 133, 145–46, 223; Babeland and, 11, 71–75, 77; feminism and, 14, 172; Good Vibrations and, 219; rebranding, 96, 237n33; sex-positive brand community, 66, 71–75, 86, 167

Briarpatch philosophy, 57–62

Bright, Susie, 28, 60, 185; founding/column at *On Our Backs*, 10, 13, 54–56, 141; work at Good Vibrations, 51–58, 95, 118–20, 122, 127, 140–41, 144, 176. *See also Herotica* book series; *On Our Backs*

*Broad City*, 223

Bronstein, Carolyn, 6, 54

Brown, Helen Gurley: *Sex and the Single Girl*, 4

Brown, Rita Mae, 93

Burawoy, Michael, 230

Burruss, Kandi, 3. *See also* Bedroom Kandi

business models, 89; Babeland, 69–70, 78, 83, 85–86, 147–49, 188–91, 194–95, 198–99, 203–9; Eve's Garden, 191–92; Feelmore, 168; Good Vibrations, 7–9, 13, 21–24, 43, 45, 47, 50, 52–53, 57–62, 66, 69, 79–83, 92, 97–99, 118, 123, 154–55, 170, 178, 192–97, 202–4, 209–10, 212–15, 218–21, 223–27, 230; Self Serve, 133–34, 138, 173, 215. *See also* Briarpatch philosophy

butt plugs, 36, 64–65, 113, 124, 132, 146, 153, 160, 179; Tristan, 125–26

Cal Exotics, 113

Califia, Patrick: *Doc and Fluff*, 79

California, 27, 43, 131; Berkeley, 82, 108–9, 146, 166, 177, 203; Los Angeles, 30, 230; Marin County, 97–98; Oakland, 7, 166–68, 189, 218, 230. *See also* San Francisco, CA capitalism, 13–14, 153; labor under, 87, 215–18; uneasy relationship with feminism, 155, 188–221, 227. *See also* entrepreneurship; profit

Cavanah, Claire, 62, 63, *70*, 125; co-founding/running Babeland, 66, 69–71, 75, 93, 103–5, 142, 147–49, 189–90, 199–200, 207–8, 216; on feminism, 169–70; on Good Vibrations, 7, 62; on queerness, 180, 182–*84*. *See also* Babeland

Center for Sexual Health Promotion, 140

Center for Women and Enterprise, 137

Chalker, Rebecca, 21

China, 128, 131, 133

Clark, Dana, 71, 74, 148, 183, 208

class, 3–4, 8, 46, 54, 187, 201, 205; contact encounters, 186; definition, 93; intersectionality and, 139, 163–64, 167–68, 171, 197, 202–3, 217, 232; in sex-toy retail, 12, 14, 43, 89–112, 127, 163–64, 167–68, 174, 177, 192–93, 202. *See also* class vs. crass discourse; cleanliness aesthetic; distinction; respectability politics; sleaze discourse

class vs. crass discourse, 13, 92, 103–9. *See also* distinction; respectability politics; sleaze discourse

cleanliness aesthetic, 50, 92, 97–101, 109, 120, 226

Clement, Chris, 127. *See also* NJoy

Coalition against Toxic Toys, 131

cock rings, 64, 74, 118; Rude Rabbit, 115

condoms, 3, 76, 145, 167–68, 232

consciousness raising, 6, 16–17, 19, 22–23, 27, 46–47, 53; feminist sex-toy stores as, 13, 35–36, 41, 49–50, 69

contact encounters, 186

contraception, 5, 46, 53. *See also* condoms

*Cosmopolitan*, 40

Cottrell, Honey Lee, 51, 141

cultural production studies, 12

cultural studies, 8

Danish Environmental Protection Agency, 131. *See also* toxic toys

Davidson, Leigh, 245n27

Davis, Angela, 163

Davis, Janell, 143, 154, 170, 178

Days, Coyote, 180, 220–21

*Deep Throat*, 6, 11

Dees, J. Gregory, 196–97

Delany, Samuel, 186

DeLong, Greg, 127–29, 224. *See also* NJoy

Denk, Rebecca, 78, 207–9

Deysach, Searah, 102, 115–*16*, 138, 151, 172–73, 183, 199–200, 203, 213–14. *See also* Early to Bed

dildos, 10, 56, *60*, 63–64, *70*, 77, 117–18, 136–37, 145, 150, 167, 198; branding, 72, 128; history of, 223; manufacturing, 13, 124–25, 130–31, 133, 160, 230; for men, 36, 158, 182; packaging and display, 1, 89, 96, 103–4, *106*, *132*; politics of, 54–55; Pure Wand, 128; role in mission, 78, 142, 168, 179–80; Scorpio Rising, 36–*37*; Venus Rising, 36–*37*. *See also individual manufacturers*

distinction, 99, 102, 105–7, 109, 115–16, 122, 126, 156, 195. *See also* branding; class vs. crass discourse; cleanliness aesthetic; respectability politics; sleaze discourse

diversity, 29, 93, 107, 112, 115, 122, 164; racial, 115, 164–68; sexual, 27, 54, 137

Doc Johnson, 2, 113

Dodson, Betty, 1, 19, 22, 24, 26–27, 40, 157–58; *Liberating Masturbation*, 6, 9, 23, 28, 32; *Love Picture Exhibition*, 25; masturbation workshops, 15–16, 23,

Dodson, Betty (*continued*)
28–29, 47; NOW Sexuality Conference
talk, 15–16, *17–18*, 191, 224; *Sex for One,*
*144. See also* Bodysex workshops
Dorfman, Ken, 2
Down There Press, 48, 56, 240n35
Doyle, Ben, 195
Drayton, Bill, 196
Dr. Ruth, 36, 143
du Gay, Paul, 229
Duncan, Gosnell, 36
Duran, Andy, 164

Early to Bed, 7, *116*, 138, 172, 199, 213, 215,
230; products, 115; sex education, 151,
183, 203; store design, 99, 102
Earth Erotics, 133–34
Eberwein, Robert, 157
Echols, Alice, 35, 163
Ehrenreich, Barbara, 4, 5
Ekstrom, Jessica, 196
empowerment, 14, 22, 151, 166, 172;
feminist sex-toy stores encouraging,
12, 33, 35, 41, 63, 66, 71–73, 77–78, 84,
86–87, 142, 148, 206, 210, 227, 230;
masturbation and, 27–29
entrepreneurship: feminist, 7–8, 14, 19,
32, 44, 62, 213–15, 225–26, 231; sex-
positive, 2, 5, 13, 69, 125, 127, 135, 166,
200, 209; social, 66, 196–98
Equal Rights Amendment, 38
erotica, 10, 42, 60. *See also* pornography;
*and individual presses, producers, titles*
Estevez, Roma, 103, 144, 170, 204,
245n27; on Good Vibrations
customers, 98, 179; on pornography,
120, 123
ethnography, 8–11, 63–66, 198–99, 229–
33
Evans, Sara, 4

Eve's Garden, 7, 29–43, *31*, 175, 197, 226;
business model, 191–92; catalogs,
*32–34, 36–37,* 39–42; customers, 36,
38–42; women-only policy, 162–63
Evil Angel, 155, 157
extended case method, 230–31

Faderman, Lillian, 236n11
Fatale Video, 55, 120–22; *Bend Over*
*Boyfriend,* 11, 13, 137, 157–60, 182
Federation of Feminist Women's Health
Centers, 21
Feelmore, 7, *166*–68, 215, 230
female hysteria, 24, 240n34
femininity, 20, 99, 108; benevolent,
202–3
feminism, types of: antipornography,
53–54; cultural, 163, 169; lesbian,
53, 93, 233; liberal, 19; radical, 20,
80, 200; second-wave, 5, 172–73;
women of color, 163. *See also* women's
movement; *and individual people,*
*organizations, stores*
feminist bookstores, 35, 43
feminist sex wars, 9, 56, 232
feminist theory, 27, 80, 162, 163
Femme Productions, 95
*Fifty Shades of Grey,* 2, 223, 230
Findlay, Heather, 54
Fine, Michelle, 138–39
First Amendment, 109
Flynt, Larry, 105, 220. *See also Hustler*
Food and Drug Administration (FDA),
5, 133–34
Forbidden Fruit, 7
Forney, Ellen, *70*
Foucault, Michel, 12, 151
Free Speech Coalition, 218
Freud, Sigmund, 19–20
Fricker, Matie, 84, *137*; co-founding

Progressive Pleasure Club, 214–15; co-founding/running Self Serve, 110–12, 136–38, 160, 173, 217. *See also* Self Serve
Friday, Nancy, 33
Friedan, Betty, 3–5, 30
Fun Factory, 128

gay and lesbian liberation movement, 5, 17, 26, 46, 181
General Video of America and Trans-World News (GVA-TWN), 211–12, 218
Georgia, 6; antiobscenity laws, 236n26
Gilovich, Paula, 170
Ginzberg, Lori, 202–3
Glickman, Charlie, 83, 96–97, *165*, 177, 180, 212; Good Vibrations sex educator training, 145–46, 152, 154
Glide Urban Center, 26
Gobé, Marc, 73
Good Releasing, 123
Good Vibrations, 112, 168, 215; advertisements, *55*, *60*, *165*; Berkeley store, 82, 108–9, 146, 166, 177; business model, 8–9, 21–24, 43, 45, 47, 52–53, 57–62, 66, 69, 79–83, 92, 123, 154–55, 170, 192–95, 197, 202–4, 209–10, 212–13, 218–21, 223–26, 230; catalogs, 51, 56, 84, 103–4, 193; customers, 45, 59, 69, 92–93, 95–99, 101, 104, 107, 119, 150, 158, 160, 179, 186; employees, 13, 50–58, 61, 70, 78–79, 95, 107, 117–20, 122–25, 127, 134, 140–47, 152, 154–55, 157, *164–65*, 176, 180, 194, 198; *Good Vibes Gazette*, 58–59; *The Good Vibrations Guide: Adult Videos*, 122; *The Good Vibrations Guide to Sex*, 10, 166; internships, 62, 69–70, 137, 213; men's roles in, 174–79; Multicultural Committee, 164; products, 44, 54–56, 55, 60, 79, 116–25, 160, 193; publishing arm, 48; racial and gender politics, 163–65; sale to GVA-TWN, 83, 211–14, 218–21; San Francisco store, 7, 10, 44–45, 52, 69, 78, 83, 146, 158, 175, 211, 227, 230; sex education, 50, 87, 118, 140–48, *147*, 154–55; sex educator training, 145–46, 152, 154; sexologists, 12, *144*; sex-positive diaspora, 13, 62, 66, 69, 83–87, 124, 137, 156; Sexuality Library, *60*, 193; vibrator museum, 51; video production arm, 122–23; worker-owned cooperative, 79–83, 245n27; zoning issues, 108–9. *See also* Down There Press; Good Releasing; Sexpositive Productions
Grand Opening, 62, 137, 174, 213, 230; unionization, 216–17
Granville, Joseph Mortimer, 24
Gray, Macy, 3
greenwashing, 134
Gunabalan, Asha, 245n27

Haave, Laura, 128, 130, 178, 197. *See also* Tool Shed
Hague, Terri, 81, 177, 194, 202, 245n27
Haines, Staci, 245n27
Hampden Village Merchants Association, 85
Hankins, Dena, 181
Headbands for Hope, 196
Heather (customer), 75, 77
Hefner, Hugh, 4. *See also Playboy*
Henderson, Lisa, 93
*Herotica* book series, 56
Hess, Elizabeth, 5
heterosexuality, 4–5, 16, 35, 55; customers and, 99, 177; norms of, 21–22, 95, 122, 249n7; queering, 158, 179–87. *See also* sexual double standard

Hite, Shere, 37
Hoeber, Marlene, 125
Holland, Kelly, 1–2
Hollibaugh, Amber, 171
home sex-toy parties, 101, 133, 238n37
homosexuality, 53. *See also* bisexuality;
    gay and lesbian liberation movement;
    lesbians; queerness; queer people
hooks, bell, 217
Houston, Shine Louise, 13. *See also* Pink
    and White Productions
*How to Fuck in High Heels*, 137
Hsieh, Tony, 73
human potential movement, 26–27, 46
*Hustler*, 105

identity politics, 8, 162, 172, 186
identity projects, 162
Illinois: Chicago, 7, 99, 102, 115, 138, 151,
    172, 213, 230
Indiana University, 3–4. *See also* Kinsey,
    Alfred; Center for Sexual Health
    Promotion
Institute for Advanced Study of Human
    Sexuality, 143
International Lingerie Show, 230
Internet, 73, 84, 86, 146, 190, 212–14, 217,
    224, 238n37; Facebook, 11, 139, 226;
    Google, 211; Instagram, 11; piracy,
    2; pornography, 123; Snapchat, 139;
    Twitter, 11, 139; Tumblr, 139; YouTube,
    139. *See also* online stores
intersectionality, 163, 172
Intimacies, 8–9, 102, 104
Irvine, Janice, 20–21, 26

Jacobs, Gloria, 5
Je Joue, 2. *See also* vibrators: SaSi
Joiner, Nenna, *166–68*. *See also* Feelmore
Jones, Jacq, 202, 204; founding/running

Sugar, 78, 85–86, 100, 102, 181, 225–26;
    work at Babeland, 78, 84–85. *See also*
    Sugar
Journey, Aileen, 8–9, 102, 104. *See also*
    Intimacies
Juawana (customer), 75–77, 108

Kamins, Rondee, 212
Kaminsky, Joel, 218–21
Kennedy, Sarah, 84, 123. *See also*
    Sexpositive Productions
Khamis, Karoline, 221–22. *See also*
    Toyboxx
Kinney, Nan, 54, 141
Kinsey, Alfred, 4, 20–21, 27
Kipnis, Laura, 105
Koedt, Anne, 20

Laqueur, Thomas, 26
Las Vegas, NV, 1–2, 7, 88, *90–91*, 108, *114*,
    166, 221–22, 226, 230
law, 12, 53, 57, 80, 143, 196, 209;
    antiobscenity laws, 5–7, 6, 236n26;
    Equal Rights Amendment, 38;
    lawyers, 81, 85; sex laws, 14. *See also*
    US Congress; US Supreme Court;
    zoning regulations
Lawrence, Robert Morgan, 175; *Bend
    Over Boyfriend* series, 11, 13, 137,
    157–60, 182
lesbians, 41, 43, 69, 171, 185–86;
    customers, 45, 56, 66, 70, 108, 122,
    173; employees, 51, 113, 161–62,
    175–76, 184; leatherdykes, 53–54;
    lesbian feminism, 53, 93, 233; at
    NOW Sexuality Conference, 16;
    pornography by, 13, 65, 120, 123,
    158, 182; pulp fiction, 4, 236n11;
    representations of, 4, 54–56, 174,
    236n11; sexual practices, 54–56,

64, 141; store owners/founders, 85, 124, 168, 183, 216; teaching people about sex, 158, 179–87. *See also* gay and lesbian liberation movement; queerness; queer people

*Lesbian Sex Secrets for Men*, 183

Lieberman, Hallie, 240n34

Love Honey, 223

lube, *60*, 64–65, 76, 115, 136, 145–46, 159, 167

Lucky (employee), 188–89

Luna, Amy, 219

Lusty Lady, 55

Macy's, 29–30, 226

mail-order catalogs, 113, 191, 232; Babeland, 63, *70*; Eve's Garden, 32–34, 36–37, 39–42; Good Vibrations, 51, 56, 84, 103–4, 193

Maines, Rachel, 240n34

male masturbation sleeves, *114*; Flesh Light, 118

manufacturing, 2–3, 8, 13, 124, 205, 230–31; branding and, 24, 105, 114, 115–16, 180; feminist sex-positive mission and, 124–30, 160, 223–24; toxins and, 130–35. *See also* China; *and individual manufacturers*

marriage, 30, 45; housewife sex-toy market, 65, 97–103; sex and, 3–4, 10, 16, 18, 23, 39–40, 120, 139, 178

Massachusetts: Boston, 62, 137, 174, 192, 213, 216, 219, 230; Northampton, 102

Masters and Johnson, 20–21, 27, 143

masturbation, 4, 46–51, 61, 148; *Liberating Masturbation*, 6, 9, 23, 28, 32; male masturbation sleeves, *114*, 118; *Masturbation Techniques for Women/ Getting in Touch*, 26–27; masturbation workshops, 15–16, 23, 28–29, 47;

women's empowerment and, 6, 9, 15–30, 40–41, 157. *See also* Society of Out-of-the-Closet Masturbators; Bodysex workshops

Mayer, Deborah, 245n27

Medical Committee for Human Rights (MCHR), 46

Men Overcoming Sexual Assault, 177

Merriman, Tyler, 113–14, 201, 208

methodology (of book), 8–11, 190, 198–99, 214, 229–33. *See also* archival research; ethnography; extended case method

Michelson, Annie, 190

Michigan Womyn's Music Festival, 84, 149

Mihalko, Reid: Sex Geek Summer Camp, 223

Miller, Laura, 245n27

Minnesota: Minneapolis, 7, 130, 138

Mirza, Alliyah, 133–34. *See also* Earth Erotics

Mitchell Brothers Theatre, 53

Modern Times, 52–53

monogamy, 5

Moraga, Cherríe, 163

motherhood, 3–5, 46

*Ms.* magazine, 28, 32–33, 192, 220

*The Multi-Orgasmic Man*, 10

Mycoskie, Blake, 196

National Organization for Women (NOW), 5, 30; 1973 Sexuality Conference, 15–19, *17–18*, 32, 191, 224

National Sex Forum: *Masturbation Techniques for Women/Getting in Touch*, 26–27

New Right, 53

New York City, 23, 30, 32, 74; NOW conference in, *17–18*; sex-toy stores

New York City (*continued*)
in, 7, 10, *31*, 40, 63, 71, 77, 84, 128, 142, 151, 169, 183, 188, 191–92, 199, 208, 213, 215, 229
New York Radical Feminists, 20
Nixon, Richard, 6
NJoy, 127–29, 223–24
nonmonogamy, 16, 18, 24. *See also* polyamory
Norton, Eleanor Holmes, 30

obscenity: antiobscenity laws, 5–7, 236n26
*off our backs*, 54, 200
OhMiBod, 3
online stores, 84, 86, 190, 211–14, 217, 238n37
*On Our Backs* (OOB), 10, 13, 54, 118, 141, 157–*59*, 182, 183, 200–201; advertisements, *55*, *62*, *147*
*The Opening of Misty Beethoven*, 122
Ottinger, Amy, 245n27
*Our Bodies, Ourselves*, 26, 28, 33

Parr, Archer, 171
patriarchy, 5, 19, 21–22, 35, 53–54, 163, 217, 249n7
Patton, Cindy, 246n7
pegging, 158, 182. *See also Bend Over Boyfriend* series
Peiss, Kathy, 205
Penthouse Media, 1; *Penthouse*, 105, 118
personal is political (slogan), 13, 161
*Peyton Place*, 4
phthalates, 130–31; Phthalate Awareness Month, 133
Pink and White Productions, 13
Pink Pussycat, 151
Planned Parenthood, 78, 85, 149, 203
*Playboy*, 4, 69, 105, 167
polyamory, 146. *See also* nonmonogamy

popular culture, 4, 11–12, 23
pornography, 1–2, 12, 89, 92, 100, 135, 178, 218, 224–25, 231; antipornography activism, 6, 9, 53–54, 69, 113; at Babeland, 64; critiques of, 39, 53–54; feminist, 10, 69, 95, 122–23, 156–60, 167–68, 201; gay male, 180; at Good Vibrations, 44, 95–96, 116–23; history of, 11; lesbian producers, 13, 65, 120, 123, 156–60, 167–68, 182; mainstream (hetero, male-focused), 28, 103, 105, 223; race and, 13, 120, 123, 167; at Self Serve, 110; women consumers, 1–2, 14, 65, 107, 167, 174, 182, 229. *See also* erotica; *and individual presses, producers, titles*
preorgasmic women, 47, 50, 243n9
Pritchett, Jennifer, 130–32, 135. *See also* Smitten Kitchen
privacy, 8, 60; gender, 163; sexual, 7, 89, 238n37
product buyers, 1, 113, 224
profit, 188–210
Progressive Pleasure Club (PPC), 214
psychoanalysis, 20–21, 33–34

Quackenbush, Marcia, 56
Queen, Carol, 109, 118, 136, 176, 178, 245n27; *Bend Over Boyfriend* series, 11, 13, 137, 157–60, 182; on Good Vibrations business model, 61–62, 212; on Good Vibrations customers, 97–98, 150; on pornography, 120–23; on sex education, 143–45; sexologist, 12, 143, *165*, 175; on sex positivity, 12–13; on sustainable sex toys, 134
queerness, 55, 123, 160, 162, 175; queering straight sex, 157–58, 179–87
queer people, 13, 85, 171, 203; consumers, 8, 64, 76, 84, 138, 146, 167, 211–12; employees, 51, 113, 161–62, 164–65,

169, 172, 175–77, 179–84, 216, 218, 233;
store owners, 85, 124, 126, 168, 173,
181–85, 204, 216. *See also* bisexuality;
lesbians
queer theory, 172

race, 14, 16, 98, 174, 187; intersectionality
and, 163, 197; marketing and, 12, 92,
98–99, 101, 112; pornography and,
13, 120, 123, 167; racial diversity, 115,
163–68. *See also* racism
racism, 35, 115, 120, 163, 165, 217
Randall, Lizz, 141, 149, 153, 170–71
rape crisis centers, 35, 149, 177
Reagan, Ronald, 53
Rednour, Shar, 55, *159*; *Bend Over
Boyfriend* series, 11, 13, 137, 157–60,
182. *See also* SIR Video
Rednour-Bruckman, Jackie. *See* Strano,
Jackie
Reich, Wilhelm, 33–34
Relles, Alicia, 1, 96, 142, 190
respectability politics, 92, 99, 102, 107–
8, 112, 120, 205, 223. *See also* class;
class vs. class discourse; cleanliness
aesthetic; distinction; sleaze discourse
Retail, Wholesale and Department Store
Union (RWDSU), 215–16
retail activism, 8, 13, 217, 231
Rinki, Christine, 150, 177
Roche, Thomas, 178
Rosen, Ruth, 18
Royalle, Candida, 95, 105, 107, 113, 122,
224. *See also* Femme Productions;
vibrators: Natural Contours
Rubenstein, Maggi, 46

safe sex, 54, 145, 157; supplies, 118. *See
also* condoms
Samois, 53–54; *Coming to Power*, 54
San Francisco, CA, 128; Fatale Video,

120; Good Vibrations store, 7, 10,
44–45, 52, 69, 78, 83, 146, 158, 175,
211, 227, 230; Japan Town, 193; Lusty
Lady, 55; National Sex Forum, 26;
*On Our Backs* (OOB), 10, 13, 54–55,
62, 118, 141, *147*, 157–59, 182–83, 200–
201; queer sex-positive community,
53, 55–56, 79; Samois, 53–54; sex
education community, 46, 50; sex
toy manufacturers, 124, 126; Stormy
Leather, 55, 175
San Francisco AIDS Project, 166
San Francisco Sex Information (SFSI),
46–47, 143, 167
Scharf, Laura, 17
Schmitt, Bernd, 75
Schrader, Carrie, 66, 68, 70–71, 74,
77–78, 188–89, 195, 206–8
Seattle, WA, 66, 208; sex-toy stores in,
7, 62, 68–71, 76–77, 94, *106*, 113, 141,
188–90, 213, 218
Self Serve, 7, 84, *111*, *137*, 183, 214, 230;
business model, 133–34, 138, 173, 215;
workshops, 136, 160; zoning issues,
110–12
Semans, Anne, 61, 80, 82–83, 98, 117–18,
*164*, 193–94, 245n27
*Sex and the City*, 2, 65
sex education, 22, 26, 37, 46–47, 91,
118; adolescents and, 138–39; retail-
based, 1, 12, 14, 44, 46, 50–57, 64–66,
71–73, 84–87, 102, 109, 112, 122–26, 131,
138–60, 162, 165, 188, 191, 197, 205–6,
209, 211–13, 216, 218, 220–21, 225–27,
230, 233; school-based, 79, 138–39;
social media and, 139. *See also* sex
educators/sales associates; sexperts
sex educators/sales associates: at
Babeland, 10, 12, 65, 85, 140, 142,
148–50, 152–53, 156, 169, 176–77, 179,
190, 199; at Early to Bed, 151; at Good

sex educators/sales associates (*continued*)
Vibrations (SESAS), 78–79, 141–43,
145–48, 150, 152, 154–56, 180–81; Sex
Educator Boot Camp, 202, 223. *See
also* sexperts
sexism, 19, 53, 113–15, 120, 169–70, 176,
216–17, 224, 249n7. *See also* sexual
double standard; transphobia
sex negativity, 12, 97, 118, 216
Sex Nerd Sandra, 223
sexology, 12, 19, 143, *144*, 175; humanistic
branch, 26–27, 34, 50
Sex Out Loud, 223
sexperts, 51, 136–60, 176–77. *See also* sex
educators/sales associates
sex-positive diaspora, 7, 50, 62, 83–87
Sexpositive Productions (SPP), 122;
*G Marks the Spot*, 123; *Please Don't
Stop: Lesbian Tips for Giving and
Getting It*, 123; *Slide Bi Me*, 123;
*Voluptuous Vixens*, 123; *Whipsmart*,
123
sex positivity, 12–13, 27, 40, 50, 66, 73, 76,
78, 83, 86, 107, 121, 145, 209, 218, 227.
*See also* sex-positive diaspora
sex therapists, 6, 7, 19, 36–37, 43, 47, 50,
141, 143
sex toys: bloggers and, 223; branding
and, 24, 105, 114, 115–16, 180; class
and, 12, 14, 43, 89–112, 127, 163–64,
167–68, 174, 177, 192–93, 202; design,
124–130, 223; feminist consciousness
raising and, 13, 35–36, 41, 49–50,
69; feminist sex-positive mission
and, 124–30, 160, 223–24; feminist
sex-toy stores encouraging, 12,
33, 35, 41, 63, 66, 71–73, 77–78, 84,
86–87, 142, 148, 206, 210, 227, 230;
manufacturing, 2–3, 8, 13, 124, 205,
230–31; packaging and display, 89, 96,
103–7, *106*, 115, 124–25, 127, *132–134*,

233; representations in media, 2–3, 65,
223; toxins and, 130–35. *See also* butt
plugs; dildos; vibrators
sexual autonomy, 5, 14, 22, 138, 151, 170
sexual double standard, 17, 20, 249n7
Sexuality Library, *60*, 193
sexuality studies, 12, 229
sexual revolution, 4–6, 18–19, 23, 26,
227
sexual vernaculars, 96, 246n7
sexual violence, 53, 177. *See also* rape
crisis centers
sex work, 45, 100–102, 109, 121, 149
Shaulis, Sherri, 235n5
Shays, Felice, 149, 161, 171, 179, 185–86,
189, 201
Shelton Electric Company, 24–25
Shulman, Alix, 20, 22
Silva, Saul, 172
SIR Video, 13, 158
sisterhood, 32, 35, 38, 163;
entrepreneurial, 214; erotic, 36
Skeggs, Beverley, 99
sleaze discourse, 87, 92, 93–97, 100–101.
*See also* class; class v. crass discourse;
cleanliness discourse; distinction;
respectability politics
Smith, Barbara, 163
Smitten Kitten, 7, 130–35, *132*, 138, 215
social media, 11, 139; Facebook, 11, 139,
226; Instagram, 11; Snapchat, 139;
Twitter, 11, 139; Tumblr, 139
Society of Out-of-the-Closet
Masturbators, 48
Society for the Scientific Study of
Sexuality, 36, 69
Solow, Lena, 216–18
Sparks, Theresa, 211
speculums, 21, 53
Stagliano, John, 155, 157
Stormy Leather, 55, 175

Storr, Merl, 101
Strano, Jackie, 13, *159*, 219; *Bend Over Boyfriend* series, 11, 13, 137, 157–60, 182. *See also* SIR Video
Streeter, Caroline, 245n27
Sugar, 7, 78, 85–87, 100, 102, 181, 215, 225
Sundahl, Debi, 54, 141
*The Survivor's Guide to Sex*, 11

Tantus, 127–28, 130, 134–35, 140, 223–24
Taormino, Tristan, 142, 181; butt plug, 125–26; *Chemistry*, 2; *Down and Dirty Sex Secrets*, 156; Sex Educator Boot Camp, 202, 223; *The Ultimate Guide to Anal Sex for Women* (book), 10–11, 126, 137, 155–57; *The Ultimate Guide to Anal Sex for Women* (film), 137, 155–57, 159–60
Taylor, Brandie, 204, 209
Taylor, Grant, 23–24
Tedlock, Barbara, 233
Texas: antiobscenity laws, 6–7, 236n26
TOMS, 196
Tool Shed, 128, 178, 197, 230
toxic toys, 124, 130–35. *See also* phthalates
Toyboxx, 221–23, *222*
Toys in Babeland. *See* Babeland
Transgender Law Center, 203
transgender people, 2, 84, 203; customers, 45, 173, 186; employees, 216, 218
*Transparent*, 223
transphobia, 115
Trojan, 3
Twitchell, James, 73

unionization, 215–18
Unite Here, 216
University of California, San Francisco (UCSF), 43, 47

US Congress, 6, 131; Commission on Obscenity and Pornography, 6; Senate, 6
US Supreme Court, 5

Venning, Rachel, *70*, *184*, 218; co-founding/running Babeland, 2, 62, 66, 69–71, 93, 103, 114, 189–90, 200–201, 208, 216, 224–25; on feminism, 169, 174; on sex education, 148–50, 205; on sexual empowerment, 63, 237n33. *See also* Babeland
vibrators, 1, 3, 14, 54, 59, 89, 91, 104, 110, 113, 158, 167, 186, 211; branding, 73, 75, 95, 99; criminalization, 6–7, 236n26; Gee Whiz attachment, 125; *Good Vibrations: The Complete Woman's Guide to Vibrators*, 49–50; history of, 24–*25*; Hitachi Magic Wand, 24, 29, 32, *44*, *55*, 125, 193, 226; masturbation workshops and, 16–*17*, 23, 28–29, 47; Natural Contours, 105; Oster, 24; Panabrator, 24; Pocket Rocket, 75; Prelude 2, 32, 40; Prelude 3, 39; quality, 127–28, 130–31, 133; Rabbit, 2, 11, 65, *184*; sales of, 36–40, 43–45, 50–53, 56–57, 198, 230, 232, 235n5; SaSi, 2; sex education and, 10–11, 41, 60–61, 64–66, 68, 115, 140–41, 145, 152–53, 179; sex-positive feminism and, 19, 30, 32–33, 42, 49, 63, 117, 147–48, 197, 221, 224, 229; vibrator museum, 43, 51
Vixen Creations, 13, 124–28, 134, 160
Voss, Georgina, 229

Warby Parker, 196
Warne, Gary, 57
Warner, Michael, 14
Waxman, Jamye, 140, 189
Weide, Laura, 99, 182, 185, 206

Wenning, Judy, 15, 19, 32

Whiptail, Ziadee, 188

*The Whole Lesbian Sex Book*, 64

Williams, Dell, *31*, 197; founding/
running Eve's Garden, 29–43, 77, 91,
162–63, 191–92, 226, 231; on women's
sexual liberation, 18–19, 23. *See also*
Eve's Garden

Winks, Cathy, 83, 93, 107, 122, 125, 127,
*164*; on Good Vibrations business
model, 50, 58, 61, 118, 193–94, 204; on
Good Vibrations customers, 98, 104;
on Good Vibrations worker-owned
cooperative, 81–82, 245n27

Wisconsin: Madison, 100, 133, 178, 214,
230; Milwaukee, 128, 178, 197, 230

A Woman's Touch, 100, 133–34, 178, 214,
230

Women Against Violence in Pornography and Media (wavpm), 53–54

women-owned v. women-only, 162, 175,
187

women's and gender studies, 9, 85, 131

women's health centers, 21, 35

women's movement, 6, 17–18, 21, 23,
30, 32–33, 163–64, 191, 217. *See also*
feminism, types of

worker-owned cooperatives, 79–83, 141,
198, 220, 245n27

worker rights. *See* unionization

XBiz Show, 230

Zappos, 73

zoning regulations, 85, 92, 108–12, 167,
221